THE GREAT WAR AND CANADIAN SOCIETY

THE GREAT WAR
AND
CANADIAN SOCIETY
AN ORAL HISTORY

Compiled By:

Gus Richardson
Lori Rotenberg
Bradley Adams
Deirdre Gallagher
Russell Hann
Gregory S. Kealey
Catherine Macleod
Sharon Mintz
Pauline Pytka
Karen Rotenberg
Mary Tate
Richard Wright

Edited by Daphne Read

With an Introduction by Russell Hann

New Hogtown Press
Toronto

Canadian Cataloguing in Publication Data
Main entry under title:
The Great War and Canadian Society
ISBN0-919940-01-3 bd. ISBN 0-919940-02-1 pa.

1. European War, 1914-1918—Personal narratives, Canadian. 2. European War,
1914-1918—Canada. 3. Canada—Social conditions. I. Read, Daphne. II. Hann,
Russell.

D640.G742   940.3`71   C76-017173-4

Design by Cathy Carroll
Cover Design by Cathy Hobart
Photographs from the James Collection, courtesy of
the City Hall Archives, Toronto
Typeset by Dumont Press Graphix and the members of Victor Hugo Assembly
Printed and bound in Canada
New Hogtown Press receives financial assistance from the Ontario Arts Council

CONTENTS

PREFACE

The War and Canadian Society Project began its work in the summer of 1974 under the Opportunities for Youth Programme sponsored by the federal government. Our goal was to produce an oral history of World War I which illustrated the impact of the war on Canadian society from the viewpoint of those Canadians whose voices are seldom heard in traditional historical writing. We felt that it would be possible to construct a richer portrait of this dramatic period of social change from taped interviews with ordinary Canadians than one that could be composed from more conventional research.

World War I suggested itself as a topic for a number of reasons. There are few who would deny that the war was a watershed in Canadian history. In addition to involving Canadians in a massive, costly, and bloody international conflict for the first time, the war also spurred industrial concentration and urban growth. While the genesis of Canadian industrial society lies in a period long before the war, the intensity of the changes in the war years rendered much of the common experience of early industrialization sharply discontinuous with the new ways adopted in the stress of wartime. The forces stirred by the war determined the particular character of the modern society that would emerge in the 1920s. Those who had experienced these rapid changes at formative times in their lives naturally possessed vivid insights into the complex of events that constituted the war experience. By 1974 the war had been over for more than half a century. Survivors with first-hand memories were dwindling. No one seemed interested in recapturing their reminiscences about World War I. The fact that most of the people who had experienced the war were relatively advanced in age made it imperative to begin work as quickly as possible.

The summer's work resulted in the preservation of more than 200 taped interviews which ranged in length from one hour to four hours and covered a wide variety of themes. While the war was the primary focus, the interviews dealt with many aspects of the first two decades of the twentieth century that had little connection to the Great War. Despite interviewing only in Toronto, we still managed to find in that former bastion of English Canadianism a surprisingly diverse group of older Canadians eager to talk with us about their experiences. While we did not intend to assemble a scientific sample of Canadian society at the time of World War I, the group of people recorded on tape is generally representative of the spectrum of ethnic and regional identities that made up English Canada in 1914. This book contains edited transcripts of the interviews which we thought best described the way ordinary Canadians' lives intersected with the broader historical forces at work. By prior agreement with the interviewees, their names have been changed to guarantee the privacy of the memories they readily shared with us; in the selection of pseudonyms, however, every attempt was made to preserve the ethnicity and general character of the real names. The entire collection of tapes has been deposited in the Sound Division of the Public Archives of Canada and is available to all interested researchers.

A project of this kind could only have succeeded with the goodwill and efforts of many people. Without the existence of the Opportunities for Youth Programme, a needless and lonely casualty of the Liberal government's war on inflation, our work could not have taken place. To the many people who worked for that programme we offer our most profound thanks. Project supervisor Bob McArthur of the Toronto office of OFY not only took a genuine interest in our work, but also provided much generous assistance and encouragement which helped make possible the publication of this book. Leo LaClare and Richard Lochead of the Sound Division of the Public Archives of Canada supplied blank tape cassettes and later a substantial grant that enabled one of the project members to attend the Annual Conference of Oral Historians in St. John's, Newfoundland. They were both always ready to advise us in a variety of areas. Jill Conway was an early and steadfast friend to the project. She took time from her many other responsibilities to support the initial application of the project and shared with us her knowledge of the role of women during the war. She also arranged for the project's University of Toronto office. Senator Eugene Forsey and Michael Cross also generously supported the initial application. Richard Lee, Bill Courtede, Craig Heron, David Millar, Wayne Roberts, Peter Warrian, Desmond Morton, and Michael Bliss were kind enough to share their research and methodological insights with project members in a series of short presentations. Krys Dobrowolski of New Hogtown Press assisted the project in many ways. Ray Sonen of CFRB and Bruce Smith of CBC Radio in Toronto provided us with the much-needed publicity that enabled us to make contact with many people in the Toronto area who had something to tell about the Great War.

Finally, we would like to thank all those who allowed us to interview them and who gave so freely of their memories. Their patience and good humour in the face of sometimes blunt and often naive questions put us at our ease and helped direct us to what was most important when our formal training failed us. This document which we compiled with them augments the historical record in important respects. We dedicate this book to all those who warmly welcomed us as guests from a different generation and hope that it may suggest to the reader other dimensions of Canadian history that can only be recovered through sympathetic dialogue with those who have lived it.

Gus Richardson

CHAPTER ONE

INTRODUCTION[1]

New attempts to 'bring back ordinary working people from their long exile on the margins of Canadian history' are being made with increasing frequency.[2] The sources for such history in Canada and elsewhere have generally been external to the subjects lived experience until quite recently. Historians interested in dealing with popular experience have based their work on research in those materials that have survived to the present, consisting largely of statistics collected by social investigators and government agencies, reports from the daily press, the records of formal organizations and popular political parties, the papers of popular leaders, and the reflections and observations of interested onlookers. The histories written from such materials have helped to cast light into some of the murkier corners of past societies and have radically altered general conceptions of the role of ordinary people in history.

However, no matter how dedicated the historian is to the task of exploring popular history through such sources, he encounters many difficulties that originate in the nature of the evidence itself. For instance, the popular leaders' papers which have survived provide the basis for most of our knowledge of popular political activity; unfortunately, they have generated biographies which celebrate the accomplishments of the leader more frequently than studies of the nature of their popular support. Other historians have seen in census data and other statistics a more democratic kind of source by which to avoid the elitist bias that plagues the student of leadership. Statistics, it is claimed, level out the platforms from which Great Men addressed the masses and direct the

9

researcher's attention to the common concerns of ordinary people. However, too often their finished work resembles a hollow commentary on aggregate patterns of mating, residence, and consumption and ignores the complex textures of everyday life and the deeper cultural meanings of the experiences described.[3]

Despite the variety of research into popular history that has been undertaken, for the most part, the people themselves remain silent. Only infrequently do we hear the authentic voice of a humble actor describing in his own words his role in and his perceptions of history. Few historians have ventured into the broad and uncharted regions of everyday life where the best witnesses are the participants themselves. Where there are no surviving witnesses, it is understandable that historians should concentrate on data that describes the common life of the community.[4] This strategy often leads to the notion that history happens *to* the bulk of the populations and drastically underestimates the contributions of the ordinary members of the community. Those in the ranks who became history's victims were rarely formless putty in the hands of the powerful. Even when the protests of the powerless failed most completely, they constantly forced the dominant to modify their most cherished schemes. Most of the time they led a highly autonomous existence and the best evidence as to the independent nature of their lived experience is undoubtedly their own testimony.

As Raymond Williams has demonstrated, the careful study of aspects of everyday life, including the spoken language, leads to significant discoveries about the nature of the larger society:

We find here [in the realm of lived experience] a particular sense of life, a particular community of experience hardly needing expression, through which the characteristics of our way of life ... are in some way passed, giving them a particular and characteristic colour. We are usually most aware of this when we notice the contrasts between generations, who never talk quite 'the same language,' or when we read an account of our lives by someone from outside the community, or watch the small difference in style, of speech or behaviour, in someone who has learned our ways yet was not bred in them. Almost any formal description would be too crude to express this nevertheless quite distinct sense of a particular and native style. And if this is so, in a way of life we know intimately, it will surely be so when we ourselves are in the position of the visitor, the learner, the guest from a different generation: the position, in fact that we are all in when we study any past period. Though it can be turned to trivial account, the fact of such a characteristic is neither trivial nor marginal: it feels quite central.[5]

Folklorists, anthropologists, and other social scientists have always considered information gathered from participants central to any effort to learn about popular customs and practices. They have long considered it part of their normal scholarly endeavour to collect and transcribe spoken testimony and have developed a sophisticated methodology for dealing with oral evidence. Unfortunately, historians have been insulated from this growing sophistication in dealing with oral evidence. The stress on documentation that dominated the early years of the development of history as a scholarly discipline led historians away from the common people whose thoughts and aspirations were seldom recorded. Businessmen, politicians, and men of ideas who produced documentary evidence as an integral part of their daily activity became the natural subjects for the historian.

It is instructive that historians coined the expression 'oral history' and developed it as a new technique for gathering evidence only at that time when the documentary productivity of the historians' traditional subjects seemed to be on the wane. Historians involved in the first collecting, specifically labelled oral history in the United States, were motivated by their sense that political and business leaders in the twentieth century tended to produce far less evidence in the form of introspective diaries and revealing letters than had the major nineteenth century figures. The first oral historians ignored the methodology developed by other disciplines concerned with the oral tradition and used the technological advances in convenient tape-recording equipment after World War II to produce the same kind of evidence that their traditional subjects had hitherto provided in writing. The major difference between traditional documentary evidence and the new oral evidence produced by major figures lay in the fact that the historian conducted the oral interview. Historians who have conducted such interviews claim that important new facts are elicited by the tough questioning of the experienced interviewer.[6] However, some recent experience would seem to undercut this claim. The one thing that Richard Nixon's major experiment in oral history did prove conclusively was that politicians are far more candid in the absence of court historians.

The most recent work in oral history has moved away from the transcription of the reminiscences as a primary aim and has been more informed by the methodological sophistication developed in the other social sciences concerned with the oral tradition. More fully exploited than in interviewing various kinds of leaders, oral history can help us broaden our sketchy knowledge of many ill-defined areas of our past. The first tentative steps to use oral sources in the writing of a new kind of history have begun to appear.[7] This introduction will attempt to place oral history in a larger context by describing and analysing historically the various approaches to the oral tradition in Canada and by examining the work of oral historians which influenced our own work in gathering and arranging our materials on the impact of the Great War on Canadian society.

I

In Canada the oral tradition has been less extensively explored than in other countries where ethnic homogeneity allowed investigators to examine popular culture more easily. Because of the conquest of New France in the eighteenth century and settlement and immigration patterns in the nineteenth century, Canadians engaged in the creation of a national cultural tradition could not find one particular folk culture to serve as its foundation. Even in English Canada a stubborn ethnic heterogeneity prevailed. It is small wonder that the guardians of our cultural tradition chose to ignore the astounding array of dialects, customs, and usages of the cultural mosaic and decided instead to emulate the concerns and style of English high culture.[8] To the historian who is now undertaking to study the strange and complex reality of everyday life in nineteenth century Canada, the standard tools of Canadian social and cultural analysis offer little that will enable him to progress beyond simple description to an understanding of the integral role that this 'invisible culture' has played in our national life. Canadian scholarship is only beginning to recover the sense of hearing that led a handful of nineteenth century figures to record and transcribe the few popular voices that speak to twentieth century observers from the midst of the crowd. In the time since these pioneer efforts, there have been few careful listeners in the ranks of Canadian men of letters. It has been a long and tortured process by which we have once again found it both possible and fruitful to 'listen to the inarticulate' through the techniques of oral history.

Canadian attitudes toward the oral tradition emerged from the origin of Canadian culture in European society. Before the nineteenth century the guardians of high culture in Western Europe seldom acknowledged the popular origins of the great works and sacred writings over which they watched.[9] Their scholarship served the interests of the dominant in their society and they continually sought to efface and emasculate popular traditions that clashed with their teachings. In the anonymous world of the common people, the oral tradition flourished without the services of scribes and teachers. When scholars and teachers did begin to take an interest in the education of the common people, they did so with reference to a highly restricted curriculum of approved writings. Popular values which came into conflict with such teachings were denounced as blasphemous. However, until the disruptions of the late eighteenth and early nineteenth centuries, popular values and speech did not often inspire fear in the powerful and could be safely ignored.[10]

The turmoil of the nineteenth century sparked a new interest in popular traditions. As the foundation on which the new nation states of Western Europe were being built, folk traits became an important field of study for those who spearheaded the rebellion against traditional political authority. In the search for the true voice of the pople, enthusiasts discovered writers and poets of humble origins whose familiarity with dialects and traditional speech patterns formed much of their appeal. Faithfully rendered popular speech patterns permeated the periodical press and, as the century wore on, the literary theories of realism and naturalism brought the speech of the people into the new novels which purported to reflect the real world. By the end of the century the same impulse had led folklorists to make the first efforts to record and collect popular stories, customs, and beliefs on an organized scholarly basis. Their new anthropological approach to cultural activity discovered in the stuff of everyday life artifacts worthy of loving preservation and careful scholarly analysis. Throughout the nineteenth century popular cultural forms won a new respectability as the basis for new kinds of political organization and new styles in art and literature.[11]

The sweeping changes wrought by industrial capitalism provided another source of interest in the words spoken by ordinary people. In addition to their picturesque speech and customs, the new working classes were also the best informants on the deprivations they suffered under the new industrial order. As industrial abuses became more acute, reformers summoned those who suffered to testify and record their experiences for posterity. The government commission and the parliamentary committee were places where many hitherto unheard voices were first listened to and recorded. In Canada, the Royal Commission on the Relations of Labor and Capital of 1889 proved a sympathetic forum for the victims of some of the grisliest abuses of Canadian industrialization to tell their tales of woe. When governments were not interested in the plight of the powerless, journalistic investigators (often called Commissioners in the latter half of the nineteenth century) sought them out and faithfully recorded their testimony. Sympathetic reporters, such as Henry Mayhew in England and Phillips Thompson in Canada, compiled moving accounts of the suffering that accompanied the shock of industrialization. These accounts owed much of their vividness to their ability to capture the genuine tone of their informants' speech patterns. The material that they recorded provides contemporary social historians with a valuable source of knowledge about the period.[12]

However, neither testimony about the horrors of industrial capitalism nor research into romantic folk customs precisely captured the complex quality of working class life. Most nineteenth century workers regarded themselves neither as tragic victims nor as charming exemplars of folk culture. With the general rise in literacy in the course of the century, many of the newly literate and more confidently articulate left behind a record which provides us with a quite different picture. When given a free hand to record their own feelings about their lives, they used their newly developed writing skills to produce autobiographies that detail the richness of their experience and their stubborn determination and independence before the powerful of their society.[13] The growth of unions and other protective associations provided public forums where these skills could be used. The records, newspapers, and journals associated with such movements created vehicles for the recorded articulation of a more general discontent with the social order.

The wholesale rise in literacy in the course of the nineteenth century added new dimensions to the popular oral tradition which previously could only be recorded by outsiders. A more widespread literacy gave rise to a body of popular published material which grew from the living community. In villages and towns local poets produced works with an intimate connection to the oral traditions of the locale while fulfilling some of the functions of the minstrels of a preliterate age. The new print media were adapted by the formerly inarticulate to record and preserve older cultural forms.[14] However, industrial capitalism also spread its control over the literary world, transforming cultural enterprise into business enterprise. As the mass of the population became literate, it was transformed from a forum of participants into a reading public and a market of consumers. The growth of widely circulated periodicals initiated an important change in the cultural relations of industrial society. As moulders of opinion, journals with wide circulation came to view their readers as relatively passive clay to be shaped by the persuasive arts of the publicist. The contexts for popular self-expression shrank drastically as the circulation of the media grew.[15]

As mass circulation periodicals grew in number there were some notable attempts to use popular speech patterns and dialects as the basis for humour and satire. Following British examples, newspapers in large American cities seized on the reporting of the police court as a source of humorous columns. These satirical commentaries on low court proceedings relied on a faithful rendition of various ethnic and regional speech patterns as a source of humour. This practice helped establish phonetically rendered dialect humour as a staple of American humorists throughout the nineteenth century.[16] In Canada the story is similar. In fact, T.C. Haliburton's Sam Slick was in many ways the same stock comic character who was found everywhere in the American press following the initial appearance of Seba Smith's Jack Downing letters in the Portland *Courier* in January 1830.[17] In the world of Toronto journalism in the latter half of the nineteenth century the columns of John Ross Robertson's *Telegraph* which covered the police courts were the earliest place where a dialect-based humour was found.[18] Other papers followed suit and in the 1870s and 1880s the columns of many Toronto and Ontario papers were filled with the regular contributions of such funnymen as Jimuel Briggs (Phillips Thompson), Sandy McSneshin, and the Sun-skit urchin. The very fabric of the puns, conundrums, and repartees that comprised their humorous writings and lectures was a sense of the richness and variety of Canadian dialects and the hidden meanings embedded in the way a particular speaker turned a phrase.[19]

While the contributions of popular humorists to the daily press were frequent and widely read, Canadian dialect humour reached perhaps its highest form in *The Grip*, a Toronto weekly composed of humour and cartoons and edited by its chief cartoonist, John Wilson Bengough from 1873 until 1892. Bengough was, like his idol Charles Dickens, trained in shorthand reporting as a young journalist. This may explain his uncanny ability to render a variety of ethnic and regional speech patterns so faithfully. He frequently ran a column entitled 'Talk of the Street' which was the simple record of bits and snatches of speech overheard on a busy Toronto street corner.[20] Bengough also brought to *The Grip* a large group of writers with similar interests. The most notable of these was Phillips Thompson who became a constant contributor in the late 1880s and eventually became editor of the publication after Bengough left in 1892. The range of English Canadian dialects offered a fertile field to the Canadian humourist and Thompson was interested in the assumptions and outlooks that were implicit in the spoken language. In the course of an imaginary 1891 *Grip* forum on the question of 'English as She Is Spoke,' Thompson summoned four expert commentators. Chomondeley Perkins, a wheezing English emigré, anxious to present himself as ill at ease in 'this blawsted coloney,' claimed that only the English aristocracy spoke proper English. This claim was hotly contested by Mr. 'Arry 'Olborne, late of 'Lunnon,' and Mr. Timothy Milligan, late of Dublin, who claimed respectively that the true sites of the best spoken English were ''Amstead 'Eath' and 'Dublin, the home of min av shuparior intelligence and janius.' The final contributor to the colloquium, Isaac Brock Secord, a loyal Canadian-born school teacher from Mephramagog Township, disagreed with everyone, claiming the highest honours for his own carefully tutored students: 'You bet, there ain't no flies on young Canadians when it comes to pronouncing correct.'[21] As the *Grip* humorists constantly demonstrated, the spoken language of Victorian Canada teemed with hidden meanings that could easily be turned to satirical purposes.

By the turn of the century the style that *Grip* had represented in Canadian journalism was on the wane. Little by little, dialect humour disappeared from the daily press to the extent that in 1894 Phillips Thompson composed a lament on 'The Decline of Dialect' ('Each quaint rustic simile/ Sonn will all forgotten by/ An' the speech in which i've sung/ Be a dead unspoken tongue....')[22] The influx of university-trained reporters into the profession of journalism further strenghtened this trend. The humour that replaced that of the local funnyman came to the newspaper as syndicated features, often already set up as boilerplate: it created nationally recognizable stereotypes rather than reflecting local usage. The slang that was found in the newly segregated sports pages consisted of expressions newly coined by writers rather than carefully preserved popular speech patterns.[23] In many ways they correspond to the rationalization that was taking place in every other area of North American business and professional life which Robert Wiebe has termed 'the search for order.'[24]

However, it is also evident that the genesis of a new standard English was also the outcome of a particular political and social programme. The superiority of the King's English was long and loudly promoted by a series of commentators on Canadian English. The Canadian version that they heard in the street and read in the daily press was to them a distressingly unfit language for a people loyal to Britain and destined for imperial service to speak. Most commentators on Canadian English linked corruptions that were slipping into the language with American influences. In 1884, the loyalist novelist William Kirby looked forward to the day when it would be possible to 'get rid of the foul foreign ingredient that has been imported into the Toronto press,' ending the liberties taken by these 'Bohemians' with the Queen's English and the sarcasm they constantly heaped on truly loyal Canadians.[25] An earlier critic, Reverend A.C. Geikie, had pointed out the many ways in which 'lawless and vulgar' American innovations were adopted by Canadians in 1857: 'New words are coined for ourselves by a process similar to that which calls them into being in the neighbouring states; still more, they are imported by travellers, daily circulated by American newspapers, and eagerly incorporated into the language of our provincial press.' He called for educated men, common school teachers and newspaper writers to stand on guard against 'the corrupt dialect growing up amongst our population' so that the Canadian experience would not 'produce a language as unlike our mother tongue as the Negro patua, or the Chinese pigeon English.'[26] Others who surveyed the state of the Canadian language later on made similar warnings about creeping Americanisms: Andrew MacPhail, searching among the various tendencies in Canadian English for the elements of a truly Canadian language even suggested the general adoption of the soft vowels of the Negro dialect of the Windsor area as an alternative to the unsavoury American tendency of most other English Canadians to flatten their vowels.[27]

In the struggle to purify Canadian English, such charity was rare. In general, most observers felt that any native Canadian innovation was a corruption of the imperial language to be guarded against. When Arnold Haultain made an excursion into the Ontario countryside in 1903 he made the following observation:

It is not a little strange how in this English colony English customs provoke a state. Among all but the educated and travelled classes in Canada an Englishman is a foreigner. His speech is a matter of merriment, his apparel a matter of comment, but smacking rather of scoff and scorn.... I am not ... speaking of the upper and Anglified classes of the larger towns.... But certainly among the populace American habits, customs, and manners prevail. Canadian slang is American slang. Proper nomenclature and phraseology are American. The college ground is a 'campus,' the local drill hall is the 'armories,' vans are 'expresses'; one never makes haste, one 'hurries up'; trains are never punctual, they are 'on time'; people 'ride in rigs,' not drive in carriages. In the open spaces of cities are seen going on in summer, games of 'ball'—namely baseball—a game which draws its thousands, while cricket barely draws its scores. Newsboys offer you papers priced a 'nickel.'

Haultain claimed that there was a growing and influential number of Canadians who looked to English usages for their inspiration and he hoped that they would be able to encourage an admiration for correctly spoken English. A contemporary of Haultain, the Canadian historian George M. Wrong, also turned a deaf ear on Canadian English. In preparing for his teaching career at the University of Toronto he took voice lessons from an actor lest the stubborn traces of 'provincial nasalism' betray the anglified refinement suggested by his penchant for snuff, spats, and a tortoise-shell pince-nez.[28] While such cultural anglophilia did not succeed in making cricket our national sport, its influence was considerable in wiping out local colour and inculcating a nervous respect among educated Canadians for correct usage and loyal spelling. The menace of American influences waned in the early twentieth century when the continuing waves of non-English-speaking immigrants aroused Anglo-Saxon fears that the Canada of the future would be 'the Babel of nations.' A generation of English-Canadian volunteers, working through such institutions of *kulturkampf* as Frontier College, the YMCA, and church organizations, feverishly threw itself into the project of engendering respect for Canadian institutions among the foreign-born by teaching them English and effacing the 'foreignisms' that coloured their speech.[29]

Throughout the formative years of English-Canadian culture, the genteel tradition in arts and letters emerged not only as an artistic style which emphasized respect for proprieties, but also as a strategy in the struggle for imperial homogeneity. This conservative cultural outlook, reinforced by political and social reaction, resisted attempts to displace it much more stubbornly than did the defenders of the American genteel tradition which included important figures who were often political radicals.[30] When the new generation of American writers grew impatient with the narrowness and sterility of the genteel tradition in the early twentieth century, they began a search for the other voices upon which to base an alternate tradition in the arts and letters. By the early 1920s great strides had been made in unearthing the basic materials of the American oral tradition. Constance Rourke, a major figure in this effort, suggested that the future American writer would be able to 'steep himself in the gathered light' of this tradition and would rediscover a 'relationship with the many streams of native character and feeling.'[31] This rediscovery of popular roots provided the source for many new directions in American arts and letters in subsequent decades.[32] In Canada the long history of imperial disdain for popular traditions and fear of foreign linguistic and political subversion made it more difficult for those Canadians uncomfortable with the genteel tradition to begin a search for the native grounds on which to found a distinctively Canadian tradition in the arts and letters. For instance, one Canadian critic who was well equipped for the task was W.A. Deacon. In the 1920s, as a disciple of Walt Whitman before his consecration by 'the literary archbishops,' he attacked the 'Canada-faking' of one Canadian novelist whose notion of a typical Canadian locale was virgin wilderness. However, in his only work on popular traditions, *The Four Jameses*, Deacon was unable to transcend the imperial outlook. While he wrote briefly and with sympathy of the host of minor traditions in Canadian culture, he devoted the book to a Menckenesque satire on four absurdly minor poets whom he had rescued from a well deserved obscurity.[33] Contemporary critics interested in the exploration of popular Canadian traditions make the revealing distinction between the 'more important... tory tradition' and the 'vulgar tradition' of 'all our beautiful failed heroes.'[34] In Canadian arts and letters those who sought to discover the elements of a national tradition through patient listening have continually foundered on the rocks of the imperial tradition.

One must look beyond the world of Canadian *belles lettres* to discover the first intellectual interest in the traditions embedded in the spoken tongue. The first Canadian scholars in the new academic disciplines in the social sciences relied upon careful observation and recording of oral materials. Interest in ethnology and folklore fostered widespread exploration into the realm of folk customs and oral traditions. The pioneers in this area were largely gifted amateurs and popular writers outside the university community.[35] Their substantial work in carefully recording certain parts of the oral record centered chiefly on the folk customs, tales, and music of the most primitive peoples of Canada. The first and most 'exotic' to undergo anthropological examination were Indians and French Canadians.[36] Gradually other peoples were studied as professional anthropologists took over the work of the amateur and the popularizer. Franz Boas sponsored field work among the Northwest Coastal Indians and the Royal Ontario Museum, under David Boyle, and the National Museum, primarily under the direction of Marius Barbeau, organized folklore sections and sponsored research.[37] Museums have been the major focus for most Canadian folklore studies, and their archeological orientation has been highly influential in forming approaches to the study of the oral tradition.[38] They have continued to be interested in archaic survivals rather than the history of the relatively recent past. While areas such as the Maritimes with its quaint bluenose magic, the West with its multitudes of recent immigrants from the last agrarian areas of Europe, and even Northern Ontario have joined French Canadians and Indian peoples as worthy of investigation by Canadian folklorists, south central Ontario remains a region relatively untouched.[39] When it has been studied, folklorists have ignored the major themes of urbanization and industrialization, preferring to search out the isolated and atypical community or those areas described by Edith Fowke as 'far enough from the main industrial centres to have developed slowly.'[40] Despite the growing sophistication of international folklore scholarship, Canadian folklore studies remain wedded to the relatively simple search for and classification of archetypes.[41] While contemporary notions of Canada as a multi-cultural society have reinvigorated the study of various primitive folk characteristics, unfortunately the folklorists' academic tasks in serving such a society remain relatively uncomplicated consisting largely of the isolation and preservation of the components of our multiple ethnic identities.[42] The result has been a failure to show how these various identities are actively used as resources in a modern industrial society.[43]

As members of a tiny academic profession which has seldom enjoyed even the prestige of a distinct academic department in the Canadian university, folklorists hardly bear the major responsibility for this failure. In fact, the more richly endowed disciplines in Canadian social science have contributed to the understanding of the role of folk culture in modern society. The work of the anthropologist Horace Miner and the Chicago-trained sociologist Everett Hughes was partly inspired by the rich body of folklore research undertaken by Marius Barbeau and others at the National Museum.[44] However, they brought to their studies of French Canada a sterile, unilinear theory of history which focused on the stages of social development.[45] Both Miner and Hughes sought to demonstrate the features of modernization in French Canadian society and used their oral material as evidence of the gradual transition from the stubborn conservative ways of a French agrarian way of life to an urban, anglicized society. In their work, modernization appeared to transform gradually the old rural customs, superstitions, and speech patterns. The preoccupation with transition gives their studies a simplified and ahistorical view of the role of culture in society: culture, however, is not an artifact which evaporates in the natural process of modernization.[46] As one student of eighteenth century British society has shown, traditional customs were the 'normative weapons' of the people in their struggle against the powerful; these customs were often 'forcibly undermined' by men of property and seldom fell into disuse as a 'natural' process.[47] The reliance on modernization theory as a means of understanding social development leads away from an examination of the oral tradition as a realm of inquiry relevant to modern social history.[48] Canadian social science has failed to suggest directions in oral research that transcend the collection and classification of primitive survivals and the most basic study of the variation of these forms over time.

Canadian historians have been even less innovative. The grandly conceived 'staples approach' of Innis did not lavish much effort on the development of communities or identities in Canadian history.[49] The uneven social and cultural remnants of the old national history have recently been bound together as a mosaic of 'limited identities.' While such an approach encourages oral research into the various identities, it does not step beyond the parameters already staked out by Canadian folklorists.[50] A Canadian social history that could suggest new perspectives for oral research is still in its infancy and interest in oral sources is even less developed. Only a short time ago Great Men still frolicked merrily through the pages of Canadian history and ordinary people played peripheral roles in their 'lives and times.' Crowds of common people usually filled the function of a Greek chorus, generally roaring approval at the *bon mots* and spell-binding oratory of the Great Man, or, less often, grumbling an undirected discontent when times were hard. When an impudent member of the audience had the boldness to heckle or shout abuse, his ill manners were usually turned aside by cleverly devised repartee.[51]

Recently the contours of a more serious examination of the popular role in Canadian history have begun to appear.[52] In this new history, the cultural world of ordinary people is seen as a complex realm which sympathetic scholars have studied with great profit. As anthropologist Sidney Mintz has demonstrated, culture is not simply a lifeless 'collection of habits, superstitions and artifacts,' but rather a resource that is used by people.[53] This anthropological viewpoint has made historians aware of the analytical potential of oral materials in approaching the history of ordinary Canadians.[54]

II

The growing body of recent work which is described as oral history traces its concern with the oral tradition to the documentary impulse of the 1930s rather than to ongoing work in folklore or anthropology. Flourishing under the patronage of the state throughout Europe and North America, the documentary tradition left its most important legacy for contemporary North American oral historians in the achievements of the Federal Writers' Project which functioned from 1935 to 1943 as a branch of the Works Projects Administration of Franklin D. Roosevelt's New Deal. Confronted with an army of unemployed that included artists and writers, as well as factory workers, New Deal administrators succeeded in finding funds to support the arts and to encourage creative activity which had a public involvement. The members of the Writers' Project produced a wide variety of imaginative material which included many efforts to record and collect oral materials, both as folk history and as models for artistic expression.[55] To some extent, this new enthusiasm for 'worker narrative and other vernacular literature' emerged from the Left's efforts to find and give a voice to revolutionary working class aspirations.[56] The various projects sponsored by the WPA continued to support the collection of such material without the cogency of left politics. An important focus of such collection was the American South. Efforts to depict the quality of southern life through the recording of oral history resulted in the 1939 collection, *These are Our Lives*, which presented the oral record as short stories. Taken together these stories constitute one of the first attempts to depict the social life of a region on the basis of oral sources.[57]

The most important single bequest of the WPA programmes to modern oral history was the collection of slave narratives. A brief but popular selection from these narratives, *Lay My Burden Down: A Folk History of Slavery*, was compiled in 1945 by the Project's folklore editor, Benjamin A. Botkin. More recently historians of slavery have used the newly published complete version extensively.[58] The ten thousand pages of narratives, despite the fact that they were often gathered by overtly racist fieldworkers, provided a remarkable testimony to the abilities of the aged to produce coherent life histories under the most difficult of conditions. The recent historical treatments of slave culture would be immeasurably poorer without them.[59] Unfortunately, the Writers' Project fell victim to changed spending priories in the early years of World War II and the bulk of the time-consuming research into popular traditions lapsed. The Left followed the lead of the state, shelving its interest in worker narrative and putting its energy into the war against fascism. In the economic boom that followed World War II in North America there were few initiatives to renew public programmes to aid beleaguered writers. In the years of the Cold War most of the energies of the Left were expended in defending itself against prosecution and there was little opportunity to cultivate a taste for vernacular literature.[60] As a result there was a long hiatus in the collection of oral history dealing with the lives of ordinary people.

In the 1960s efforts to discover what the world looked like 'from the bottom up' led social historians back to the oral tradition.[61] While many of the new oral historians took their cue from the work begun in the 1930s, they were not as well versed in the methodology of the oral tradition as the pioneers they emulated.[62] Indeed, much of the new collections relied on a methodology which was in some ways diametrically opposed to that which informed collecting under the Writers' Projects. The influential Oral History Research Office set up at Columbia in 1948 by Allan Nevins inspired new collectors to pursue a different kind of data. Nevins believed that the biographers of future Great Men would have a difficult time reconstructing careers that were increasingly conducted by telephone and air travel; the bulky correspondence and reflective diaries which had made it possible to write scintillating biographies of the prominent nineteenth century figures were no longer a part of the lives of modern Great Men. Nevins proposed to offer these titans of our time the opportunity to record on tape the inner reflections that they had not had time to set down on paper. With these records, the biographers of the future would have a surer guide to the past than if they tried to sift through the tons of uninformative paper invariably left by these Great Men to line the shelves of archives.[63]

Those who worked on the Columbia project quickly discovered that they needed an interview technique radically different from that used by folklorists or anthropologists. With recalcitrant subjects who usually insisted on complicated restrictions, the interview usually developed into a type of cross-examination or a narrow search for particular facts. The relationship which this type of interview engendered can be measured by examining one popular manual on oral history which contains a section on ethics dealing primarily with liability under the libel and slander laws.[64] At their worst, programmes inspired by the Columbia model divert the meagre resources available for oral history away from work with those who have valuable stories which they would freely tell to projects treating the lives and times of retired, reticent politicians who have had many

other opportunities to place their thoughts in the historical record.[65]

The interview based on the Columbia model challenges the subject while it gleans information. While such cross-examination would be confusing to most of the people the social historian would choose to interview, work in some areas of social history has proved that the Columbia interview technique can be effective. In the delineation of radical political or labour movements where the obscurity of failure or the rancour of old antagonisms have conspired to leave a slender or contradictory written record, the oral historian has been able to uncover a vast array of data which renders the story more comprehensible.[66] In other areas, the written record is simply deliberately misleading so that the participant is a more accurate source than the most carefully compiled statistics. For example, living informants have helped to cut through the euphemistic descriptions in the official military reports of the British army during World War I in which mutinies among labour companies were recorded for posterity as 'disturbances' and where the 'drastic measures' employed to quell these disturbances included firing upon and killing mutineers.[67] In other cases, where the documentary sources suggest the bare outlines of an event, oral sources have been used to fill in important detail. The dramatic contours of an early twentieth century vigilante episode in Texas were vividly reconstructed by Lawrence Goodwyn who augmented the fragmentary written record with material gathered through interviews with participants.[68] Used imaginatively, such oral history techniques can unearth new evidence which the social historian cannot find in the surviving record.

A second major variant of oral history which derives its methodology from the work done in the 1930s and which is enjoying a new vogue is the life history. Compiled from the oral reminiscences of the subject who is guided by a sympathetic collaborator, life histories do not attempt to fill in the uncertain or non-existent data of a particular area of historical research. Instead, the subject and his collaborator attempt to piece together the subject's autobiography. Efforts are made to incorporate into a coherent and revealing narrative the elements of an essentially oral culture.[69] One of the best recent examples of the genre is a life history compiled by Theodore Rosengarten, *All God's Dangers: The Life of Nate Shaw*. Shaw, a black Alabama sharecropper, told his story at the age of eighty-five, shortly before his death. This dramatic narrative provided a remarkably rich and detailed picture of the social and cultural world of an agrarian community in the American South. As a member of the Alabama Sharecroppers Union, Shaw joined in armed resistance to eviction proceedings being carried out against a neighbour in 1932. He was arrested and spent the next thirteen years in prison. *All God's Dangers* combines two elements which make it an excellent life history: it provides a rich sense of the mental processes and oral expression of a typical, non-literate sharecropper whose story could be told only in this way, and it offers a highly interesting story. Few other life histories combine these two almost contradictory elements so well. Often, the most typical subjects are neither the most interesting nor the best narrators; the best narrators often prove to be highly atypical. A series of recently published Canadian life histories conducted by Rolf Knight provide important information on aspects of the social history of the Canadian west coast, but unfortunately lack both the drama and the rich picture of community life that Shaw was able to communicate.[70] Perhaps the weakest aspect of the life history as a form of social history is that the best ones tend to originate from agrarian settings where the oral historical finds an ally in cultural patterns which encourage narrative by community patriarchs. Few North American life histories reflect the predominantly industrial society in which we live as central themes. While Norwegian researchers have made imaginative attempts to record the life histories of the first generation of industrial workers in that country, North Americans have largely remained content to search for their subjects in rural settings.[71]

A recently published work by Peter Friedlander, *The Emergence of a UAW Local, 1936-1939: A Study in Class and Culture*, has brought certain of the elements of the life history to bear on the history of modern industrial society, combining them with techniques derived from the Columbia model to produce a quite different kind of oral history. Instead of relying on the narrative powers of Edmund Kord, a former executive officer of the union local, Friedlander chose to engage in a 'critical dialogue' in which Kord was constantly challenged when he offered unconscious or casual interpretations and his 'extensive narrative' was interrupted by the 'intensive' questioning of his collaborator. While the method does not produce anything in the way of an authentic narrative, it does demonstrate that oral history is a most trustworthy method that can produce significant data on 'aspects of social life that never leave sufficent traces in documents....'[72] It also shows the wide gap between oral historians who use the memories of union organizers to answer important questions and those who have uncritically offered organizers' reminiscences as the highest form of oral history.[73] The texture of 'extensive narrative' often provides important clues to the undocumented aspects of social life especially when one moves from leadership figures to the rank and file, the participants rather than the leaders.

The works of oral history that have most influenced our approach have combined the methods of the life history narrative and the search for unrecorded facts. In the examination of a general social phenomenon like the Great War, it was necessary to find many informants to speak on various aspects of wartime experience; even the most critical dialogue with a single trusted informant whose memory was keen and comprehensive could not provide persuasive evidence of the Great War's impact. Instead, we followed the example of those oral historians who have used a number of different informants to compile a general portrait. The popular books by Studs Terkel, *Hard Times* and *Working*, suggested that by careful arrangement and instructive juxtaposition, narrative materials could create their own critical dialogue. However, the interviewing techniques described by another popular collector, Barry Broadfoot, in his oral histories, *Ten Lost Years, 1929-1939: Memories of Canadians who Survived the Depression* and *Six War Years* seemed excessively uncritical: 'an interview would begin with the man or the woman laughing off the depression, saying they could not remember anything—and then suddenly coming up with a hell of a story....'[74] While we did not wish to approach our subjects as if we were conducting a cross-examination, the life history technique still required the active participation of an interviewer, familiar with the broad themes to be explored and able to draw the subjects into the areas of experience which they shared with other interview subjects. We combined approaches which consider oral history as a source both of new kinds of historical information to augment the traditional record and suggestive data on the lived and spoken experience of a particular time and place. The distinction made by Terkel in his modest description of *Hard Times* as a 'memory book, rather than one of hard fact' was a false one.[75] The oral record adds new dimensions to hard data and when it makes possible the gauging of popular attitudes, it becomes something more than quaint reminiscences which impart only a vague sense of the flavour of an era.

An approach which incorporates these two basic orientations to the oral record has resulted in the publication of oral history which is neither obsessed with provable facts nor overly reliant on one remarkable narrator.[76] One of the most fruitful programmes of oral history research has grown up around the History Workshop of Oxford University's Ruskin College. The fruits of this research have served as the basis for a number of important articles in the *History Workshop Journal* as well as two published volumes of a projected multi-volume series of studies of village life and labour in late nineteenth and early twentieth century England.[77] The most ambitious and synthetic piece of oral history to appear to date is Paul Thompson's *The Edwardians: The Remaking of English Society*. Modestly described as a report on an ongoing project which has conducted over 500 hundred interviews with Britons born between 1872 and 1906, the book uses oral evidence to depict the 'untidy reality' of British society during a period of transition. Thompson has gone far beyond any other oral history project dealing with a general theme (including this one) in attempting to control his interview sample against the demographic and geographic characteristics of the period to be studied. His work has shown that oral history can help provide a fuller picture of the ways in which social reality is interconnected with personal experience. In his work the national economy is reflected in the family budget, and the socialist vanguard and the trade union movement become part of the thrust for self-improvement on the part of individual members of the working class. Thompson has also been responsible for the journal *Oral History* which has served as an important forum for those working in oral history.[78] In

Canada, Jane Synge has embarked upon a promising project in Hamilton informed by the same methodological rigour as Thompson's project.[79] The oral record can suggest new meanings for social developments that could only be poorly sketched with the most artfully managed statistical data or the most sensitive probing of ideology.

III

In making the social impact of the Great War on Canadian society the primary focus of our interviews, we selected a chronologically limited period which enjoyed both scholarly and popular recognition as a watershed in Canadian history.[80] Few Canadians can pass through our public schools without encountering the text-book mythology of the war: a youthful nation rallied loyally to Britain's side in 1914; Canadian troops proved their mettle time after time on the corpse-strewn battlefields of France and Belgium, winning international recognition for their valour at Ypres and Vimy Ridge; on the homefront the country rallied to support her troops overseas and withstood the last wrenching trauma of adolescence in the form of the Conscription Crisis; and gradually modern Canada emerged as a mature nation-state, first in the Imperial War Cabinet and finally at the Versailles Peace Conference. Despite the efforts of contemporary Canadian historians to explore more fully the social history of the war, this unfortunate identification of the Canadian people with the Canadian state remains a popular view of the meaning of the war. The rough, grating textures of the original events, which included violent death, brutal political repression, and breathtaking social transformations, are deftly blended into a national picture of a smooth ascent to full political autonomy. The silence of the war generation has allowed the experiences that jarred and shocked it to become for posterity a national war effort, selflessly and gladly given by men and women who never questioned their duty. It becomes easy to forget that Canadian soldiers won, along with their reputation for bravery, a richly deserved international reputation for unmilitary insubordination off the battlefield.[81] In 1977, it is no longer necessary for the sake of maintaining morale for the war effort to deny the facts of wartime strikes by Canadian workers on the homefront or the camp mutinies of 1919 in which thousands of Canadian soldiers participated.[82] Yet the persistent conception of the heroic, national meaning of the war seems to deny that such events ever took place. When the war generation is encouraged to speak in its own words about its experience of the war, the complex, discordant quality of those years becomes immediately evident.

Most Canadians, either at home or overseas, do not remember the war as a diplomatic or military adventure. Rather, everywhere the wartime period was a highly disruptive social experience. On the eve of the Great War, Canada was well along the road to becoming a modern industrial society. Yet, throughout the country many traditional styles and ways still stubbornly resisted the assault of change. The war did not introduce any startlingly new social trends; rather, it acted as a catalyst, greatly accelerating certain processes already underway. By 1914 industrial capitalism was highly advanced in Canada. Manufacturers had long been consolidating production in larger and larger corporations and striving at the same time to eliminate traditional workplace inefficiencies in their efforts to produce cheaper goods for a larger national market. With the coming of the war and the sudden demand for unprecedented amounts of standardized goods, the ongoing thrust for efficiency in production was given a boost that was jarring for those who had recently entered the workplace. Traditional artisanal prerogatives, which had long been under managerial assault, now came under the pressure of the patriotic sanction to produce at a faster rate. New efforts were made by management to break down jobs into simplified tasks. In the industries spawned by the war, such as munitions, no artisanal traditions prevailed in the quickly organized factories staffed by women and 'green' employees. Here even more radical departures from the older ways were initiated. The war effort served to break down walls of resistance against which a generation of industrial modernizers had hurled themselves in vain.[83]

The new techniques of persuasion that had gradually been transforming advertizing in Canada before the war were mobilized by government to produce a highly effective propaganda machine that grew more sophisticated as the war continued. As popular enthusiasm for the war waned, display advertisements subtly reminded the recalcitrant that their duty lay in enlisting, working harder, digging gardens, buying war bonds, or being thrifty. Even a tentative Canadian Tin Pan Alley was pressed into service and provided such memorable tunes as *When You Boy Comes Back to You* and *The Ammunition Girl: A Real Live Marching Song and One Step*. If anyone did tire from exhortations to 'do his bit,' a vigilant Press Censor monitored the Canadian press, ferreting out even the casually disloyal and warning the offending parties.[84] As well as pressing into the service of the war effort the latest arts of publicity, many aspects of community life were also transformed to serve the war effort. Quilting bees were promoted by semi-official Patriotic Societies as a means of raising money.[85] Women with relatives or loved ones overseas were encouraged in white-feathering able-bodied males still at home and presumably shirking their duty.[86] Even the solemnity of religious services was invaded when it suddenly became acceptable to do volunteer knitting in chruch.[87] By 1918 the continuing pressure of new demands at home combined with the losses of human life at the front to eradicate the last vestiges of the social ways of Victorian Canada. The new world that was forged in those years bore little resemblance to what had gone before.

The changes wrought by the war were felt first and most violently at the front. In 1914 the large numbers of volunteers who enthusia 'ically flocked to enlistment centres had no way of knowing what they would encounter in France. Canadian experience in British battles of the nineteenth century had been slender enough to allow a Kiplingesque notion of the empire at war to prevail. On the day that war was declared in 1914, a veteran of the Egyptian Campaign gathered volunteers together to drill in front of the Town Hall in Southampton, Ontario; a year later it would be evident to any Canadian recruit that anything a veteran of the battle against the Mahdi might have to say about modern warfare would be simply irrelevant.[88] The Canadian soldier soon learned that the modern techniques of war offered little opportunity for individual acts of valour in combat and no chance to escape from the presence of promiscuous, meaningless death. During the days and nights of waiting in the cold and rain and mud of France and Flanders, the Canadian recruit found much to ponder about the meaning of a civilization to whose defence he had been summoned. At the front the German whose barbarism he had enlisted to defeat often seemed less ominous than the pretensions and incompetence of his own officers whose privileges in this war often meant the difference between life and death. The 'enemy to the rear' became as easy an object for the resentment of the fighting man as the enemy on the other side of no man's land.[89] In a world where hesitation to obey could be interpreted as treason, there were even fewer ways for ordinary soldiers to resist than there were for the civilians at home. However, mutiny and rebellion were not so infrequent among Canadian troops as the official record implies.[90] Sarcasm was one means of resistance that many an ordinary soldier could effectively use with impunity. When an officer's photographs were released to the press purporting to depict Canadian soldiers 'going over the top' during the Battle of the Somme in 1916, the men he had photographed 'in action' at a training school in England remembered the deception and sneeringly asked him if he wanted any further 'fakers' whenever he visited their units.[91] Usually there was little to assuage the harshness and loneliness of the soldier's situation and even less to remind him of the world he had left behind. The society which he reentered at the war's end, was greatly, if not violently, altered during the course of the war years. However, it was the returned veteran and the 60,000 Canadians who never came home who ensured that the post-war world could never return to 'normalcy.'

The drama of the war years was the formative experience for a generation of Canadians now in their seventies and eighties. The interviews which we conducted in the summer of 1974 with over 200 members of that generation then living in the Toronto area are a vivid testimony to the impact of that experience. In interviewing our subjects we attempted to tread a delicate line between a concern for the integrity of the narrative form and an interest in the informative value of the particular areas of their experience. We tried to combine the role of the collaborator in a life history with the role of the historical investigator. Project members consulted relevant literature on the wartime period and continued to meet weekly throughout the summer in order to compare the varied material that was being collected and to discuss techniques that were proving fruitful in individual interviews. Efforts were also made to keep track of the ethnic, occupational, and geographical representation in our sample.[92] We attempted to encourage the narrative form by having our collaborators give some account of their lives and activities before the war. In general, this was the way that the members of the war generation themselves remembered the war. We canvassed for our collaborators publicly, using word of mouth, leaflets, the radio newspaper, and magazine advertisements. Our collaborators had both clear memories of the period and a high degree of candor in revealing their own experiences. The document that we have assembled from these interviews was arranged so that the character of their collective experience could be communicated to the reader.

The oral history of the war generation is rich in detail and feeling and covers a wide variety of areas and themes. The general nature of these areas and themes can be readily perceived from the organization of the book. A thematic introduction acts as a guide to the subject matter of each chapter. What remains to be discussed is the question of the oral history of the war generation as historical evidence. It is a difficult problem which can be approached in many ways. If oral history is to become a recognized and reputable resource in modern historical methodology, then questions as to its reliability as evidence must be convincingly answered. Unfortunately, some professional historians have approached the question in ways that suggest an unreconstructed Hobbesian notion of social psychology in which the subject of the interview guards his 'truly significant material' behind a 'defensive veil that the interviewer must penetrate.' The historian in question suggests that the natural penchant for mendacity in the interview subject should be broken down under cross-examination by two or, even better, three professional interrogators and allows only that popular oral histories conducted by means of a one-to-one interview relationship (as this oral history was conducted) 'do little permanent harm and they do serve to collect anecdotes and colour which might otherwise be lost....'[93] Such off-hand condescension is all too common in the corridors of history departments and is based on a view of human nature with which those who sneer so easily might well feel uncomfortable if they chose to examine its implications more critically. In examining the material we now present, we discovered a variety of evidence. Some was quite straightforward. Other evidence flew in the face of what we had assumed to be true from published works based on the documentary record. Still other evidence dealt with areas of life and experience on which the documentary record was notably deficient. However, even when some of the evidence that we gathered seemed at first glance to be flawed by fabrication, misinformation, or faulty memory, none of it could be blithely consigned to the rubbish heap because to preserve it would do 'permanent harm.' We learned many things by subjecting such evidence to the closer scrutiny of the second glance. When sympathetically considered, almost every piece of evidence we collected contributed in some way to a deeper understanding of popular experience during the Great War.

In judging the oral record of the Great War as historical evidence at its most basic level, our collaborators provided a great deal of traditional evidence of the kind that historians have usually found in documentary sources. As such, little in the way of methodological innovation is required in using it as evidence, since it treats questions with which historians are already familiar. However, the oral record of a period when the freedom of publication and information—the real basis of a balanced documentary record—was severely curtailed by government often contains valuable data on various kinds of oppositional or socially unacceptable activity where none or little exists in the documentary record. For instance, the wartime suppression of reporting of events such as strikes and mutinies or of candid reporting of life at the front left an artificial void in the record which can be rectified by the information of actual participants whose reminiscences would have normally been well-documented in other contemporary sources.[94] Because such evidence is based on memory, it is often approached with a scepticism based on the notion of the degenerative effects of old age on memory.[95] While this data should be scrutinized as carefully as any other kind of data, it should not be subject to any special doubt simply because it is generated by memory. The best modern research on memory suggests that memory is one of the most unshakeable features of the human mind, preserving the experience of the individual with remarkable accuracy to advanced age, despite even severe organic impairment or, in one extreme case, psychosurgical intervention which inadvertently destroyed the capacity to remember, but left the patient's memory up to surgery intact.[96] At any rate, it should be clear that the memories of survivors of the Great War are far less suspect than the historical sensibilities of the wartime Press Censor who was responsible for the incomplete documentary record of the war we now possess.

The oral record moves from these ordinary areas of historical documentation to those aspects of everyday experience about which the documentary record has had little to say. What evidence is recorded often conspires to create a picture of many aspects of past society in which those actors who left substantial documentary records come to occupy roles quite at odds with their actual significance. For instance, it is generally understood that ideas on the role of women were substantially altered by the wartime experience. However, when historians interested in these questions consult the documentary sources, the papers of the leaders of the women's suffrage movement loom large and provide the easiest method of studying how 'manpower shortages meant increased female employment in hitherto unfeminine jobs.'[97] At that point, however, the newly unsheltered Canadian woman who became a munitions worker can no longer be conveniently studied in the papers of the suffrage leader. Thereafter, our knowledge of the smallest details in the lives of suffrage leaders proliferates, despite the fact that Canadian female munitions workers contributed far more to revolutionizing the consciousness of women's capabilities than did suffrage propagandists dealing in doctrines that had already been in general circulation for over half a century. The oral history of the female munitions worker contributes to a broader understanding of the social history of this significant change in women's work during the war. The war effected many other important changes that temporarily, but acutely, altered patterns of home, workplace, and community; oral history can lead us to the particular meanings that such alterations wrought in the everyday lives of the Canadians who experience them and help us place the commentary of reformers and community leaders in a more proper perspective. For example, there is a vast body of recorded evidence on the high martial spirit of English Canadian community leaders. In reviewing this record, a recent history has concluded that the wholesale restriction of 'aliens' by the federal government can be understood as a benevolent policy designed to hold in check 'the unrestrained enthusiasm of native Canadians to persecute their fellow citizens.'[98] The oral record suggests that the state was far less successful as a 'regulator' of nationalities than this judgement claims. Popular excess did not emanate solely from the pulpit and rostrum. In the neighbourhoods of Canadian cities there were outbreaks of Anglophobia which no one even recorded, let alone controlled. There is probably no other extant account than that of Howard Ainsworth (p 196) of the wartime tarring and feathering in Toronto of the German carpenter, Frederick Spade. His public humiliation at the hands of an English Canadian mob in Clinton Street provides us with graphic evidence of how limited federal order could be. We search in vain for the rule of law, or even an inquiring reporter from the daily press at the scene of the outrage. The humiliators quickly melted back into the community, invisible to their contemporaries and unrecorded for history. Of lasting significance is perhaps one area on which the oral record of the war must for the present remain silent. No surviving German Canadian contacted by our project in the summer of 1974 was willing to talk of his experience in Canada during the Great War. Even in silence there is significance.

Finally, the oral record of the war greatly expands the area of inquiry to the many aspects of cultural and social history which are embedded in the spoken language. The whole complex of manners, rhythms, and usages which makes up the spoken language remains one of the strongest marks of identity in modern society, providing clues to a varied cultural past even where modernization seems to have created a social conformity. When read or listened to carefully, the testimony that makes up this book yields a vast array of subtle data on ethnic, regional, and class identities. During the Great War, the consciousness of Canadians was confronted by a variety of messages communicated through the new and evolving forms of persuasion. The shock of events at home and overseas was experience in a new kind of language. As one writer has expressed it, 'New phrases and words ate into the mind and burrowed there like moles....'[99] These words and phrases have remained a real and largely unexplored part of the wartime heritage. They formed a vivid part of the memories of those who contributed to this collection. Study of the new styles of expression engendered by the war requires great care. Often, what seems to be a memory slip or a simple error can provide new information on an old problem. One notes the imprecise way in which the various words, 'conscript,' 'draftee,' and 'volunteer' are used in some of the interviews (pp 106-107). As everyone knows Conscription was not enacted by the Union Government until 1917, yet the word 'conscript' obviously came to mean much more than can be communicated by a sterile history of dates and institutions. This was clear to all young Canadian men during the war years; hounded by white-feathering, harangued by recruiting officers, and pressured by family and friends, they knew that there were no 'volunteers' after the fall of 1914. Many other aspects of the subtle shifts the campaign for the war effected, or the stubborn resistance it encountered can be gleaned from the words and usages of the war generation. This new and revealing language is the most unique resource that the oral record of the war can offer to history.

The latest historical work on the early twentieth century stresses the final victory and ratification of the institutions and methods of corporate industrial capitalism.[100] When we began our interviews with members of the war generation, it was assumed that oral history would help confirm this emerging picture of the hegemony of a mature industrial order. In recording interviews with ordinary Canadians who experienced the period, a slightly different picture emerged. It is true that there could be no doubt that the few overt contemporary challenges to the rule of corporate capitalism were resounding failures. However, the world that our collaborators helped us reconstruct was not quite the world we expected to encounter. Those Canadians who might seem the most fully 'incorporated' by the sway of industrialism to the quantifier of acts of resistance proved quite independent when interviewed. Even while the victors in the long struggle to impose industrial capitalism were dictating their peace treaties to the defeated parties of 1919, new spaces in which to live and from which to resist were being staked out by the defeated. For Canadian soldiers, who seemed the most completely accommodated to the status quo of 1914, the war was a deeply unsettling experience which led, not to a confirmation of the world as it was, but to a profound questioning of the worth of industrial civilization. At a time when much of our social criticism is engulfed in pessimism engendered by the cultural and economic crisis of late twentieth century capitalism, oral history is one resource which can provide us with a quite different and more hopeful sense of our history. When this book was planned in the spring of 1974, it was not intended that it should be a magisterial volume answering the last question about the Great War and Canadian society. It was conceived as a tentative work which would suggest the possibilities of doing oral history with older Canadians on important themes which were then being neglected. It is now offered in the hope that our experience will serve others planning to explore the many worlds and feelings which only oral history can recapture.

Russell G. Hann

NOTES

1. In writing this introduction I have profited from discussions with all members of the original project and from consulting the various working papers by Bradley Adams and Gus Richardson produced during the life of the project. Krys Dobrowolski, Craig Heron, Bryan Palmer, Daphne Read, Wayne Roberts, and Richard Wright read various versions of this paper and their comments helped sharpen many aspects of the final version. Special thanks are offered to Brenda Hann, Gregory Kealey, and Gus Richardson who provided more than can be briefly listed here. Without their intelligent criticism, pertinent information, and constant encouragement, the introduction would be poorer in many ways. I would also like to acknowledge personally the contributions to my own work on this project of the late Elgar Houghton, who told me many things about life in early twentieth century Canada, and of the late Margaret I. Cowan, who taught me the many things that could be learned from patient and sympathetic listening.
2. Gregory S. Kealey and Peter Warrian (eds.), *Essays in Canadian Working Class History* (Toronto 1976),7; for a review of recent trends, see Russell G. Hann and Gregory S. Kealey, 'Documenting Working Class History: North American Traditions and New Approaches,' *Archivaria*, 4 (1977), 92-114.
3. For an important discussion of the distortions of quantitative history informed by modernization theory, see Bryan D. Palmer, 'Modernizing History,' *Bulletin of the Committee on Canadian Labour History*, 2 (1976), 16-31.
4. This is not to suggest that it is impossible to treat popular history with sympathy and understanding from the fragmentary records we do have. The work of Edward Thompson has demonstrated that eighteenth and early nineteenth century sources can yield many insights into popular experience when carefully and sensitively examined. See his, *The Making of the English Working Class* (New York 1963); *Whigs and Hunters: The Origin of the Black Act* (New York 1975); and, with Douglas Hay *et al.*, *Albion's Fatal Tree: Crime and Society in Eighteenth Century England* (New York 1975). See also, Richard Hoggart, *The Uses of Literacy: Aspects of Working Class Life with Special Reference to Publications and Entertainments* (Harmondsworth 1958) for a sensitive account of popular life in more recent history.
5. Raymond Williams, *The Long Revolution* (Harmondsworth 1965), 63-64.
6. Peter Oliver, 'Oral History: One Historian's View,' *Canadian Oral History Association Journal*, I (1975-1976), 13-14.
7. See Raphael Samuel, 'Local History and Oral History,' *History Workshop Journal*, 1 (1976), 191-208.
8. Brian Stock has correctly argued that in Canada the Great Tradition that we have did not emerge from a native oral tradition in 'English Canada: Culture versus Experience,'

Canadian Forum, LVI (April 1976), 6-9. However, the fact that the founders of the Great Tradition in Canadian arts and letters chose to follow European models does not mean that there was no popular oral tradition. As Stock himself has previously argued, the many popular traditions which do exist in Canada are in many ways more vibrant than our Great Tradition. See 'English Canada: the Visible and Invisible Cultures,' *Canadian Forum*, LII (March 1973), 29-33. See also David Arnason, 'Comment,' *Journal of Canadian Fiction*, II (Spring 1973), 1-2.

9. Walter Benjamin, *Illuminations* (New York 1969), 223-224.

10. Natalie Z. Davis, 'Printing and the People,' in *Society and Culture in Early Modern France* (Stanford 1975), 189-226; E.P. Thompson, 'The Crime of Anonymity,' in Hay *et al., Albion's Fatal Tree*, 255-308.

11. Martha Vicinus, *The Industrial Muse: A Study of Nineteenth-Century British Working-Class Literature* (London 1974), 140-142; Richard M. Dorson, 'The Use of Printed Sources,' in Dorson (ed.), *Folklore and Folklife* (Chicago 1972), 468-470; R.M. Dorson, *The British Folklorists: A History* (Chicago 1968).

12. John Burnet (ed.), *Useful Toil: Autobiographies of Working People from the 1820s to the 1920s* (London 1974), 10; P.E. Razzell and R.W. Wainwright (eds.), *The Victorian Working Class: Selections from the Morning Chronicle* (London 1973); E.P. Thompson and Eileen Yeo, *The Unknown Mayhew* (Harmondsworth 1973); G.S. Kealey (ed.), *Canada Investigates Industrialism: The Royal Commission on the Relations of Capital and Labour, 1889* (Toronto 1973); on Mayhew see Yeo, 'Mayhew as a Social Investigator,' in *The Unknown Mayhew*, 67-72; for Phillips Thompson, see Hann, 'Brainworkers and the Knights of Labor: E.E. Sheppard, Phillips Thompson, and the Toronto *News*, 1883-1887,' in Kealey and Warrian (eds.), *Essays in Canadian Working Class History*, 35-57.

13. For examples, see M. Nadaud, *Mémoires de Léonard, ancien garçon maçon* (1895; Paris 1977); A Working Man, *Reminiscences of a Stonemason* (London 1908); and Burnett, *Useful Toil*.

14. W.A. Deacon, *The Four Jameses* (1927; Toronto 1974), 190-191.

15. M. Vicinus, *The Industrial Muse*, 159; Per Gedin, *Literature in the Market Place* (London 1977), 13-43, 16; Raymond Williams, *The Long Revolution*, 177-236; R.D. Altick, *The English Common Reader* (Chicago 1957).

16. Jack Gladden, 'Archie Bunker meets Mr Spoopendyke: Nineteenth-Century Prototypes for Domestic Situation Comedy,' *Journal of Popular Culture*, X (1976), 170; Brom Weber, 'The Misspellers,' in L.D. Rubin (ed.), *The Comic Imagination in American Literature* (New Brunswick, N.J. 1973); John M. Harrison, *The Man who Made Nasby* (Chapel Hill 1969).

17. Gladden, 'Archie Bunker,' 169; Walter Blair, 'The Popularity of Nineteenth-Century American Humorists,' *American Literature*, III (1931), 175-194.

18. Ron Poulton, *The Paper Tyrant: John Ross Robertson of the Toronto Telegram* (Toronto 1971).

19. See Hann, 'Brainworkers and the Knights of Labor,' 39; Stratford *Herald*, 8 September 1875.

20. See *Grip*, XXXVI (7 February 1891); Stan Kutcher, 'J.W. Bengough and the Millenium in Toronto,' *Urban History Review*, (October 1976), 30-49.

21. *Grip*, XXXVI (10 January 1891).

22. 'The Decline of Dialect,' *Canadian Magazine*, III (1894), 489.

23. On the 'growing demand for men better equipped with the learning of the schools' in Canadian journalism, see J.S. Willison, *Journalism* (Toronto 1899), 5-6; Hugh Duncan, *The Rise of Chicago as a Literary Center* (Totowa, N.J. 1964), 178-179.

24. *The Search for Order* (New York 1967).

25. Public Archives of Canada, William Kirby to George Taylor Denison, 18 August 1884, Denison Papers, Volume 3.

26. 'Canadian English,' *Canadian Journal of Science*, II (1857), 345-355, 353.

27. W.D. Lightall, 'Canadian English,' *The Week*, VI (1889), 581-583; A. MacPhail, 'Our Canadian Speech,' *Saturday Night*, L (29 June 1935), 1-2.

28. Arnold Haultain, *Two Country Walks in Canada* (Toronto 1903), 16-17; Alan Bowker, 'Truly Useful Men: Maurice Hutton, George Wrong, James Mavor, and the University of Toronto' (unpublished Ph.D. thesis, University of Toronto, 1975), 75, 106; Williams, *The Long Revolution*, 237-253.

29. Alfred Fitzpatrick, *Handbook for New Canadians* (Toronto 1919), 1-3, 119.

30. Henry May, *The End of American Innocence* (New York 1959), 3-8; for an interesting look at continuities in the social and family backgrounds of the new generation of rebels, see Kenneth S. Lynn, 'The Rebels of Greenwich Village,' *Perspectives in American History*, VIII (1974), 333-377.

31. Constance Rourke, *American Humor* (New York 1931), 302; Joan S. Rubin, 'Constance Rourke in Context: The Uses of Myth,' *American Quarterly*, XXVIII (1976), 575-588.

32. See Alfred Kazin, *On Native Grounds: An Interpretation of Modern American Prose Literature* (New York 1942).

33. W.A. Deacon, *Poteen. A Potpourri of Canadian Essays* (Ottawa 1926), 97-101, 51-62; and *The Four Jameses* (1927; Toronto 1974).

34. David Arnason, 'Comment,' *Journal of Canadian Fiction*, II (Spring 1973), 1-2.

35. For reports of early popular writers on folklore, see 'Folklore Scrapbook,' *Journal of American Folklore*, XI (1898), 159-161.

36. For an example of an early investigation of French Canadian folkways by an amateur, see William P. Greenough, *Canadian Folklife and Folklore* (New York 1897); see Marius Barbeau, '"Totemic Atmosphere" on the North Pacific Coast,' *Journal of American Folklore*, LXVII (1954), 103-122.

37. M. Carole Henderson, 'Folklore Scholarship and the Sociopolitical Milieu in Canada,' *Journal of the Folklore Institute*, X (1973), 98,133; and 'The Ethnicity Factor in Anglo-Canadian Folkloristics,' *Canadian Ethnic Studies*, VII (1975), 11-12.

38. F.J. Alcock, 'Folklore Studies at the National Museum of Canada,' *Journal of American Folklore*, LXVII (1954), 99-101.

39. For an excellent bibliography of works relating to Canadian folklore see Ruth Dyck (comp.), 'Ethnic Folklore in Canada: A Preliminary Survey,' *Canadian Ethnic Studies*, VII (1975), 90-101; on the Maritimes and Newfoundland see A.H. Fausett (comp.), 'Folklore from Nova Scotia,' *Memoirs of the American Folklore Society*, XXIV (1931) and Helen Creighton (ed.), *Bluenose Magic: Popular Beliefs and Superstitions in Nova Scotia* (Toronto 1968); for a good description of the relatively recent Newfoundland folklore programme at Memorial University, see H. Halpert and N.V. Rosenberg, 'Folklore Work at Memorial University,' *Canadian Forum*, LIII (March 1974, 31-32; on the West, see R.B. Klymascz, *Folklore Narrative Among Ukrainian Canadians in Western Canada*, Mercury Series: Canadian Centre for Folk Culture Studies, No. 4 (Ottawa 1973); on Northern Ontario, see Edith Fowke, 'Lumbering Songs from the Northern Woods,' *Memoirs of the American Folklore Society*, LV (1970); an exception to the general ignoring of settled, industrial Ontario by folklorists are the special numbers of the *Journal of American Folklore*, XXXI: 119 and 120 (April-June, 1918), which focussed on Ontario folklore; however, the National Museum collector and member of the Geological Survey, W.J. Wintemburg, who contributed work to these numbers on Grey County, Toronto and vicinity, Oxford County, Waterloo County, and other places, betrayed

attitudes which might have served him well as a member of an expedition to recover Indian relics on the Pacific Coast, but which made it difficult for him to observe patiently the dynamics of the industrial society in which he was a participant observer. The results of his work are a series of disjointed discoveries wrenched from their context, making it difficult to know how they were used in their particular social setting.

40. On the tendency to seek out atypical archaisms in Ontario folklore studies, see Edith Fowke, 'Notes,' *Folk Songs of Ontario*, Folkways Records, Album no. FM 4005 (New York 1958), unpaginated. One early collector confessed his own preference for the atypical regions of Ontario where one did not encounter the 'horrible colloquialisms, nasal twang, and wonderful idioms' which coloured ordinary rural speech; on this quest to find folk who spoke like real folk, see C.A. Fraser, 'Scottish Myths from Ontario,' *Journal of American Folklore*, VI (1893), 185-198.

41. See Linda Dégh, *Folktales and Society: Story-Telling in a Hungarian Peasant Community* (Bloomington 1969), 49; and Dégh, 'Folk Narrative,' in R.M. Dorson (ed.), *Folklore and Folklife*, 77-78; see R.M. Dorson, 'A Theory for American Folklore,' *Journal of American Folklore*, LXXII (1959), 197-215 and 'A Theory of American Folklore Reviewed,' *Journal of American Folklore*, LXXXII (1969), 226-244 for attempts by an American to establish a relationship between the study of American folklore and the study of American history; for interesting attempts to apply the methods of the folklorist to eminently modern industrial situations, see Bruce E. Nickerson, 'Is There a Folk in the Factory,' *Journal of American Folklore*, LXXXVII (1974), 133-139 and Alan Dundes and Carl R Pagter, 'Urban Folklore from the Paperwork Empire,' *Memoirs of the American Folklore Society*, LXII (1975), 220-223.

42. Henderson, 'The Ethnicity Factor,' 15-16.

43. H.G. Gutman and G.S. Kealey, 'Introduction,' in Gutman and Kealey (eds.), *Many Pasts*, I (Englewood Cliffs, N.J. 1973), 4-5. For a fine example of the ways in which folklore materials can be used to write social history, see L.W. Levine, *Black Culture and Black Consciousness: Afro-American Folk Thought from Slavery to Freedom* (New York 1977).

44. Horace Miner, *St. Denis: A French-Canadian Parish* (Chicago 1939) and E.C. Hughes, *French Canada in Transition* (Chicago 1943).

45. S.D. Clark, 'Sociology in Canada: An Historical Over-view,' *Canadian Journal of Sociology*, I (1975), 228-229.

46. For a particularly cogent discussion of some of the ways in which modernization theory can vitiate historical analysis, see Christopher Lasch, 'The Family and History,' *New York Review of Books*, XXII (13 November 1975), 33-38 and 'What the Doctor Ordered,' *ibid.*, (11 December 1975), 50-54.

47. Robert W. Malcolmson, *Popular Recreations in English Society, 1700 - 1850* (Cambridge 1973), 116-117.

48. For instance, see D. Riesman, 'Oral and Written Traditions,' in Carpenter and McLuhan (eds.), *Explorations in Communications* (Boston 1960), 110-114.

49. For an assessment of the effects of such theory on Canadian historiography, see Russell G. Hann *et al.*, 'Introduction,' in *Primary Sources in Canadian Working Class History* (Kitchener, Ontario 1973), 9-12.

50. J.M.S. Careless, 'Limited Identities in Canada,' *Canadian Historical Review*, L (1969), 1-10.

51. For an evocation of the history of Great Men and crowds, see J.M.S. Careless, 'Donald Creighton and Canadian History,' in J.S. Moir (ed.), *Character and Circumstance* (Toronto 1970), 12-13.

52. See the first two volumes of *Labour/Le Travailleur* (1976-1977), as well as other books

and articles cited above.

53. Sidney Mintz, 'Forward,' to N. Whitten and J.F. Szwed, (eds.), *Afroamerican Anthropology* (New York 1970), 1-16.

54. See Bryan D. Palmer, 'Most Uncommon, Common Men,' *Labour/Le Travailleur*, I (1976), 7-9.

55. Linda Dégh, 'Folk Narrative,' in Dorson (ed.), *Folklore and Folklife*, 77-79; William Stott, *Documentary Expression in Thirties America* (New York 1973); Jerre Mangione, *The Dream and the Deal: The Federal Writers' Project, 1935-1943* (New York 1972); M.N. Penkower, *The Federal Writers' Project: A Study of Government Patronage in the Arts* (Urbana, Illinois 1977), 144-147, 152-154.

56. See Stott, *Documentary Expression*, 4; for an example of the way political struggle provided an impetus to the collection of oral material, see Theodore Dreiser *et al.*, *Harlan Miners Speak: Report on Terrorism in the Kentucky Coal Fields Prepared by Members of the National Committee for the Defense of Political Prisoners* (1932; New York 1970), 91-228, which consists of the testimony of miners as to repression in the region, and Chapter 9, 'The Free Speech Speakin's' compiled by John Dos Passos as courtroom testimony.

57. See *These Are Our Lives: As Told by the People and Written by Members of the Federal Writers' Project of the Works Progress Administration in North Carolina, Tennessee, and Georgia* (1939; New York 1975); Mangione, 12.

58. *Lay My Burden Down* (Chicago 1945); Mangione, 256-257; a useful collection of some of the slave narratives is found in Norman R Yetman (ed.), *Voices from Slavery* (New York 1970) to which Yetman has appended a helpful introduction, 'The Background of the Slave Narrative Collection,' 339-355; a complete edition of the typescript narratives edited and introduced by George P. Rawick has been published as *The American Slave: A Composite Autobiography* (Westport, Conn. 1972), 19 Vol; a discussion of the narratives as historical evidence is C. Vann Woodward, 'History from Slave Sources,' *American Historical Review*, LXXIX (1974), 470-481.

59. See, for instance, Eugene D. Genovese, *Roll, Jordan Roll: The World the Slaves Made* (New York 1974).

60. Mangione, 329-374; in fact, in the years following World War II, important sections of the non-Stalinist American left, notably those associated with *Partisan Review*, were openly hostile to the ways in which Stalinists used the fruits of research into the vernacular heritage and began a concerted defence of *avant garde* styles in the arts. See R.H. Pells, *Radical Visions and American Dreams* (New York 1973), 334-336; in Canada, the rapid evaporation of the concerns and styles of the 1930s in the 1940s is one of the most puzzling aspects of Dorothy Livesay's memoir of those years, *Right Hand, Left Hand: A True Life of the Thirties* (Erin, Ontario 1977), 278-279.

61. Staughton Lynd, 'Personal Histories of the early C.I.O.' *Radical America*, V (May-June 1971), 49-76.

62. To gain some insight into the magnitude of the contemporary effort, see the far from exhaustive catalogue of 230 North American research programmes by A.M. Meckler and R. McMullin (comps.), *Oral History Collections* (New York 1975); for a guide to the literature on contemporary oral history, see M.J. Wasserman (comp.), *Bibliography on Oral History* (New York 1971); for a discussion of recording techniques and standards, see W.J. Langlois, *Aural History Institute of British Columbia Manual* (Victoria 1974); despite the explosion of guides in interviewing techniques, one of the most useful guides to collecting we consulted was D.D. Baker, *Local History: How to Gather it, Write it, and Publish it* (New York 1944); for those interested in the proliferating new literature on oral history, it is conveniently reviewed in Ronald J. Grele, 'A Surmisable Variety: Interdiscipli-

plinarity and Oral Testimony,' *American Quarterly*, XXVII (1975), 275-295.

63. Elizabeth B. Mason and Louis M. Starr (eds.), *The Oral History Collection of Columbia University* (New York 1973), vii.

64. William W. Moss, *Oral History Program Manual* (New York 1974).

65. Flagrant uses of oral history by politicians engaged in memoir-writing are many; for a particularly absurd example of the diversion of the resources of oral history away from more logical subjects, see Bruce M. Stave (comp.), *The Making of Urban History: Historiography Through Oral History* (1977).

66. See Irving Abella (comp.), 'Portrait of a Jewish Professional Revolutionary: The Recollections of Joshua Gershman,' *Labour/Le Travailleur*, II (1977), 184-213, for a fine example of what such an interview method can yield. See also, Abella, 'Oral History and the Canadian Labour Movement,' *Archivaria*, 4 (1977), 115-121.

67. Douglas Gill and Gloden Dallas, 'Mutiny at Etaples Base in 1917,' *Past and Present*, 69 (November 1975), 88-112.

68. L.C. Goodwyn, 'Populist Dreams and Negro Rights: East Texas as a Case Study,' *American Historical Review*, LXXVI (1971), 1435-1456.

69. For a description of basic methodology in the life history, see: S.W. Mintz (comp.), *Worker in the Cane: A Puerto Rican Life History* (New Haven 1960), 6-10, and T. Rosengarten, *All God's Dangers: The Life of Nate Shaw* (New York 1975), xiii-xxv

70. See Rolf Knight (comp.), *A Very Ordinary Life* (Vancouver 1974); with Maya Koizumi, *A Man of Our Times* (Vancouver 1976); and *Stump Ranch Chronicles* (Vancouver 1977).

71. Edward Bull, 'Autobiographies of Industrial Workers,' *International Review of Social History*, I (1956), 203-209.

72. *The Emergence of a U.A.W. Local* (Pittsburgh 1975), xi-xxxiii.

73. *Ibid.*, xxvi.

74. *Hard Times* (New York 1970); *Working* (New York 1972); Broadfoot, *Ten Lost Years* (Toronto 1973), v-vi; *Six War Years* (Toronto 1974); Barry Broadfoot was interviewed by two project members in the fall of 1974 in *The Varsity*, 29 November 1974, 8-9.

75. *Hard Times*, 17; this project learned many things from a suggestive review of *Hard Times* by Michael Frisch, 'Oral History and *Hard Times*: A Review Essay,' *Red Buffalo*, 2-3 (no date), 217-231.

76. *Oral History*, published from the University of Essex, is the most interesting journal that specializes in oral history. See also *Sound Heritage* published by the British Columbia Provincial Archives.

77. Raphael Samuel (ed.), *Village Life and Labour* (London 1975) and *Miners, Quarrymen, and Saltworkers* (London 1977).

78. *The Edwardians: The Remaking of English Society* (London 1975).

79. For a preliminary report on her work, see Jane Synge, 'Immigrant Communities,' *Oral History*, 4 (Autumn 1976), 38-51.

80. R.C. Brown and R. Cook, *Canada, 1896-1921:A Nation Transformed* (Toronto 1974), 212-320.

81. See, for instance, an account of a 1917 brawl between Canadian and Australian troops in Bill Gammage, *The Broken Years: Australian Soldiers in the War* (Canberra 1974), 234-235.

82. See the major role played by Canadians in camp riots at Kinmel Park and elsewhere in Dave Lamb, *Mutinies, 1917-1920* (London 1977), 8, 21-27.

83. See Gregory S. Kealey, '"The Honest Workingman" and Workers' Control: The Experience of Toronto Skilled Workers, 1860-1892,' *Labour/Le Travailleur*, I (1976), 32-68; Herbert G. Gutman, 'Work, Culture, and Society in Industrializing America,

1815-1919,' *American Historical Review*, LXXVIII (1973), 531-588; David Frank and Donald Macgillivray (eds.), *Echoes from Labor's War* (Toronto 1976), 15-16; Craig Heron and Bryan Palmer, 'Through the Prism of the Strike: Industrial Conflict in Southern Ontario, 1901-1914,' *Canadian Historical Review*, LVIII (1977), 423-458; R.C. Brown and R. Cook, *Canada, 1896-1921: A Nation Transformed*, 228-249.

84. Unfortunately, the full story of the selling of the war in Canada remains to be written. Even a casual perusal of the most available materials suggests that the Canadian effort was both as imaginative and as concerted as those in Britain or the United States. For a revealing piece of Canadian propaganda, see H.M. Wodson,*Private Warwick: Musings of a Canadian in Khaki* (Toronto 1915). For the titles to these songs and many others, see Huronia-Canadiana Books, *Catalogue*, List 64 (May 1976); Public Archives of Canada, Dept. of Secretary of State (Canada), Chief Press Censor's files, RG6E1, 1915-1920; see also W. Entz, 'The Suppression of the German Language Press in September 1918,' *Canadian Ethnic Studies*, VIII (1976), 56-70.

85. Norman McLeod, *The History of the County of Bruce* (Owen Sound 1969), 45-46.

86. See below, pp 93, 103-104.

87. Wealtha A. Wilson and Ethel T. Raymond,'Canadian Women in the Great War,' in *Canada in the Great War*, VI (Toronto 1921), 176-177.

88. McLeod, *History of the County of Bruce*, 42.

89. For a perceptive analysis of the effects of the extreme situations of life at the front on British soldiers, see Paul Fussell, *The Great War and Modern Memory* (New York 1975), especially Chapters II and III.

90. See Lamb, *Mutinies*.

91. Peter Robinson, 'More than Meets the Eye,' *Archivaria*, 1 (Summer 1976), 33-43.

92. No attempt, however, was made to assemble a perfectly balanced interview sample. We were interested in finding in a relatively short time as many interesting interviews as possible.

93. Peter Oliver, 'Oral History: One Historian's View,' 13-14, 17; a useful corrective to such attitudes about the 'harm' that is done through collecting popular materials is R.M. Dorson's 'Oral Literature, Oral History, and Folklore,' in Dorson, *Folklore and Fakelore* (Cambridge, Mass. 1976), 127-144.

94. Gill and Dallas, 'Mutiny at Etaples Base in 1917,' 88-112.

95. For an example see William W. Cutler, 'Accuracy in Oral History Interviewing,' *Historical Methods Newsletter*, III (June 1970), 1-7.

96. Howard Gardner, *The Shattered Mind* (New York 1975), 176-219, and Colin Blakemore, 'The Unsolved Marvel of Memory,' *New York Times Magazine*, 6 February 1977.

97. V. Strong-Boag, 'Introduction,' to N.L. McClung, *In Times Like These* (1915; Toronto 1972), xiii.

98. Brown and Cook, *Canada, 1896-1921: A Nation Transformed*, 224-227.

99. Phillip Child, *God's Sparrows* (1937; Toronto 1978), 108.

100. See, for instance, David F. Noble,*America By Design: Science, Technology and the Rise of Corporate Capitalism* (New York 1977), or Stuart Ewen, *Captains of Consciousness: Advertising and the Social Roots of the Consumer Culture* (New York 1976).

CHAPTER TWO

A RURAL WAY OF LIFE

On the eve of the Great War Canada was well on the way to becoming a modern industrial society. A majority of Canadians, however, still lived on farms or in the rural communities that served them. While Canada boasted one of the world's most advanced agricultures, many early communal forms persisted in the textures of rural life alongside the newest implements of agrarian technology. Steam engines and thrashing machines were easily integrated into communal work patterns descended from the pioneer bee. Many kinds of work were traded between neighbours. Children and adolescents formed a considerable part of the workforce on the predominant family farm. The structure of work and leisure corresponded more to the rhythms of days and seasons than to an externally defined efficiency. Rural churches and schools were the underpinning for this stable society, providing a shared way of life for those who stayed in the community and easing the transition to an urban society for those who left.

Mrs Sally Hill

She grew up on a farm near Alliston, a small town in southern Ontario.

We grew up very happily. We used to have square dances. The farmers around would invite us all, and there'd maybe be 50-75 people. They'd clear the kitchen and have it there. The grandmothers and grandfathers, right down to the little tiny babies would come. The babies would be all comfortable in a big bed, and the clothes would be put in another bedroom, and everybody would dance and talk. There was no liquor at all, and if any boy had it on his breath or was the worse of it, the girls would boycott him and not dance with him at all. We wouldn't have anything to do with him. Isn't that funny?!*(laughs)*

Was that just because of the town you were raised in?

I don't know if it was or not. Yes, it may have been. They were very God-fearing people. They weren't what you'd call religious fanatics exactly, but they were very upright and honourable in every way. I often look back and marvel at the way everybody could trust everybody else. You were dealing with people that, if they said, 'I will do this and you can depend on it,' you could depend on it, and they didn't let you down. And if you bought something from them, you knew it was exactly what they said it was and didn't have some hidden defect. The hardest thing in the world to get used to now is the fact that you can't trust people's word or you can't trust their motives. At least that's just my idea. But that's the way I found it in my life. As a general rule, we always took people at their face value, and we believed in them, and we didn't expect any underhand moves from them. I can't say that I've suffered too much from that, so perhaps I shouldn't mention it. But there is a noticeable lack of that in these later years.

After the First World War, the world changed. It was just like a waltz before, just like a Strauss waltz. Nobody had too much money, but everybody seemed to be able to bring their children up and educate them. I'm not trying to make it out as ideal or anything like that, and I don't know anything about the city where things might have been terrible. But out where I lived, everybody was God-fearing, and if you knew that somebody didn't have anything, if they were sick or there was an accident, automatically you went and helped them and brought them things and did their work for them, and you never thought anything about it. That was just part of what everybody did. And that's the truth as I remember it.

Jim Robertson

His family emigrated from Scotland to Canada in 1907, in response to a cam-paign for farmworkers, and settled in Woodstock, Ontario.

I remember the threshing operation in the very early days. Two houses shared the feeding of the men. They used to come over to our house and mother would see that they had plenty of food. The talk was very free and friendly, and you heard the different accents. We heard the Scottish accent and the English accent. Then there was one family that I remember very particularly: they had come in the early days by oxen from Vermont. Even a meal at threshing was really quite a thing. People gathered on those occasions. Life was much slower paced, and conversation was a very important thing. On occasions of that kind, people really set their sights at finding out where people had come from, what they did. 'Do you like it here, Mrs So-and-So, as well as you did back in Scotland?' The whole atmosphere was very genial and very colonial. I remember it all very clearly. I think I'll write a novel about it very soon, before it fades away.

Do you recall whether the people who came for the threshing were from the area, or did the farmers hire people seasonally from outside the area?

From what I can recall, they were all just neighbours. They helped each other, and the thing sort of equalled out, maybe not quite consistently, because some crops were heavier than others, and some farmers had more acreage than others. But it was a very welcome experience. It was perfectly charming, as I recall. Of course, sometimes memory enhances everything.

Growing of turnips was quite a marvellous thing—of course, I'm seeing it as a child. The men would get up early in the morning in November; the mist was on the meadows, and the cobs were on the corn—I'm not launching into poetry —but it was beautiful, as some of the poems suggested. Hired help were always very courageous and full of humour because they knew that they would have a very good meal, I suppose. They wrapped packing around their trousers to keep their feet dry, because of the spreading of the turnip leaves. They went down the turnip rows systematically with a sickle and whacked off the leaves and dropped them maybe two or three rows into one. Then somebody would follow with a wagon with boards on the side, and fill it up and haul it out to the root cellar. The root cellar was under the barn bank; a window was removed and the turnips were forked in, I believe. In other situations, in my imagination, they drove the wagon up the barn bank, and there was a chute and they just let them all slide down, and they would pop into the root cellar.

What machinery did your father have?

By that time I think that machinery was already in good use. The corn-binder was a marvellous piece of machinery. It's so commonplace I can hardly describe it. It was just a thing that went up and down the corn rows. This is for the corn on the cob. Corn in Scotland is wheat and oats and barley. The corn was tied mechanically with a string, then it was dropped down into the bag. The cobs were cut up when the sheaves were put on the cutting blocks. They were cut and elevated into the silo by steam power, before the days of tractors.

The man who owned the cutting blocks owned the 'Black Maria', which is the steam engine. It was a marvellous thing with a terrific personality. There was always an element of fear that this wonderful steam engine would set fire to a place, and sometimes it did.

He would bring it around to the farms?

Yes, they took their turns. Some people cut their corn a little earlier than others. The same went for the threshing too. The man who owned the threshing machine owned the cutting blocks. He had his clients, you see. He was a very good man, but then there was some competition. This thresher always had no trouble getting all the families he needed.

The arrival of the machinery was like a great day. No circus could come up to the arrival of the threshing machine, and the hauling of the machinery and setting it up in the barn or outside the barn.

When was this?

About 1913, I think. But from then on it was an annual event, right on to the Roaring Twenties.

Frank Bell

He grew up in Lancaster, a town in eastern Ontario with a mixed French and English population.

There was a certain amount of animosity between the original French and later Scotch settlers, and this was based on the school curriculum. First of all, the school was in English—we only had one school in those days, a public school —and the history was English. When I first started to school they didn't teach Canadian history. It was only when I was in the last grade, which would be called the eighth grade nowadays, that they brought in Canadian history, and I was fascinated with it. It was written in a sort of storybook form. History was always my best subject, I always excelled in it. We got a new teacher one time who was teaching history. I was in junior fourth at the time, so I promoted myself to senior fourth—the senior fourth and junior fourth were in the same room. She didn't know the difference and none of the pupils ever told her. When she found out I guess it didn't matter anymore. I used to answer most of the answers in the senior fourth class, although I was in the junior fourth, but this was because I read extensively in the library. And all the library books, or the ones I read anyway, had to do with British history. They were adventure stories. I re-member one was called *Soldiers of the Queen*, which fascinated me. The result was we got the impression from these books, whether it was intended or not, that one Englishman could lick about 20 Frenchmen. Now sometimes I tried to put that to the test, and it didn't work out because the French kids in the school were just as tough as we were, and perhaps tougher, because to a certain extent they were discriminated against, especially in the teaching. The result was, I think, that generally speaking the French children were a year or two behind in school, because they spoke French at home and when they went to school they had to speak English. I remember one fellow who was in my class—Herbie Parent. He was head of the class, I think. But when it came to the entrance examinations he failed. And what he failed in was spelling. The principal of the school took this up with the Department of Education and he was allowed to take the examination over again with her giving him the exam. Apparently the teacher they had brought in for the exam had a Scotch pronunciation, and Herbie couldn't get it. So the result was a lot of words he didn't spell at all. Anyway he was graduated, he didn't lose his year. But his father was one of the hotel-keepers and was one of the prominent citizens around there, and I'm not sure that some of the others would've got the same break.

Mrs Judith McKay

Her father, a Methodist minister on the country circuits, was a 'hell-fire preacher, a real pulpit-pounding preacher.'

Did you go to Sunday school?

Oh boy, did we go to Sunday school! Sunday was church of some kind all day, and it just depended on your age how often you went. Sunday morning was church, and in my father's household you got a little preview of the sermon at breakfast. Then you were all got ready for church. Dinner was put in the oven so it would be ready when you got home, and all the children would be got ready in spotless Sunday attire. There was usually a baby, and it was left home with the hired girl. All the shoes were cleaned up Saturday night. Nothing, not even a thing like that, would *ever* be done on Sunday. Then we had church, and believe me, you must pay attention. Nothing was worse than having your father look down from the pulpit and say, 'Judith!' because you were fidgeting.

Ben Wagner

He was born in Paisley, Bruce County, in 1897.

The church served as much more of a social centre in those days than it does now. Very often the only time the farmer's wife spoke to someone through the week was in church. She didn't get out to visit neighbours—occasionally, but not very often. The church was your social centre, and you met people there. If you didn't go to church, you were almost out of it.

Alex Boulton

His family farmed in South Fredericksburgh which, according to him, was the smallest township in Ontario in the early 1900s. Most of the 300-500 people in the township were the descendants of United Empire Loyalists.

The concept of love was an entirely different concept than it is today. In those days, remember, people coming out of the Victorian era were very strict in their conduct. It was never even admitted that sex existed. That was regarded as a dirty word. In those days pregnant women would stay completely out of sight. No one would ever admit how the child came into being, but since the baby arrived, why, that was wonderful! Well, I don't know who they thought they were fooling, but nowadays that's common knowledge. In those days the approach between boys and girls was the old-fashioned courtship approach. It was more a social type of contact. There's far more physical contact between boys and girls now than there was in those days. That was taboo. Anything in the way of sex stimulation was taboo. It was thought impure, bordering on immorality. But there was a lot done that wasn't admitted, because there were a few illegitimate births around too. But wherever those occurred, the mother was treated as an outcast or next thing to it.

How did you get to know a girl?

You'd usually invite her to go somewhere on some event. After church service on Sunday mornings was a usual meeting place, and you'd see the girls home. That's the usual approach. The church was the meeting place, the social centre of the community.

Mrs Sally Hill

She laughs now about her parents' avoidance of the immodest subject of sex.

Did your mother talk to you about sexuality?

No, never. I was taught in high school. We had physiology and hygiene, and those were the first published textbooks on it. I wish I had them now. About what happened, there were no lectures where the boys and girls sat together and looked at each other's reproductive organs or anything like that,believe me. I didn't know a thing about it, because I was an only child and was brought up on a farm. Of course I saw animals but not to any great extent. My father was very modest. We had plows, and sometimes the point that runs through the ground breaks if it hits a big rock. My dad would say to me, 'you go up to town and get me a plowshare.' I never said, 'Dad, what kind?' He'd hand me a little piece of paper, and you know what they were? Cockshutt plows. He wouldn't say that word to me, and I wouldn't dare say that to the man. I was supposed to give him that piece of paper. Isn't that amusing!

Frank Bell

Saturday night in Lancaster.

My father was a barber and his shop—it's hard to describe—was just what you would call today a cubbyhole, I guess, but it was about ten feet wide and maybe 30 feet long or 20 feet long and had two barber chairs in it. He had a sink with a drain out the back. His shop was downtown at the village and our house was over at the edge of the village. He was also the local tobacconist. I don't think in those days everybody sold tobacco. I think it was just done by a tobacconist, who was usually the barber. I remember a lot of cigars were sold in those days, and people smoked pipes a lot. We were a lumbering community, and although I don't recall it, because I was too young to smoke, there must have been a great many restrictions on smoking, because it could be very disastrous in our community.

In those days you could get a shave for ten cents, which was fairly good because you could hire a man for a dollar a day. So you might say ten cents was an hour's pay for a labourer. So labourers didn't get shaved by the barber, of course! But the businessmen usually did. There was another barber whose name was Denis. And the businessmen made it a point to be shaved by one or the other every day. The farmers quite often shaved themselves or saved their whiskers until the weekend, and then came in and expected them to be taken off for ten cents. But this was their weekend treat.

I remember one man, a farmer by the name of Fraser. He used to come into town, and he would sit in the barbershop and listen to the local gossip. Saturday night you used to have to wait quite a while, but they didn't mind it; they enjoyed it because it was a chance to meet and talk to people. This man was clearing his land and, like most people around there, was very poor, and had to live frugally. But on Saturday night he got a shave and he bought a ten-cent cigar. That was his week-end bust-out! He didn't drink. Some of them would drink, but he didn't, and I remember my father remarking how he never saw a man enjoy a cigar so much. He would sit and roll this cigar, and puff on it, and look at it, you know. He wouldn't dare smoke at home because of the danger of fire, even if he could have afforded it.

There was another fella, an old bachelor who lived with his mother. I say 'old'. He seemed old to me at the time because he never seemed to be shaved or anything. Probably he was a middle-aged man. But he lived with his mother on a farm back there and he used to come in on Saturday, and, oh, he would sell a few chickens, or take a pig to the stockyards (we shipped a lot of stock from Lancaster to Montreal). He would head for the hotel, and he would get drunk, and when he got kicked out of the bar—which was when he ran out of money, because his credit was no good—then he would come to the barbershop and get his weekly shave, see. He usually came in drunk, not that he couldn't walk or anything like that, but feeling good. His memory was bad, and sometimes when he'd get there he wouldn't have the dime for the shave. Next week, when my father would try to collect the dime, he would swear to God that he had paid it, and my father was trying to put something over on him. So he had to be put on a cash basis. So he got into the habit that he would always save this dime. Before he got thrown out he put it in a separate pocket, I guess. When he got thrown out of the bar-room, he could always come down and get a shave. So this night, he must've sold a pig or something, because he had quite a bit of money and when the bars closed at twelve o'clock, he still had money, so he came down to get a shave. But what he didn't remember was that he had also come in at nine o'clock and got a shave. He had the money, and he wanted to flash it, see. So about ten-thirty he came in again, and he wanted to show that he had plenty of money, and he wanted a shave. Well, my father tried to explain to him that he'd already had a shave, but there was nothing on God's earth could convince him that he'd been shaved, so my father shaved him a second time, you see. Well, those were the days when you shaved with a straight razor, and my father's razors were pretty sharp, and when you shaved a man a second time there wasn't much left on his face. So when he came in that third time, it was just hopeless. You couldn't shave him because you would've taken the skin off. So my father put him in the chair and lathered him up and everything, and then shaved him with the back of a comb, and he never knew the difference!

We had what they called an 'Indian list' in those days. As you probably know, the Indians were not allowed to buy whiskey, because they weren't supposed to be able to handle it. Well, there were a lot of other people besides Indians that couldn't handle it, and these people were put on what they called the Indian list. Now I don't know who put them on, I guess maybe the local mayor or something. But anyway, these people were forbidden to drink, and since in a small community like this the bartenders knew everybody by their first name, it was easy to put anybody on the Indian list. And there were a number of people who would get drunk and start fighting, and they were put on the Indian list, and they had to just quit drinking or get somebody else to get a bottle for them. Which wasn't easy, because fighting wasn't encouraged too much.

It was rough. There was a lot of hullabaloo. You got a few drinks, and you did a lot of hooting and hollering and stuff, but actually there wasn't much fighting. The lumberjacks would come in, and they would get liquored up, and perhaps they would have an argument with the millworkers and so on, but if a fight started, usually somebody stopped it. I never remember anybody being hurt. We had a local constable. He was a clerk in the hardware store, and he had no real authority, and I don't think he ever got any pay—I don't know what he got for his job. But anyway, if a fight developed, they went to get this fellow. His name was Dougall Macdonald. He certainly was no fighter, but he did have the authority of the people behind him, and when he stopped a fight, it stopped and that was it. Nobody ever questioned his authority that I know of.

Unfortunately, this Saturday night carouse had a bad effect on my father because these guys would get a few drinks in them and if they had a bottle of their own when they came into the shop they would always insist on my father having a drink. And into the back room they would go, and he would have a drink. How he kept from cutting their throats I don't know. But apparently he must have knew when to quit, because although I have seen him feeling pretty good, I never remember him cutting anybody.

Richard Mills

He had a strict Baptist upbringing on a farm near Sarnia, Ontario.

There were all kinds of people around us. There were people much like our household. My father was a very religious man. We'd call him a *very* religious man today; in those days I don't think he was—he was just another religious man. There were a lot of families just like ourselves, raising their children, going to Sunday school. They were pretty decent people. We had a contrast. We had a group—I shouldn't call it a 'group'—it was scattered people who went to town every Saturday night and got *tight*, really tight. They were *out* Sunday morning. You'd see them in the summertime lying in the gutter, in the back of the livery stable, just out since they'd drank so much. So we had this awful contrast. I often said that I saw more drunkenness as a boy than I've ever seen since. There's more drinking now by far, but it's taken in moderation. In those days you were either a temperance person or else you went out to get tight. There was nothing in-between at all.

What kind of person got 'tight'?

The ditchers were the ones that got tight. It was very flat country, and there were ditches all over. There was a group of ditchers lived here and here and here. (*gestures*) They didn't have a farm; they had maybe ten acres and a little house, and they would ditch all summer.

What did they do in the winter?

Oh, I guess some of them stole. I mean, they weren't very high class people. Some of them had families. They were a hard living group of people. We had one good farmer near us. His name was Billy Fleming. He was a good farmer, but he was a bachelor, and he was a drinker! He was a Saturday night boy, too. But he was the only farmer that I recall who was a heavy drinker. The others ones were these ditchers and threshers. There were some people, all they did was threshing. They had their tractors and separators and they had buzz saws for cutting wood. We all had wood, you know. They cut for the winter. They were of the other type who drank too much. They were rated at a lower social level than we were.

Ben Wagner

Was there a Women's Christian Temperance Union in Paisley?

There was, I think. Mother was against the use of liquor and father didn't drink, but I don't think mother belonged to it. The Women's Christian Temperance Union had a name for extremism, with all these speeches about demon rum, and the Scotch folk tend to be a little careful going about that.

The story of prohibition in Ontario is a very mixed-up affair. The local bar had become the meeting place in the little village, where men went and met people while their wives went shopping. But they were also enticed into drinking, not so much drinking, into spending money. We can only afford alcohol today because we're a very affluent society. We couldn't in 1914. We just plumb couldn't afford it. And that was why the feeling throughout Ontario was in favour of prohibition.

Was Paisley a dry town?

No, it had three hotels—three bars. Incidentally, two of those hotels folded up as soon as prohibition came in. They were living on alcohol. I take the odd drink myself and I always keep liquor in the house for my friends, but I recognize it's a thing for an affluent society.

Prohibition came to Paisley with a thing called the Prohibition Act on which you could vote. Each local area could vote whether or not they would allow bars. It was very wisely set up because you had to have a 60% majority to carry it, then you had to have a 60% majority to overturn it. So you couldn't have it going and coming on a few votes every year. But then general prohibition came to Canada. It was a war measure in 1916 to allow grains to be used for other purposes. It was a federal measure, and it was more or less respected because it was a war effort. Sometime on in 1920-21, they decided that the war was over, and the federal law lapsed. Then the provincial people took it up, and they carried prohibition in Ontario. But by that time there wasn't this onus to win the war, so the Prohibition Act was very much winked at, and it became smart to have a bottle of whiskey in the house.

Mrs. Judith McKay

What kinds of rules did Methodists have about behaviour?

They were *very* strict: no dancing, no cards, no liquor. My father was a great leader in the Temperance Movement, and I can remember stories about when we lived in Victoria Harbour. I was too young to know, but I can remember stories about the liquor interests trying to set fire to the barn, because he used to preach against them.

Was your mother ever involved with the WCTU?

Oh, of course, oh my dear, she was the *minister's* wife. She always wore her little white bow, a tiny little white bow of baby ribbon which every WCTU woman wore.

Alfred Nevin

The telephone creates a new kind of social life for people in rural communities.

My father was one of the first originators of the Beeton Telephone Company. He and a local doctor, with two or three others who lived in Beeton, started it. The doctor was complaining because he couldn't get in touch with his patients and the patients with him in an emergency. Something was said about 'We should have a telephone,' so father said, 'Let's have one!' The doctor was the originator of the idea because of his particular need in Beeton. So they formed the Beeton Telephone Company, which turned into quite a large company. Actually they had 1200 subscribers. Then, with the change in technology in telephones, you had to put in new exchanges, and the Bell Telephone Company had a stranglehold on all of these small companies, because they took the lion's share of all the long distance calls. My father was president till he was 80, and then the company was taken over by the Bell. The company was established in 1911.

You didn't have a telephone until then?

No. There was a telephone in Beeton, and there may have been one in the store in Bond Head, but there was nothing throughout the country. So father and the other directors built up a line that had 1200 subscribers. The rate at that time was eighteen dollars a year.

We had, at one time, fourteen people on our line. It used to be a little annoying; you wanted to get through what you thought was an important call, and you'd pick the phone up and hear somebody talking. Now it didn't take you long to find out who did the gossiping. You couldn't help but recognize most of the voices, you see. Mother was very anxious one time to make a call. So she picked up the phone, and she'd listened in two or three times, and these were young people that were talking. The boy on the phone was supposed to transmit a kiss to this girl, and he said, 'Did you get it?' And Mother said, 'Yes I did, and I didn't like it!' *(laughs)* And both hung up, so she got her line. Mother had a great sense of humour. There was another person on the line that had a clock, and she was a great talker. If you listened too long, you'd say, 'Now if Mrs. So-and-So would hang up, I'd like to use the line.' There was a lot of fun in it, but it used to be a little annoying. It was kind of a social life for people.

CHAPTER THREE

CITY STREETS

Life in urban Canada before the Great War was a more variegated experience than life in rural Canada. Industrial society had produced a range of economic and social groups. Real disparities between the comfortable and the poor were reflected in radically different lifestyles in various neighbourhoods. Economic necessity made working class family life a world apart from the world of the more comfortable middle classes. Young working class women became domestics, and helped create surplus leisure for middle class children, while their brothers hawked newspapers after school and gradually drifted into the work force at an early age. Urban leisure activity among the middle and working classes differed sharply in kind and in quantity, but a larger amount of it was enjoyed outside the home and family context than in rural Canada. Church and school helped recreate and stabilize the society. However, a variety of urban institutions — the mission, the settlement house, and the industrial school — reflected new styles of social control imposed by the more powerful sector of the community on the lower orders. Unresolved social tensions prevaded both the struggles of the poor to provide a decent life and the inexorable search of the powerful for new institutions of social control.

Les Beauchamp

His family came to Toronto from London, England in 1912 when he was six years old.

I was living in Toronto in the spring of 1913. We settled on Wilton Avenue, now known as Dundas Street East. The neighbourhood was very good. There was the old Cabbagetown school, Park School, very well known in those days. It was quite handy for us then. Not everybody had bathrooms in the house, but the Harrison's Bath House over at Regent Street and Sackville was always handy for us to go and get our weekly baths. In fact, when we went to Park School, in the junior classes, they used to parade us over there either Thursday or Friday afternoon. Make sure us kids did get a bath. But it was very nice. It was a largely Anglo-Saxon area, Scotch and Irish and English, mostly English.

We went to the Little Trinity Church on King Street East. I was Anglican at that time. That was the handiest for us at that time. I understand it's the oldest Anglican church in Toronto now. And we attended there for the war years. But we also attended a settlement house called the Evangelist Settlement, at the corner of Queen and River Street, which was always open, seven days a week, and it had gymnastic classes and cooking classes. My mother went there for the gym classes. It was activity for us. We did exercises, gym work, and we could also take up other types of sewing classes and cooking classes when you reached a certain age. My mother attended those. There was an Ear, Eye and Nose clinic there, for what you might call the working poor of that time. And they had a back area where we used to learn to play softball in those days. We did a lot of cork work. Have you ever done cork work with pegs? We used to do a lot of that and make rugs and whatnot.

My mother was a God-fearing woman, and we used to attend ten o'clock Sackville Street Mission, come out of there at eleven, and run like mad to Queen and Jarvis Street to the Fred Victor Mission. We used to go there for another session for an hour, then we used to walk back to Queen Street East. Then in the afternoons, we'd go to our regular church Sunday school. This was a typical Sunday for us. At night, we went to the Evangelist Settlement where they had reading classes. Different people would read good books to us. I think that's where I first heard about the *Wizard of Oz*. Some lady read it in episodes. Then we would go upstairs to the hall and sing hymns and singsong up there and listen to a talk. That was our Sunday. The only big thing is, being youngsters at that age, between eight and fifteen, we had the advantage of four picnics a year and four Christmas parties. *(laughs)* But in those days for Christmas there was no-thing doing as far as we were concerned. Welfare was unheard-of in those days. St George's Society was very good to us for about the first two or three Christmases; they sent along a roast of beef. But the Star Santa Claus Fund was very handy; they used to send this box along, with a sweater, a pair of socks, a toque, two or three toys, candies, and an apple. That was always well received by our family.

What was the St George's Society?

We came out under a scheme through the St George's Society. It's an English organization and it has a Canadian affiliate out here. Through them, I think, my father went up and applied, let them know that these Anglicans, these British people, were over here.

The part that strikes me is how you got by when you were poor. My dad never earned more than $25 a week in all his life. But as kids we just dug in. We could see the earnestness in the way my mother would do it. At the time we had a little kitchen stove and we'd burn coke. Coke was cheaper than coal. You'd get a whole bag of it for eight cents I think it was, go down to the bottom of Berkeley Street on Front, and get a bag of it. You felt pretty big holding it up to the chute and the guy pulls the chain that fills the bag up. But sometimes you didn't have eight cents. So we used to find out when they were dumping it around the back. They would burn so much coal to get the gas. So we used to go around picking it. You would be down there scrounging around, trying to get the best pieces of coke out of that. It would be no good and somebody would come along, saying, 'Oh, it's better over at Broadview.' And we had these little pushcarts, two-wheel things, and my brother and I would race like mad across Front Street over the old Don bridge and get down to coke. And there was better pickings over there at Broadview. But this is what we had to do. Things was very tough and cold in the wintertime. We never knew what cold was until we came to Canada. As kids I can always remember doing that, running and trying to get as much coke as we could, so we wouldn't have to go on the cold days.

Then there was the little jobs we used to try to do around, like newspapers and trying to sell as many of those as you could. You couldn't go around to any of the corners. Most of the corners were already occupied, so we always had to slide up the side streets. Going up the side streets you would come into different working offices, and the man would lean out the window and whistle, 'Hey, got a paper, boy?' And I'd run in and I said, 'What kind do you want?' 'Oh, two or three. Can you come by every day?' 'Fine.' I was delivering four or five dozen. It took all my time to carry four or five dozen. The trouble is I had to watch the corner boys as I came along. I had to duck down back alleys. Well, they knew I was cutting in on their trade. I used to work at Yonge and Wellington and walk all the way down to Queen and River Street. It's about a good mile, but I had to go all through the back alleyways to get along that way to avoid the main corners, in case these other fellas...

Did the corner boys work full-time?

Most of the big corners were held by regular newsboys. They would buy hundreds of papers, you see. But it got on that I would be picking up four or five at this street, and about another block or two further along I'd be getting rid of two or three papers. I'd wind up at the corner of Sumach and Queen Street. I'd have three papers. I thought, 'Here's six cents. I'd better try and sell them.' I may have been half an hour late getting home, and mother would give me the dickens for being late for supper, but I'd made the six cents. There was little things like that we used to do at that time. But I can remember my mother: she had to go out scrubbing floors and whatnot. I thought, well, if my mother has to do that, well, we have to dig in, you know. Our rent then was ten dollars a month, and it was pretty hard to come by at times.

Mrs Anne Whitelaw

She was the second of ten children. Her father made deliveries with a horse and wagon, and his income was high enough to afford a nursemaid for the children. The family moved several times, looking for better places to live.

Did you come from a religious family?

Well, I don't know what you would call a religious family. We always went to church. We went to mass at St Paul's, I tell you, and back up to Fred Victor Mission, then back up at 6:30 at night. St Paul's used to be going to kill me because I was going to Fred Victor Mission. My mother belonged to Fred Victor Mission, see. St Paul's didn't like it because I was a Catholic and Fred Victor Mission was Protestant. But my mother just told them she'd send her children where she liked. They were hers, and they were in a good place when they were in church.

I loved the Fred Victor Mission, more than St Paul's. At St Paul's you went in your seat and then you stayed there and you didn't move. The nuns were there, and you didn't move and didn't turn your head or anything else. But we went to Fred Victor where they had what they called a children's service. You could sing, and they had movie pictures of the Bible and that. And it was early at night and you could get home. I think it was six o'clock or something we used to go. We'd run like dickens to get up there in the back room of the Mission. It was a lot more fun. We were able to go there to what you called kindergarten. They had none of that in the separate schools. And up at the Fred Victor Mission you had cooking school. You could go to the gymnasium on the top floor to play basketball and different things like that.

You'd do that after school?

Yeah, and we'd get out of school and run. Oh, we'd be so perfect so that we wouldn't get kept in. And if you got kept in, you were kept in till four thirty or something and you'd get to the mission late. And half the time you were kept in really for nothing in my opinion. I don't know whether it's better or worse in the schools today.

In the junior third class, do you know what I was kept in for? I was getting to the stage that I noticed boys. St Paul's School was the girls' school and the boys' school was separate. Well, I was on the second floor. Now the platforms they had there were just wooden ones; there was two steps. One day I stepped out sort of towards the fire escape, seeing one of my boyfriends, and says, 'Yoohoo!' I had to kneel for two whole days on them wooden steps. I thought my knees were going to break. Oh, we got the strap for next to nothing. Now in front of me there was a girl sitting. Her name was Sabina. Her father had a wallpaper business on Parliament Street. She lived on Berkeley Street, see, away from Parliament Street. She really thought she was nice. She was the only child. She was always sort of dressed a little bit. Now I wore my hair in braids. I had long hair and wore it in braids with a couple of ribbons. She wore hers in curlets, ringlets. *(laughs)* You know what I done? In the desk there was an inkwell, so I stuck both her curls into the inkwell. *(laughs)* She was so stuck on herself, and she didn't like sitting in front of me, you see. Do you know what the punishment for me was for that? As I say, there were two steps and I was made to kneel on them steps for two days. My poor knees!

Did she think she was better because she had more money?

She thought she was better, and she seemed to be the teacher's pet. Sabina never done anything wrong, no, no. So I'm going to fix Sabina and I got fixed!

Did you ever go to any of the short movies or to vaudeville or anything like that?

I remember my aunt taking me to a movie, and it was up around Bay Street some place. And when things moved, they scared me. *(laughs)* I got scared. The first movie we went to anywhere was when St Paul's built the hall which is at Sackville and Queen and which is called the Good Shepherd Home now.

Father Hand was a visitor at our house. Him and my father used to like to talk over the races, and if my father was going to the race track over at Dufferin, he was taking us up on the wagon to the Dufferin race track to watch the races over the fence. *(laughs)* He bet on them, but I think he lost more than he bet. But one time he won $100. My God! I thought Parliament Street—I can't remember, but I think he was going crazy. *(laughs)* The name of the horse, I can still remember, was Mustard Seed. My mother used to get mad because he was taking the money and going to the races. Well, it was money being taken out of the house and if you didn't win any, you lost it all. Come home with nothing in your pockets and sometimes had to walk. It was money going, yeah. Oh, they had more arguments over them horse races! She wouldn't want to give him the money to go to the races. You see, my mother handled the money. My father'd get his pay and give her so much for the house, and then he had his spending money, whatever it was.

What did your parents do for entertainment?

Well, I guess my mother's entertainment was going to the Fred Victor Mission. They had a Tuesday night club, and then they did have a mothers' meeting, you see. They played little games, the same as what we did, and had a religious service first. Sometimes I had an awful fight to get out of this house to go to the things I wanted. I can think of the fights that she had too. Oh, gosh! They'd go at each other. My father didn't want her to go out. He'd say something about picking up other men or something. Oh, I got it too. She says, 'Listen, after having you, I don't want to pick up any more men. I want no part of them.'*(laughs)*

What about your father? Were there drinking places around where you lived?

Oh, yes. The Hotel Rupert was at the corner of Parliament and Queen, yes. That was a very good stamping place. And the Chadwick House was on Sherbourne Street, and we used to take pails over and get them full of beer. Just a tin pail. You could buy it and take it out.

Barry Richardson

He got his first job at age ten (by lying about his age) as a 'tobacco boy' for the Imperial Tobacco Company in Montreal. He and the foreman were the only English-speaking people out of approximately 120 people in the department. Most of the workers were women.

When I worked in the Imperial Tobacco Company, the company gave each employee, if you were in the cigarette department, five packages of cigarettes a week to keep them from stealing. If you were in the cigar department, you got so many cigars, or in the tobacco department you got tobacco. I used to change my cigarettes for tobacco and take the tobacco home to my father. He was a pipe smoker.

Did it stop people from stealing?

I don't know about the men. It didn't stop the women. In those days the women wore bloomers. There was two men always stationed at the entrance to the factory, looking you over as you went by. And if they saw you walking a little awkwardly, you would be taken to one side, and invariably they'd find that the ladies had their bloomers packed with cigarettes. *(laughs)*

Did they smoke them or sell them?

They'd sell them. Invariably they'd catch one or two a day. You'd see them go to the line, and then you'd hear afterwards that somebody was caught stealing, you see. You couldn't steal very well once they got the government seal on them because that was the government stamp. But before it got to that stage, you could pick them up very easily off the machine, single cigarettes or in a package. You couldn't sell them to the stores, but you could sell them to friends.

Eric Rosen

He joined his family in Canada in 1909 when he was eleven, and worked in a pant factory in Trenton. He was the youngest of about seven boys working there.

The bulk of the staff were girls. At that time it was a little different to what it is now. The machines were operated from one motor and there was the wheels all underneath. It was one of my jobs to fix the belts when they broke. Of course, when I got down under there, you could bet the girls would be jumping. I always got blamed for any mischief, I don't know why!

I got three dollars a week and worked a fairly long week, Saturdays and all. I'd got up to six dollars a week when I left there in 1914. During the slack period I went and got a job with a contractor and he set me to work tearing down the plaster because they'd had a fire in this house. At the end of the week he said, 'How much do I owe you?' So I thought for a minute, and I know I shouldn't have done it, but I told him I was getting eight dollars a week. I lied to him. So he gave me ten.

What were the working conditions like in the factory?

Nothing to really shout about. You did what you were told. There was no such things as unions. The boss was the man. Many times he was going to give me a raise, but I didn't get it. You'd go in and tell him and yes, he'll do it, but you know! That was the way it went. Mind you, in those days we didn't know anything about talking back as we do today. I think it's gone a little bit too far. I find it very difficult to see what happens in these days. And yet I don't like the way in which we were almost ground down. You just did it, that was it. You didn't think. We weren't disturbed then by the things that we are disturbed with today. I don't think we sat down and grumbled about it that much. Oh, I'd say, 'I don't know why he doesn't give me some more money,' or something like that, but that was it. It didn't eat me up.

Oh, some of the supervisors were alright and some weren't. Some were very temperamental people, but you had no recourse to anything. If they said you were wrong, you were wrong. That was all there was to it. I don't mean to say that I was unhappy, because I've never been like that too much. But it wasn't ideal, let's put it that way. You went to work because it was the thing to do. You had to go to work, you needed to go to work, and you sort of took it as it came.

Larry Nelson

As a child he lived comfortably in downtown Toronto. His father had been in the horse business in the west.

I always felt that, as far as Toronto is concerned, I don't think you could have a better city for a boy to grow up in, in that period. Because there was no sense of being organized. If I wanted to play baseball, I went out on the street and played on the corner lot. I played hockey and shinny on Small's Pond down on Queen Street, over on the other ponds and even on the Don River. I've swam in the Don River down by Riverdale Park. Those were happy, carefree days. A friend and I had two shetland ponies that we used to race in the wintertime, from Yonge Street to Church Street. That was a lot of fun. Nobody ever held out inducements for us to get out and amuse ourselves. No, we did it spontaneously. In the wintertime we'd go sleigh riding in High Park or Riverdale Park. There was no skiing, of course, in those days. If you wanted to swim, the city ran a boat from over at Fisherman's Island down to the bay, and you could swim in the icy waters of Lake Ontario if you wanted to. Otherwise you didn't swim; the cops got you. Of that generation there were remarkably few good swimmers. You had no place to swim.

I lived on Gloucester Street, running off Yonge Street. At that time it was a nice, quiet, middle-class street. Now it's a street of cheap rooming houses. We had wonderful neighbours. I'm a Protestant myself, but most of my neighbours around there were Catholics, and consequently most of my friends of that particular period were Catholic.

I think that there was quite a lot of snobbery in Toronto. Of course I was what you might describe as middle middle class. I don't remember school ever drawing any lines of social structure in the schools at all. Jarvis Collegiate drew from Rosedale and Jarvis Street as well as from what we used to call The Ward and Cabbagetown now. There was no distinction at all that I recall. The same when I went over to Riverdale Collegiate too.

I think perhaps you do look back through rosy spectacles on those days, but times were bad at certain periods too. I can remember that in the summertime typhoid fever was epidemic when I was a boy, always in summertime. I had typhoid fever when I was twelve; I was out of school for a year. So did my sister; she almost died. And I had scarlet fever when I was about fourteen. Well, I survived all those things alright.

Do you remember what books you read?

I remember two periodicals or annuals which were commonly read or were popularly read by boys, youths probably from the ages of ten to fifteen or so. That was *The Boys' Own Annual* and *Chums*. These both were frequently given, at least in my case, as Christmas presents. Both the annuals had a great deal in common, and most of the boys were paragons of manliness. They had sections dealing with hobbies such as sailing, and what we would call handicrafts, and many other activities. Looking back on them now, they were pretty splendid reading for boys. Some aspects of it, in this permissive age, seem a bit ludicrous. For example, I remember I wondered what it all meant at the time when they used to speak of 'secret places' and of a common phenomenon that every boy knows about—wet dreams and nightly emissions and so on—as sapping the strength and loss of virility and so on, that we know is a bunch of nonsense these days. The panacea at the time was cold baths, a great deal of strenuous exercise like cross-country running, and so on. But on the whole, as I said before, the books did have quite an influence on us as boys.

Of course, there were the Henty books. Once again the boy was a paragon of virtue and manliness and bravery in his books too. But on the whole, I can remember some of them which were quite well done as far as the historical background was concerned.

Did these influence you?

Yes, I think so. I don't think you can ever get rid of those mores as you go out and get older. I think it has some influence all your life. It's quite true it fades off as you get older, but I don't think you ever entirely forget it or throw off what you derive from those books. There was another type of book too that was very popular and was rather significant too. That was the American books. There were two books that I can remember that were popular with boys, and that was the Frank Merriwell series—I don't know whether you ever heard of them or not. He was a great all-American athlete. He played rugby and football and baseball. Baseball seemed to be his great sport, and he always won. He always won, nothwithstanding the dirty tricks of his opponents. The other was Horatio Alger, a poor but honest boy who starts at the bottom and who by industry and loyalty to his employer rises to the top and eventually marries the employer's daughter. A lot of garbage now, we think it is, but as I get older I'm not so sure. Looking around among some of my friends, I can see that some of them did perhaps model themselves on some of the characters in the books that we read.

Mrs Sally Hill

When you were fourteen you were initiated into the gentle art of getting your tummy all squeezed. But I was taking music lessons and Mrs Heath was my music teacher and she had gone to a very progressive girls' school in the States, so she made me a rebel. She said, 'Don't let them put you into corsets. It's not necessary. The human form is not meant to be constricted like that!' And when it came my day, I said to my mother, 'I'm not going to wear a corset, you know.' 'Why not?!' she said, although she never squeezed herself. 'Because I don't want to.' But I've seen my cousins actually tie themselves to the bedpost and walk away so they could be pulled in. Their waist would be small enough so you could take your two hands and span it around. But I never had to. I wore a ferris waist. It was about two thicknesses, and it was corded, and it had the suspenders so you could fasten up your stockings. It was a great innovation then, because it was always round garters, you know. They used to knit the round garters. The girls would be knitting garters for themselves, and they used to twist them somehow around their legs, but I didn't do that. These waists had buttons on the shoulders so you could kind of adjust them. They were great big, flat buttons with two holes in them (they looked like ivory) and instead of thread sewing them on, there was tape that went through the two holes. I've never worn corsets. I escaped.

I guess the spirit of change was coming into effect even then, because, I was just thinking, I had my hair first cut short 50 years ago. It was so hot and my hair was so heavy. I could sit on my hair. So in desperation and not telling my husband or anything, I went and had my hair cut. Oh, he was wild! Oh, he was so mad at me he wouldn't speak to me for about a week! But oh, my hair felt so nice. My head just felt painfully heavy because I used to have it twisted up in a huge great big lump on the back of my head. So I've never worn long hair again. That's another thing I escaped—the heavy head of hair.

My mother used to have a pompadour over what they called a rat, and this rat was a round, artificial hair thing, it looked like a snake. They just brought it round and pinned it, and then they brushed their hair over it and made a great big knot on top.

I remember when I was young, we used to tease our hair. We had hygiene, of course, and things like that, and physiology. They used to tell us never to tease our hair, we were breaking it, and then it would never grow in right. We used to get scolded, but we used to tease it. We used to have two big lumps like beehives, one over each ear—must have looked awful funny! That was when I was in high school. But in public school I just wore it braided halfway down my back, with a bow on the end of it and then a curl.

How long did you wear floor-length dresses?

I didn't. I'll tell you, I had dresses probably down to there (mid-calf), it was the most I ever wore them. Then, by the time I got to be fourteen, do you know what came in? The hobble skirt. Did you ever hear of the hobble skirt? It was 20 inches around the bottom, and it was curved up the front. Underneath you wore a cerise or a paddy-green, frilled, taffeta petticoat, or if you couldn't afford the whole thing, you just wore a piece. You could actually buy the piece to put in underneath there. You could not get that skirt above your knees under any circumstances! It was terrible to get onto the streetcar, because many and many a time two men would take you and hoist you up onto a streetcar. You just hobbled. It really was a hobble skirt—and peg-topped. They had pleats in the top, and then you wore a vest with it. And you just hobbled!

Edward Thompson

Courting? You didn't go too far to court. You would take in one of the nickel shows, for instance, and sit with the arms around the neck probably, and sneak the odd kiss or something like that. But courting generally wasn't as wide open as what it is today, in that if you went to somebody's house usually there was a piano, and you would play and sing on the piano. Then you would take her home and stand on the veranda for about five minutes before the old man'd say, 'Hey, Elsie, come on in. Send that guy home.' It's quite different. I mean, it was more polite—I don't know what expression to use. But it was considerably different to today. There seemed to be something more real about it, like the Santa Claus parade. It used to be along Bloor Street. It seemed more real as a Santa Claus than what it does today. Today it's like a fantasy or a carnival or something like that. But in those days you had a feeling that there was something genuine or real about it. And this realness is what's gone out of the lives of we people from away back, as I see it.

Mrs Agnes Fairbanks

Her father was in real estate. Since her mother 'had a horror of public schools and collegiates' she was sent to a Presbyterian girls' school (despite the fact that the family was Anglican), and then to university. In her own words, 'my family wanted to protect me.'

Courting was mostly done at the skating rinks on Saturday afternoons or in the evening when they would have a band, and you would know people, and they would offer their arm, and you would take it. I found I couldn't skate without somebody's arm. And we'd go round and round to the band, and then it would stop, and then you'd talk, and then another tune would come along. We spent a great many Saturdays at the rink. There were lots of parties too. In those days young girls were 'brought out.' Mother had a huge reception one afternoon, and I stood beside her, and all her friends came. It didn't matter so much about mine, but they came too. All mother's friends accepted me, and we had a lovely time. Then later in the winter, father gave me a beautiful dance. I think it was called Sage's Parlours. It was just along here on College, just east of Spadina Avenue. Of course, that was delightful—a real party all my own. I was nineteen then.

What did 'coming out' mean exactly?

That they had a daughter old enough to come out into what you might call 'society.' That, I suppose, is when we started having our little cards. I can remember mother's little cards with her name on, and you'd go calling and leave a little card. There was always a dish in the front hall of any home that would accept these little pieces of card. I think mother's days were every second Thursday, and people would come in and have a cup of tea. That's all so different now.

Mrs Helen Gloucester

Born in Wales in 1890, she and her husband came to Canada in 1911 and settled in Toronto.

My first baby was born in the General Hospital up by Riverdale Park. The doctor put me in the hospital two weeks before she was born, on account of being a stranger in Canada. I had no friends, and my doctor thought that I'd be safer in the hospital than listening to all the neighbours that were telling me different things and scaring me.

Did people tell you what it was going to be like when you had your first baby?

No, they scared you half to death. Of course, I didn't know anything. In the old country we don't know nothing like the kids do today. We don't know nothing what's going to happen. We don't even know where the baby's coming from. Oh, it was frightening. That's why the doctor put me in the hospital, because he found out I didn't know which way the baby was coming. I thought I had to be cut. Of course, they didn't talk about those things in them days. Oh no, that was out!

Mrs Sally Hill

Did pregnant women have to hide themselves?

There was a certain amount of leering, and women were very modest. The very fact that they were pregnant seemed to them to show what they'd been up to, I guess you might say! They didn't go out very much; they went for walks at night.

There were no maternity clothes at all. We had to make do the best we could. I used to make dresses out of a navy blue heavy print, which was about the least conspicuous thing I could get. But I remember that women did not go out as they do now, in and out of stores and shopping. People got things for them, and they went for walks on their husband's arm at night. That was the modest thing to do. He just looked as if he didn't know what to do with it, but he had to acknowledge it. It was his fault! *(laughs)* Then everybody made a big fuss after it was all over. We used to have a joke. In the books they'd say, 'She whispered in her husband's ear that there was going to be a little stranger.' In other words, he was the last one to know! *(laughs)*

Mrs Roberta White

Her family came from England to Toronto in 1905. Her mother had worked in a factory in England as a blouse and pinafore designer, but in Toronto she was well known as a midwife.

My mother was a midwife. Everybody thought that she was pretty wonderful. Her grandmother, my grandmother, or my great grandmother was a nurse, and in England my grandmother was a nurse, but my mother never had any training that I recall. She had practical experience.

Didn't doctors deliver babies?

Oh yes. If they got there in time, they delivered them, alright. But there was always the ten days the woman spent in bed, and the other children to be taken care of, and the husband to be fed, and a nurse wasn't above that sort of thing. Mother was a strong, healthy woman, and she stepped right in there and took the mother's place until the mother was able to take over herself.

Did doctors look down on midwives?

I don't know whether they did. I didn't really know doctors all that well. But my mother certainly looked up to the doctors. But she was never subservient. She was always capable and quite herself, you know, a person in her own right. I remember one time she had a run-in with a doctor because he hadn't properly removed the afterbirth. He tried to wiggle out of it by excuses, and she just told him off, which she would, of course. It was her patients she cared about, not the doctor's feelings. She had doctors, that I was more aware of as I got older, that thought the world of her, thought she was wonderful.

Mrs Edith Thomas

She came to Toronto with her husband in 1905, because of the job shortage in England. She had worked in a factory, but in Canada she worked at raising her thirteen children and as a midwife. Women in her neighbourhood did not go to the hospital when their babies were born.

How did you become a midwife?

Because I had so much knowledge of it. I got my information from the old midwife, and then I learned lots of things. You learn when you go around from one place to another. And then the doctors got to know me, and so they used to send me out. The women had to pay for it. They didn't pay much money because the poor things didn't earn much. It was mostly poor people like myself—they didn't have the money to give you. Some I took and some I didn't, because I knew they wanted it, and I was not too bad off then, because I was doing alright myself. And I said, 'No, you get something for the baby.' And many, many a time I've had to take things out of my home and give to the poor people to help them out.

I went to one woman at three o'clock in the morning. She was sitting in the washroom there, and the husband come for me, asked if I'd come to see his wife. He said, 'Liza is very sick, will you come over and see her?' So my husband says, 'You better get dressed and go and see what's the matter.' She had a little premature baby. Well, she wasn't ready for it because she was only about six months. She wasn't near her time. So when I went and seen her, I went home again and packed my sheets to make diapers and different things, and the doctor wouldn't come. But the baby come, and I had nothing to put it in, see. So when he come at seven o'clock in the morning, he was surprised. 'Oh,' he said, 'that won't live.' I said, 'It's doing alright.' I put it in a little wash basket on the floor near the heat going through. Wrapped it up in a blanket, it was only a little thing. That's a guy that's six foot two now! I dressed it and fixed it up. He said, 'It'll never live.' He's an old doctor too. I said, 'Yes, it will, I'll look after it, so stay there.' And I went home. I had to tell my husband what happened, you know.

Eric Rosen

His wife came to Canada under the auspices of the Barnardo homes. These homes were responsible for collecting and choosing suitable children (usually orphans) to send to Canada as domestics and agricultural labourers. Mrs Rosen's plight as an overworked servant was typical of many Barnardo children.

My wife really shouldn't have been a Dr Barnardo girl, because her mother was in England. How she managed it I don't know. She got her into the Barnardo home. She came out here in 1914 as a girl of fourteen. She was put into homes here where they were supposed to let her do some work and then have some schooling. But they never sent her to school. They treated her very unkindly, and she had no friends. The woman she worked for during the war got her a job at munitions at Dufferin and King at night, and then she'd do the housework. The person that she worked for just at that time carried on so much that one night I was seeing her home and she started to cry. It was half past nine and she was afraid to go in. So I said, 'Look, enough of this!' So I phoned my mother. She said, 'Bring her home.' So I brought her home, and mother went out and got her clothes the next day. They didn't have the supervision in the Barnardo homes that they do today. People got away with things. The kids were not looked after as they should have been.

How did your wife get into the Dr Barnardo homes?

I guess her mother worked it through somebody, I don't know. You see, I had always imagined that you had to be an orphan, and of course, she wasn't an orphan because she had a mother. I was so provoked with her when she used to tell me. I'd said to her several times, 'How did you used to feel when you came to this country and you didn't have anybody? Did it not get you down?' 'No,' she said, 'I just took it. I thought nobody cared.' You know it makes my sons boil when they think of it.

What kind of work was she doing?

Housework, and boy, it was housework too! Scrubbing floors and scrubbing walls and stripping wallpaper. When I wouldn't let her go in, and I took her home, my mother went over the next day and told the woman, 'Now you have Gladys' clothes ready tomorrow, and my son will come over and pick them up.' Well, I went over, they lived on Lynd Avenue. There was a tin trunk on the veranda, and her clothes were strewn there. At that time she wore those corset things, and there they were, laying out there. I had to gather everything up, and the woman wouldn't even come to the door.

Mrs Sally McAffrey

Her family had very little money, yet they had a live-in maid and a washerwoman who came once a week. Her father's salary as deputy registrar of the county was too small to support five children, and he was forced to moonlight as a secretary.

At that time it was the thing to have a maid, and even though we had very little money, mother had a maid for a long, long time. Wealthier people would have more than one maid. People who had larger houses and more money to spare would have more than one, but as a rule, it was just a maid of all work. It must have been at the same time mother had a washerwoman once a week. But as we got older, that sort of thing disappeared. I don't think we could afford it.

The maid got the ordinary wage that a maid would get. We didn't call her a maid then, we called her a servant. I don't remember how much, but it was a ridiculous amount as things would be nowadays. It was not any more than twelve dollars a month, but of course, she did get her living, her room and board.

Mrs Betty Brooks

Her family could more easily afford a maid, as her father was one of three dentists in Sault Ste. Marie.

I remember my younger sister and I used to have to do the dishes on Sundays because it was the maid's day off, and the maid had one other half day off a week. And they got about $20 a month. They were single women, and they were quite important in a household. I think that was one thing the war ended, being able to get maids to work—maybe it didn't, I don't know. I remember the maids that we had when we were children. They'd stay three or four years, and then maybe get married and leave.

Mrs Adrienne Stone

They had daycare in the old Victoria Day Nursery. My mother was on that board. They kept the children for I think it was ten or fifteen cents a day, something like that. It was privately run. I can't tell you the details because I don't know them, but I do know that it's the old story that sounds a bit like the television, *Upstairs, Downstairs.* There was a very prominent lady in Toronto who used to go out to dinner and come back with a cheque in her pocket to buy something they needed at the day nursery. It's still going and I'm not sure of the name of it. I think it's quite a well-known day centre in Toronto. But it did start as the Victoria Crèche.

Would people like your mother put you in daycare if she was going away?

No, it was strictly for working mothers. It was on the old basis of what used to be called, I suppose, charity.

Mrs Ethel Cameron

She grew up on a farm but went to the city and worked in factories.

Women did not work too much, but I don't think there was too much against them working. They were respected because, if we had to make a living, we had to do it somehow—we had to work. A lot of women went into domestic service, but it was something which I never wanted to do. I didn't think I was cut out for it. I didn't like working for other people, in other people's homes. I would rather work out, in the mill or someplace like that.

Mrs Roberta White

My very first job was in a suspender factory just this side of Sherbourne Street, and oh, it was dreadful! I hadn't much training in doing the same thing over and over again. I got three dollars a week. So I said to the man that I wanted a raise, and he said alright, he would give me a raise. So you know how much he gave me for a raise? Twenty-five cents. So I was indignant and I quit. I was so mad.

Mrs Sally McAffrey

She was a stenographer in a factory office for two years, then moved to the Daily Woodstock Sentinel Review, *one of three newspapers in Woodstock, Ontario.*

There were three newspapers in Woodstock. It was a most outlandish arrangement that there should be three newspapers in a town of less than ten thousand people. I worked for the *Sentinel Review*, and the others were the *Daily Express* and the *Times*. Eventually they both gave up and the *Sentinel Review* was the only one. I don't know if they failed or they just decided to discontinue.

When did you start working at the newspaper?

That'd be about 1910, I think, till 1916. It was quite a long time, and I did everything but wash the dishes there. The boss used to say, 'Oh look, Miss Edwards, I think you could do this.' And he'd put me into some other job. I worked in the advertising department of the newspaper. I worked on 'Rod and Gun.' I did this 'Athletic World' stuff and 'Motor Magazine.' But I ended up as a sort of sub-editor on the *Sentinel Review*. Society Editor was the title I went under, but I would help the editor of the paper. I did any typewriting that he wanted, and I worked in the news office of the paper. And it was then that Bob said to me one day, 'You know, if you weren't a woman, I'd make you city editor.' I sort of looked at him, and he said, 'Well, at least you wouldn't get drunk.' *(laughs)* He had just had a set-to with an editor he'd had to fire just like that, because he was tight most of the time.

Was it unusual for a woman to be sub-editor on a newspaper?

Well, you see, the trouble was that there were Council meetings and things of that sort that had to be reported late at night, and at that time no one would send a woman to be out till midnight by herself. That was unheard of, unthinkable! So that was that.

Was there a union in the newspaper office?

That is a story in itself. One summer there was a strike in the newspaper office, and the reason was that the boss wanted to keep it an open shop, and the Printers' Union were insisting on it being a closed shop. So for several weeks that was one of the jobs I did. The boss sent me out into the composing room, and I worked on a darn old monoline printing thing and made an awful hash of it. But I did learn to do it very well before I was through. But I broke the strike for about six weeks. It didn't bother me any, except that they called me a scab. Some of the printers who were out said, 'I wonder what the boss has on Miss Edwards. She's a sca-a-ab.' *(laughs)*

You didn't think the printers were justified in trying to . . .?

Well, I don't know. Things were different at that time. Unions were by no means so all over the place as they are now. I think everybody thought that Taylor was perfectly right in sticking out against the closed shop. As a matter of fact, he won out. They just sort of leaked back. There was no formal caving in or anything of that sort. But eventually practically all the men who had been out came back and came back on his terms.

You see, the strike was just about the closed shop. Mr Taylor was always very good about wages and hours and that sort of thing, letting them off when they needed it. And when they'd get tight, he'd sort of gloss it over.

It was before the war, it would be about 1912, I should think. It was in the summer. It lasted about two months. The first paper we got out was a joke. It was no more like a newspaper than it was like a present-day magazine. It was a dreadful looking thing. But eventually we got that we were printing not too badly.

Did they set up a picket line outside the newspaper office?

No, there were no pickets in those days.

CHAPTER FOUR

NEWCOMERS

Canadian immigration policy in the early twentieth century had been designed to recruit an agrarian population for the Canadian west. Both British and Central European immigrants were lured to the last frontier by the promise of cheap, plentiful land and high-paying jobs. Many took the publicity of the CPR and government immigration agents at face value. Some planned a brief sojourn in the new land in order to acquire the capital to set themselves up in business after returning home. Others planned a life of gentility on their Canadian estates. Still others fled repressive regimes, landing in Canada with less thought of the future than of the past they had just escaped. To some extent, no immigrant was totally satisfied with the promise of Canada. For the unhappy British immigrant, the outbreak of the war offered the chance to end his unfortunate stay in the New World. The non-British, trapped in an alien and unfriendly land, would encounter even more hostility during the war years.

I. HOMESTEADING IN THE WEST

Michael Sheehan

In 1902 Mr Sheehan went west, leaving his home in Mimico, Ontario. An unskilled labourer, he worked on farms and in lumber camps, but finally in 1910 he acquired his own homestead. He returned to Mimico, on the outskirts of Toronto, in 1914, just before the war broke out.

When I was seventeen, I went out west. The great cry in those days was 'Go west, young man,' so I did. But I had no training for anything. We didn't go in for carpentry or plumbing or anything like that. We were kind of nomads, you know, like our ancestors. We just went out and braved the world. I worked on farms and in the lumber camps, and I drove the rivers. I had a really wonderful time out in Alberta, Saskatchewan, and British Columbia. I homesteaded in Saskatchewan, 125 miles southwest of Saskatoon. It was near the county town of Kerrobert on the Biggar-La Verna railroad line. I had some very interesting experiences out there.

I was working on a farm, and a farming boy from Ontario was working opposite, and then there were a couple of boys about two miles down, near Fillmore, Saskatchewan, south of Regina. These two boys were Americans, and they had homesteads way up in northern Saskatchewan. They induced this other lad and myself to go out and take up homesteads with them. I didn't go right away, but this other lad went out and took his homestead. He wrote down to me and he said, 'Mike, come on out here, there's a homestead right next to me.' I suddenly got the idea that I'd go out and see this homestead they wanted me to take. I got permission from the farmer and went up to Regina. And suddenly I got the idea that I must have that homestead. So I telegraphed up to Saskatoon—that's where you had to register—and filed on it by telegraph. Then I went up to Saskatoon, certified the application, and paid my ten dollars. You got all this quarter section—160 acres—for ten dollars. You bet the government that you could stay on it for three years during the summer and break 30 acres. Sometimes you won out and sometimes you didn't. But anyway, I got up to Saskatoon, and I suddenly thought, 'I'm up this far, I might as well go out the rest of the way.'

There was a Goose Lake Line and an Eagle Lake Line running out west from Saskatoon. One was CPR and the other was CNR. I took the Eagle Lake Line. It was really a freight train with all kinds of supplies going out, but it had a little coach on the back end of it for any passengers. It stopped all the way along at any place where anyone wanted to get on or off, whether there was a station there or not. And we rocked along—there was no care taken of the line. Well, we got out to this little town of Mackenzie. It was named after the restaurant keeper, old Mackenzie. And I said to old Mackenzie, 'Do you know the McConnell boys up north of here?' 'Oh yes,' he says, 'I know them well. They do all their shopping here.' I says, 'I'd like to get out to see them.' 'You can go out in the morning.' 'No,' I says, 'I can't wait, I gotta go tonight.' 'Why,' he says, 'it's 25 miles!' He took me outside, and he looked out toward the north, and he said, 'Do you see the North Star? Well, you make a beeline for that, and you'll come to the McConnells 25 miles away.' I started out walking in the middle of the night. I was young and full of pep and strong as a horse. I trudged along all night long. Finally I came to the crest of a valley, and I looked away out, and there was a light away over there. So I made for this light, down hill and up. It was rolling country. Finally I came to a little shack about twelve by fourteen—all the shacks were built the same size. I knocked on the door, but nobody was there, so I just opened the door and walked in. I took off my coat and lay down on the bed. I guess I went to sleep, because I don't know how long it was till I heard the jiggling of harness and talking. Presently the door opened and in come my friends. They were astonished to see me there, and so was I, of course. There were three of them, the two McConnell boys and Bill Charming. Next morning they took me to my homestead.

I was there the next three years. I got my patent, worked the thirty acres, and planted trees around, put in a windbreak, and built the barn. In the wintertime we all did the same thing. All the homesteaders used to go up to Prince Albert and work in the woods, and then in the spring we'd drive the river, taking the logs down to Prince Albert. We were 70 miles north of Prince Albert.

Did you work on the farm alone?

Well, with the money we made in the winter, we had our 30 acres broken by a neighbour. He had a ploughing outfit, and he used to go around ploughing up the ten acres a year for all the homesteaders.

What year did you get your homestead?

1910, and I was out there until 1914. It was tough going, and there were lots who gave it up. There were some who went up north where the timber country was, and they took homesteads up there, but they couldn't clear the land and get any crops growing. It was hard work and took too much money. But down on the prairies where we were, it was much easier. We had nothing to contend with that way. All we had to do was to have the land cleared and broken up.

So many of the homesteaders never stayed on. They just proved up their homesteads, got the title from the Saskatoon office, which made them the owner of the homesteads, and then they walked out. It takes quite a lot of money to buy your horses and ploughs and put up your barns. You had to do a certain amount of fencing. There was quite a lot of machinery that you had to have to start your farming operations. One thing and another, they had all they wanted of farming during their homesteading.

The homesteaders were mostly from Ontario, but the big farmers came from the Dakotas in the States. These Americans took up homesteads and bought land. They all had quite big farms. They had money, you see. They sold out down in Dakota, so they came up loaded. They put up nice houses and barns, and they had nice equipment, horses and cows, and everything.

We had some luck, because two years after we got in there, the CPR came through from Minneapolis and Moose Jaw, going up to Prince Albert. Then the year after that, the CNR came down from the other direction and crossed the CPR within a mile from our homesteads. We had a town there in no time! Three or four years after we were in there, we had a town and shops—a blacksmith shop and groceries—and we even had a hotel, which we later turned into a hospital. Oh, it was wonderful! In the meantime, when we had to get supplies, we had to go 25 miles down to old Mackenzie. It didn't matter. It's a funny thing when you are young: nothing seems to stop you. The McConnell boys had a team of horses, and Bill and I used to borrow the horses and take the trip down to Mackenzie to get groceries. If we said we were going on Wednesday, it didn't matter whether there was a blizzard blowing or what else. It didn't matter, you just went. You walked probably all the way because it was in the wintertime or it was too cold, and you'd stay overnight and then come back the next day.

Wilfred Lamont

He was working as a junior clerk in Norwich, England, when he first heard of the opportunities for better wages in Canada.

This chap was talking about going to Winnipeg. He made such a good story, I they're advertising, anybody can get out there. They have big signs out: "Go west, young man,'" he says, 'and you can go there for, it takes about ten or twelve pounds.' I went home to my dad, and I was rather abrupt. I said, 'I'm going to Canada in about a month I hope, Dad.' He was much surprised. He said, 'You are, are you!' I eventually got twelve pounds and away I came out here. This was in 1912.

How did you arrange for employment?

Oh, the government arranged all that, you see. I supposed as I only could afford twelve pounds for my passage, they'd drop me off at the nearest big city without going farther. But I came right across Canada to this little village, Codrington, just below Brighton. I was bound by a government contract to stay at farming for a year. But I didn't like the place I was at. The old fella was a man in his sixties, I guess. He'd been a previous lumberjack. Apparently he'd had just enough money to buy this—it was a hundred-acre farm, you see. He had two horses and maybe two cows. He had weird ideas. I wanted to shave, and he said, 'No, you don't shave here. Just grow a beard.' *(laughs)* You know, I was just a young kid. And his wife run straight with him, 'Oh Harvey, let him do what he wants. That won't hurt for him to shave, get clean and that.' Well, after an argument he gave in.

Then came the time that he had to take me out and show me how to farm. He took this team that he had, and he said, 'You sit on the gate.' He had about a five-acre field. He says, 'I'll take them around, and after awhile you'll be able to handle them.' They were a little frisky in the spring. So I sat on top of this gate, about eight o'clock in the morning, and I was sleepy. And I thought, 'Where is he now?' He was out of sight—went down the hill and around, took him about half an hour to get back to where I was. And I said, 'How about it?' 'Oh, too frisky for you,' he said. 'You can't handle them.' So I waited again. After three times around like this, I made up my mind. I says, 'Okay, I'm getting out of here.' So I waited till he got over the brow of the hill, and I rushed into the farmhouse. The old lady, his wife, says, 'What are you doing?' I says, 'Oh, I'm going up to get my trunk. I'm sending it away someplace.' So I put all my stuff in and nailed up the old trunk and let it down the staircase, out into the road. They had the old milk stands, where they send the milk to the cheese factory, so I sat there with my trunk.

A fella come along. 'What are you doing? Aren't you Harv Benedict's man?' I said, 'That's me. But no more.' 'How's that?' he says. I said, 'I don't like it there.' He says, 'Well, look, I'll take you down to the cheese factory. The farmers all come and bring their milk there to make cheese. We'll see what we can do.' So he took me down, and I waited. As I was looking around, the chap that runs the cheese factory says, 'Can you use an axe?' I was told never to say no. *(laughs)* 'Sure,' I says. 'Can you split wood?' I said, 'Oh yeah.' So he took me to the back of the cheese factory, and I swear there was a pile of about 500 nasty, chunky pieces of tamarack, which is about the toughest wood that you can do. Of course I went up, and he went back in the cheese factory. I raised the axe, and wham, I hit a block of this tamarack, and I couldn't get it out. *(laughs)* I was wriggling it and wriggling it and didn't know what to do. In the meantime the fella come out of the cheese factory and says, 'How much have you split?' I said, 'This is the first piece. I can't get my axe out.' 'Ah,' he says, 'you never saw an axe before in your life.' So he says, 'Come on in the cheese factory, and you can help me to make cheese. You can stir it up.' And while I was doing that the farmers were coming and delivering their milk. A young fella come to me, 'What are you doing?' he says. 'Aren't you Harv Benedict's man?' 'Yeah, I was,' I says. 'I quit. I can't get along with him, he won't show me anything.' 'Oh well,' he says, 'how'd you like to work for us? I've got a brother and three sisters and my mother. My dad works on the Trent Canal.' (They were building the Trent Canal at that time.) And I said, 'Alright.' I had a very enjoyable time until came the fall, and I said, 'There won't be much to do around here in fall.' 'No, mend a few fences,' he says. 'We'll feed you, we don't pay you anything.' So I thought, 'My goodness, that's awful. How am I going to buy anything?' I heard there was another Englishman, he was on the farm. So I went there, and I said, 'You been out long?' He said, 'I been out five years. I've got a couple of kids.' 'How are you making out? Is that your house?' 'Oh no,' he says, 'that's not my house. The farmer lets me live there.' I said, 'You've been out here five years, and you've got a couple of kids, and that's all you've got, and you're renting this on the farm?' He says, 'Yeah.' So he was trying to be satisfied, but I started to think. So I told the Calhouns (that's the people I was with), 'I'll be leaving this fall. I can't stand still all winter.' (By the way, I was getting thirteen dollars a month and room and board.) And I came to Toronto.

The first night, I remember, I had an old English raincoat and drum hat on. I must have looked a sight. Anyhow, the people said, 'Go up to the City Hall, they might have a job.' This was in the afternoon I arrived in Toronto. So I went up. Oh yes, they could probably take me. I went to the City Hall again the next day, and they took my name. So I went back to a boarding place where I was staying, and I looked through the newspaper, and I saw this John Inglis Company on Strachan Avenue. I didn't know where Strachan Avenue was. I was boarding on a place called Ashdale Avenue way out in the east end. I took a streetcar as far as I could. I remember I ended up at Yonge and Queen. I said to a fella going by, 'Do you know John Inglis on Strachan Avenue?' 'Sure,' he says, 'it's along that way.' Of course I had no idea of the city. I looked along Queen, and it looked pretty long to me. But anyway, I walked and walked and walked. And I got to Strachan Avenue about noon, just before William Inglis himself was going out. He says, 'Hello there fella, what are you looking for?' I said, 'I'm looking for a job, sir. I read in the paper you wanted a stenographer, typist.' 'Oh,' he says, 'you look kinda muddled up. What's all that dust on your shoes?' 'Well,' I said, 'I didn't know which way it was, sir, and at a place called Yonge and Queen somebody said, "You go west there on Queen, and you'll come to it."' And I kept walking and walking, and I just got here a little while ago.' 'Oh my god-father!' he said, 'If you can walk that far looking for a job, you can start Monday.'

Neil Haiste

The son of a poor working class family in Sussex, England, he too sought a new future in Canada.

I came to Canada because I had a brother or two here; they came through a society that helped to pay their expenses coming over here. They were doing alright here, and I couldn't see any prospects over there. Finally I had the chance to borrow some money, and I came over here. I borrowed half the fare and had to pay it back in just about twelve months. I was seventeen years old and that was in 1910.

We came under the Agriculture Society of Canada, and the first job I got, they sent me down to a farmer in a little two-by-four place they call Cherry Valley. It was in between Waterford and Simcoe. It was supposed to be a fruit farm. Hell, the only fruit on that farm was about two apple trees. I was there from sometime late in June to help them get the harvest in. We had the harvest in and everything else, it was getting near fall, and the old farmer was giving me hints that I should get out and get another job in a canning factory. I said to him one day, 'What the hell's wrong with you? You want to get rid of me?' 'Well, no,' he said, 'but we've got all the harvest in now, and we've got a few apples to pick and a few potatoes to dig. We can manage.' 'Alright,' I said, 'what about this contract you got with the government to keep me here for twelve months?' 'Oh hell,' he said, 'we can get around that. You can stay for the winter, work for your board.' 'What's that mean?' 'Well,' he said, 'you can do chores around here and work around here, but you wouldn't get any pay.' 'If that's all I'm worth, that bed I sleep on and the grub I get,' I said, 'it's time I got out.'

Richard Mills

Was it common for farmers in southern Ontario to bring in outside labourers?

Oh yes, we had a lot of English people—Barnardo boys. A lot of the farmers used to get Barnardo boys and had to teach them to be farmers. Some of them were good, but most of them weren't good at all. To the point that, from my very limited knowledge, I didn't rate English people very high because my contact was with those poor English people sent out to Canada. They were, I would say, away below the standards of the farm boys brought up around here. But the one I knew personally was a good fella. He was a really good fella. He used to go to the Baptist Church.

When did they start bringing them over?

Oh, I don't know. All they were to me were Barnardos. So-and-So's got a Barnardo boy. That's all I know about it. I knew the story: Dr Barnardo felt that a lot of these poor poverty-stricken boys, with no chance at all and no family background, were wandering the streets, and he'd pick them up and send them to Canada to get a job. They'd be better off here than at home.

I don't think they were treated very well. It depended on what farmer they were with. I think some of them gave them a good chance and some of them really ridiculed them and weren't very fair. I'm sure of that. And they didn't stay around long. They didn't have to stay, you know. Some of them stayed for years, but I think a lot of them just stayed for six months or a year, then they disappeared somewhere, we don't know where. I think it was back to some town, likely. My impression was that none of them knew a thing about the country and the crops and farming, and they were just from some mining city or shingle city or London.

II. LIFE IN THE CITY

Bruce Murchison

My father was a butcher on Parliament Street, serving the Cabbagetown and Rosedale areas. He came to this country from England as an immigrant and he walked the streets all day trying to get a job. All he could see was signs in the window that no Englishman need apply. This was in the eighties. Finally towards the end of the day, he was passing a butcher shop on Parliament Street, owned by Mr Stone. He asked Mr Stone if he could work for his board and lodging until he got employed, and Mr Stone took him in. He remained with Mr Stone and bought him out and raised our family. And he never forgot the lesson of being an immigrant and how hard it was to get started. This was exemplified in the life he lived. He was a most generous man. We had a big attic, and he put beds up in the attic. And the farmers who supplied him with vegetables, produce, butter, eggs, meat, all had daughters seemingly who wanted to come to the city and have a spell of city life. And so these daughters volunteered to work with mother, doing housekeeping duties for their lodge and board. This enabled my father to go down in the butcher cart and meet the incoming trains bringing immigrants to Canada who were on their way out west to get 160 acres, which the Canada of that day was offering to settlers.

David Allan

His father lost all his money in 1910 in a bank crash in England, and subsequently came to Canada. His parents worked for a farmer in Georgetown until his father was able to find a job with a law firm in Toronto.

The most lost soul in Toronto, perhaps in the whole of Canada, is a white Anglo-Saxon, or an Englishman particularly, because when my father came out here in 1910, they had signs up on what was the old Massey-Harris Company:

'No Englishman need apply.' The reason for that was there were a poor bunch of undesirables brought out to Canada by the Salvation Army about that time, and they'd get a job at Massey-Harris (it's now Massey-Ferguson), and within two or three weeks they were trying to tell the Canadian people how to run their jobs. Well, that's a disaster, you see. They were a poor type of English people, but you've got poor types of any nation as far as that goes, and so it made it awfully difficult for anybody coming to Canada from England to get a job or be recognized or even make friends.

'No Englishmen need apply.'

Mrs Maria Pawel

What did your parents do in the Ukraine?

They were sort of a semi-peasant. My father had to supplement what we couldn't get out of a bit of land we had. He used to buy pigs—go from village to village and buy pigs, and bring them back into the little town where we lived —and he worked for commission. So he supplemented a little bit more to feed his family that way, because he had no money of his own. He had to borrow the money to buy the pigs, and then the man just would give him a certain percentage. It's hard to translate just what it was. It was sort of a buyer.

They were hardworking people. They sort of wrestled their living from the land, but they supplemented to eat a little better, to go in and work for somebody else for a few pennies a day.

I was born is 1897. I remember the most when my father came to Canada in 1907. He was sick and tired of working for somebody else, so he thought he would make enough money in Canada and come back and start his own business. So that's how he landed in Canada. When he did come to Canada, I remember him saying that it was sort of the end of some depression they had just before 1907, so he couldn't get jobs. He walked from Kenora to Winnipeg, hungry most of the time. So then he landed in Winnipeg and signed up for British Columbia to build the railway, and I don't know how long he stayed there, but he didn't have a lot of money to send to us. Anyway, from British Columbia he came to the town of Saskatoon, Saskatchewan, and he got work in the city works department, digging ditches and so on. He thought he'd make enough money and come back home. Well, what happened then: he was illiterate, so somebody else had to write his letters. So one young smart aleck wrote a letter for him, and wrote what he said, then he added on his own: 'Sell everything and come to Canada.' Dad didn't mean it that way. He didn't want us to come. He still thought he'd make enough money to come back. Well, mother didn't think twice. She sold everything she had, and we landed in Canada in 1911. He was making twenty cents an hour then and worked ten, twelve hours, digging ditches. You know, they were putting in sewers and so on. Saskatoon was just building up then. That was 1911. See, this is the history of how we landed in Canada, and we did land here, and what can you do? He was working, so somebody else came and got us from the station. There was five of us. I was the oldest.

What do you remember about the trip over? Were you excited about going?

I was fourteen, and I didn't know what it was all about. I didn't go to school until I was nine years old in our country, when it became compulsory. You see, the peasants didn't give a darn, especially for the girl. What would she want with school for? Well, you know, I grew up. When I was fourteen, I was this size already. So how you going to go to the school with kids? So I left after three years. So when I landed here, what can I do? I didn't have the language. It was terribly hard, and I had to go to work right away, because my father couldn't keep the whole family. We had to have a place to live, so we bought an old shack and bought everything on time, and bought a lot, and moved the shack from somewhere else into a lot, so we had a home, but we couldn't live out of it. The first one we lived in, there was four families in the eight-room house, all immigrants, and we had to share one stove. That's the way we lived.

The first job I ever had was in a little Chinese restaurant in Saskatoon out of the way from the main streets, like. And what can I do? To his standard, I couldn't even peel the potatoes properly. I'd never done that sort of work before. I didn't fare very well. He let me go because I wasn't to his standard, I guess. I was a kid, you know, very thin. So then after that, I got a job in another restaurant. I think it was four dollars a week, and I worked twelve hours altogether. It was a split shift, we were off in the afternoon. I was washing dishes, scrubbing floors, and everything else that came along. I left there, and I went to work in London Hotel. Gee, that was hard. It's a very, very busy hotel. That's where I began to learn all about what life is like. I worked with people that were grown up. I remember one day I was scrubbing a cement floor on my knees. I collapsed, and the girls carried me into a room, but I pulled through.

How many hours did you work at the London Hotel?

Well, it wasn't the hours. You were there steadily. You had your room and board there. You get up at six o'clock in the morning, and you went right through, maybe you were off a half an hour or so before dinner, and then you come down to dinner, and then you go again, and you work until it's finished. Sometimes it would be nine, ten o'clock at night. I worked by the month, not by the week. That's the way they worked in the hotel. I was there for awhile. Then I was without work for awhile, and I remember some woman heard about me. She had a rooming house, so she came out to the house and she took me out to help her in the rooming house. That was in 1912, in the fall. I stayed there four years, and that's where I got my schooling. She helped me a lot.

I had three brothers at that time and one sister. There was five of us. My brother Steve went to work, but you know how boys are—they went for themselves. But my younger brothers had to stay home. That's the way they started. But with me, I don't know, all my life I've never had nothing for nothing. I worked very hard and I always have to get it the hard way.

How did your parents feel about you working?

They wanted kids to go to work because they needed help. Just like we have today. If you can't keep them and the child is old enough, they see it's not enough food in the house, so they go and help out. That's the way we were.

Did your mother get a job too?

No, how could she? At the time in Saskatoon there was no industry. The only jobs you can get was the private homes, restaurants, and hotels, maybe the odd sort of gardening that you could go and earn extra money. But there was no way of getting out. We had three rooms in our shack. The whole family slept in one room. And there was another room, quite narrow. There was three wooden beds, and six men boarders on top of it. That's how she supplemented some of the money we used for food and paid for the stuff they bought—the shack and the lot. So this is the way we lived when we first came. There was a small kitchen and a little cot in the kitchen—there was a man sleeping there. On top of it all, this lot my father bought was a wrong lot. In about a year's time he had to move the shack to another lot which was originally his, where he should have moved first. When we moved the shack there, there was a great big dilapidated shack at the back of this lot. So we got rid of the boarders from the house, and mamma put them all into this shack. There was about eight of them there. And she cooked and washed and everything else for them. I don't know what they paid her.

At the hotel I got about $20 a month and my room and board. That wasn't too bad. It wasn't much, but at least I had a home. I used to come and help out, and when I could spare a couple of dollars, I used to give them to my mother. She had to struggle. I remember a lot of times she used to get up very early in the morning and go and fish, try to get goldeye we had in Saskatchewan River. She used to fish so the kids would have something to eat. There was no welfare then. I don't know how she pulled through. She used to try everything she can, including selling booze—home brew—that's the fact!

You know, I used to condemn her then, but when I analyze it now, I don't know if anybody else could have done anything else.

That was during the time when my father was in the hospital. This was the way. The people could condemn them then, but when I look back I don't. She was illiterate, very backward, my mother was, but you know, she had a skill —she was a midwife, but not registered. I'll bet you that she delivered the babies of most of the Ukrainian women in Saskatoon, and you know, the doctors tried to prosecute her. There was one doctor. He says, 'Oh no, you leave her alone. There wasn't a child that she delivered that died or a mother that died. Just leave her alone.' She had her own way of doing things with that.

What was Saskatoon like? Did you get to know a lot of people?

You got into a crowd. It's just like you see it now—the Italians stick together. So you stick together and you find your own. This man that we first came to, he was quite a progressive person in his way; he knew how to do things, we didn't. I remember he organized a choir. At the back of his house, there was a great big shack and he sort of made it into a dancing hall, and we used to gather there for recreational purposes. Oh God! You know, when I look back it's frightening, it's really frightening how these young men came as immigrants to Canada. They were all strong. They had no place to go, they had no way to get rid of their energy. You know what a young man looks for. We used to have dances. I don't remember one dance where there wasn't a terrible fight. They'd bang each other to I don't know what. It was just terrible. One day I remember, it was 1913. We were all in our own shack. In that place where they have dances there was a man killed. First thing I knew, everybody was fighting everybody. A man was killed. They killed him, they killed each other. They banged each other off the steps. Oh God, it's just terrible! They were just like wild boars! They had no education. All they knew was work and work. They worked, but you know, a young man needs recreation, and you couldn't know how to get it until a lot of people, like this man that we came to, got together (some of them for their own selfish purposes) and they began to organize them. So they had a place to go and sing; they had a place where they had supervised dancing, and it sort of cleared up. But it was just terrible then.

I remember one of my friends was getting married, I think it was in 1914 just before the war broke out. She was getting married, and there was a hall on this side and that's where the wedding was. The Anglo-Saxons used to come in a group once in awhile. They pay their way and they come into the dance, and the Ukrainian boys resented that. They come in and they would ask their own music, so the musician would play it. I remember it started this way at this wedding. They asked for them to play a square dance, and our boys didn't like it, and then it started. Oh God, what a mess! Everybody was fighting everybody. The groom grabbed his wife and away he went. When I was going home, everybody was going through the windows and everywhere. That was a fight! There was a great big ditch on the other side of the road. Believe me, there must have been about 20 young men laying there, beat up. Nobody was killed. I know one man was pretty badly stabbed, but he came out. That's how we lived, and that's the beginning of the Ukrainian immigrants in Canada—hard work, struggle.

Did the girls mind the Anglo-Saxon boys coming to the dance? Was it just the men that were fighting?

It was the men that were fighting. You know how they used to treat the girls? As an addition. The girl was nothing, she was recreation, and then a lot of it started about the girls too. The main thing was ignorance.

Were you discriminated against?

We were always called Bohunks or Galicians. Galicia is a region, but it was because the people that came from there were backward. To Anglo-Saxons it looked like they were nothing. They'd say, 'Dirty Galician!' You know, I used to hate that word. If anybody would say that to me I could kill them! I couldn't stand that, not the name 'Galician' or 'Bohunk,' but just because what they thought of us. I couldn't stand that. We had an awful time. Kids used to come home from school crying. It was not a pleasant thing.

There was a sort of depression before the First World War. I think it was 1913. It was very hard to get jobs and my father was already working and he was digging ditches. One Anglo-Saxon came up and he was swearing. He said, 'How can that Bohunk work and I'm without a job?' And just before that when the time was a little better, in 1912, Anglo-Saxons spat on him in the ditches, 'Ptui, you dirty Bohunk!' During the sort of recession they had then, this man complained to the authorities, 'How is it that the Bohunk is working and I'm not?' Bohunks did everything. They did the hardest jobs.

You take all the Ukrainian people—they all suffered. Every bit of progress we've got in our living, somebody suffered for it. Somebody went on strike and his family went hungry. Somebody's head was smashed until we got at least a little bit. We fought for every blessed inch of ground that the working people ever had.

Mrs Anna Smokorowsky

She was born in Venlaw, Manitoba in 1902, three years after her parents had come to Canada from the Ukraine.

My parents were on this homestead for eleven years. My father was illiterate, he couldn't read or write, and he felt how hard it was for him to get along in a country where he couldn't even sign his name or read what he had to. He felt, as we grew up, that he couldn't let us grow up like that with no education. So, because there were no schools there, he sold the homestead in 1910, and we moved into this little village of Gilbert Plains. We were the only ethnic family at that time in Gilbert Plains. The rest of the populace was Anglo-Saxon, and there was a few German farmers and maybe some other nationalities which at the time I didn't know.

We lived in a little two-roomed shack. That was all that we could afford. At that time there were four children, three girls and a boy. All we brought with us from the homestead was a cow because we felt that would be our livelihood as my dad had no specific trade. He was just an ordinary worker that just had his hands to offer. And we brought this cow with us to Gilbert Plains.

We lived very poorly. I remember a year or so after we were there, my brother had taken the cow out to pasture, and she turned loose and was running across the railroad track, and the train came along and killed this cow. Well, there was our livelihood! The cow was killed. My mother and the rest of us cried because we felt so sorry for this Bess, the cow that we had. But there was nothing we could do. You know, we couldn't get any compensation at that time or anything. This was one of the heartbreaking things of our life there. We had all the milk we wanted when the cow was around, and then when we had to buy, well, we just had to use a little bit of milk.

My father and mother were very strict. The ethnic people really hung on to their children. They made them obey, they made them listen. We wouldn't dare speak out to our mother if she ever was chastising us. If you ever went out, you had to be back at a certain time. I remember once in Gilbert Plains, when I was a teenager, I went to a dance at Venlaw, the place where we were born. I came back later than my mother told me. She locked us out, and she wouldn't let us in

the house. We slept in the hayloft. We thought we'd put up the ladder and get up
to the bedroom, but she heard us putting that ladder up, and she took the broom,
and she swept us right off that ladder and told us, 'I told you to be in at
such-and-such a time, and unless you learn to listen to me, then you'll not sleep
in the house.' So we grabbed some old blankets in the summer kitchen and went
up and slept in the hayloft.

How far did you get in your schooling?

I had three years of high school in Gilbert Plains, and then it got to where I just
couldn't continue because my father couldn't provide. My mother used to do
day work, and she used to get discarded clothing from people. Sometimes she'd
remake it for us and sometimes not. Sometimes just as it was, we'd put it on. And
then there was another thing that was bad! They'd recognize this clothing that
belonged to other people, and they'd call out, 'You've got Mrs Leper's dress on!
You've got Mrs Morrison's coat on!' And things like that. When you got up to be
sixteen, seventeen, you begin to notice that. And I left school and I went to work
in a hotel, of all places.

Before that, going to school, I used to wash dishes in a Chinese restaurant,
which was hard work. I'd work a week, and he'd give me a dollar and a half for
washing these dishes. It was hard water, and we had to put in washing soda to
soften it up, and I can still see that grease and that fat floating around in that
dishpan. That was hard! And then we'd pick potatoes for 25 cents a day. We
thought we would make us a few cents to buy ourselves something to go back to
school. When Eaton's catalogue came in the fall, we had maybe five dollars, but
we wanted to buy the whole thing that was there!

Frank Lloyd

*An unskilled labourer, he came to Canada from England in 1913, when he was
nineteen.*

Why would I want to come to Canada? It was quite an adventure. It just comes
down to this: it's a matter of a boy wanting to go someplace else, don't ask him
why. The word 'adventure' comes into it. And then at the same time he always
had a stomach. He always wanted the wherewithal to get by and everything like
that. But I'm very, very sorry to say that when I did come out here after all these
glowing, enticing advertisements—I know now that it was mostly done by the
CPR to get people out here to occupy the land so that, I suppose, they would get
more business for their railway. I have heard that this was the case, I don't
know.

I often think of my first moments in Toronto. The very first impression I got
of Toronto was a very large unemployment parade. I couldn't understand what

this was. I was told what it was, and I just couldn't understand it because I'd always been used to living in a country where there was *always* a lot of unemployed. But there was absolutely *no* provisions made over there any more than there was here. But the English people those days used to help each other.

Paul Sawchuk

The war was approaching. I was in Austria and noticed that there was mobilization of the army, and then they started to call the young people to the army. I decided not to go. I was not Austrian, I was Ukrainian, and therefore why should I give my life? So I tried to get out of the country and go to Canada if possible. My older brother was already here, and when I wrote him that I intended to go to Canada too, he said, 'Don't come now, because it is a very bad time.' It was 1913, it was really unemployed and very low wages.

I could not leave the country Austria, because it was my age already to go into the army. I had to borrow the passport from a younger fella, and I went on his passport to Germany. When I came to Germany, I got a job first in the smelter, in order to get money to go to Canada. I was working hard, a lot of overtime, for six months. I saved enough to pay for my ticket to go to Canada. So I left and came to Toronto in August 1913 during the Exhibition. It was hard to get a job. My brother was also without a job for awhile, but somehow it was possible to arrange enough that we could live together. Finally I got a job in a tailor shop, which was on Simcoe Street, and I worked 48 hours a week for seven dollars. That was the amount of money that I could spend. At the same time, I was sending a couple of dollars to father and mother there. It was a difficulty because there was no union; there was no possibility to get better work.

Were there a lot of other Ukrainians with you on the boat when you came to Canada?

Oh yes! There was no room on the boat. It was a cattle boat, and there were no cabins in there, just a dormitory, because they were taking the cattle one way, and the immigrants another way. When you came to eat on that, oh boy, it was terrible!

When you first came to Canada, did you picture it the way it was or did you think it was going to be better?

I thought it is always going to be better. I never believed that it would be just as bad. In Germany, there were lots of workers. They were dreaming to be masters here. *(laughs)*

Abraham Kuznetz

The harsh anti-Semitic laws in Russia forced many Jews to leave. Those who came to Canada, unable to speak English or find steady employment, faced 'a crisis.'

It was hard at the beginning. Everyone went more or less the same way. An awful lot of tailors went out peddling from door to door. An awful lot took farms. You know, all of sudden they give farms in Saskatchewan, a quarter of a section of land. The farms were probably 25-30 miles apart from one another. It rained, they froze, they were telling us what they went through. Ninety-nine per cent left the farms and returned to the city. It was a very hard life. It's all right for real farmers, they used to live like that in Europe. But with us, it was a different struggle.

Bruce Cole

His parents emigrated from Poland to England and then to Canada in 1906 in search of a better way of life. Theirs was a strict Jewish household over which his grandfather 'ruled with an iron fist.' His parents were both tailors, and his father spent the rest of his life working at Tip Top Tailors.

About 1907 or '8 we moved out to the west end of Toronto. We bought a four-room house for $2,000—$200 down and $1800. The builder built a number of these houses and started a clothing factory in the west end of the city, and that was the inducement to buy the house. And then when all the houses were sold, he sold the factory. It was created specially in order to sell these houses.

Now in the four rooms and a lean-to kitchen lived my mother, father, six children, my grandfather, grandmother, and a cousin. It was a bit crowded. My father, mother, and five children slept in the dining room, my grandfather and grandmother had the front room, my sister and cousin slept in one room upstairs, and the other room was not used because my grandfather turned it into a synagogue. It would have been a desecration to use it for a bedroom, so we slept like rabbits.

Was it after this clothing factory closed down that your father went to work for Tip Top?

That's right. He was one of the original workers for Tip Top. At that time, it was called the Berger Tailoring Company. Then the war came along, and they got munition contracts. Apparently the in-laws of Mr Dunkelman (one of the owners) were friendly with Sir Sam Hughes, who was the Minister of War at the time, and managed to land some juicy uniform contracts. And from then on everything was sailing with the Tip Top Tailors.

My father was getting about fifteen dollars a week. Prior to that he'd worked for the Lowndes Company. He was a skilled worker, a sleeve-hanger, and he used to earn about fifteen dollars a week. But then the question of work on Saturday came up, and when he refused to work on Saturday, they put him on hand-work like the girls would do—the felling, the hand sewing on piecework, and that's when he made five to seven dollars a week.

I'll never forget if I live to be another 80 the tragedy when one Friday he came home with his pay, a five-dollar bill, and lost it. I remember my mother and he walking up and down the sidewalk with tears streaming down their eyes. At that time we had six children. My uncle had this clothing place round the corner on Peter Street, and my mother would go over there and wait until they finished eating, and then whatever was left on the table in the way of bread and so on, just like the bird taking it home to the little ones, she would wrap it up in her apron and bring it over to us so that we could have something to eat. That was real tragedy.

Did your father talk at all about the working conditions at Tip Top?

They weren't bad. His main complaint was that he was forced to work on Saturday, which he didn't want to do. I interceded on his behalf at one time with Mr Dunkleman. Mr Dunkleman said, 'Well, I wouldn't want to work on Saturday myself, but we have to do it, and our workers have to do it. Each share has got to produce.' My father found it very humiliating. We were at the end of the Dundas Street streetcar, and he used to walk a mile or two before getting on the streetcar on the Saturday morning, work for half a day, and then stay downtown until nightfall before he would come back. It was a very humiliating experience. As a matter of fact, my grandfather objected so seriously that he moved out of our house and moved downtown again with another son.

Were a lot of Jewish people in the clothing industry?

Yes, the workers were mainly in the clothing industry. There was the odd tradesman that came over that was a plumber or a bricklayer or a sheet metal worker or a roofer, but I would say most of them were in the needle trades industry.

Were there women working at Tip Top?

Yes, always. There's always women in the clothing industry. They do what is called the felling—the hand sewing and the buttonholes. That was before they had buttonhole machines. The men did the cutting and the pressing and the main seams and the sleeve-hanging and so on—anything done by machine. The women did mostly the hand sewing.

Were the men more skilled than the women?

Maybe. Now my father for instance was a sleeve-hanger. That was considered a very skilled job, because the sleeve has to be gathered in such a way that it will hang properly. Felling, that is hand sewing, is skilled work as well, but it was a division of work rather than a division by skills.

Morty Stein

He came to Canada in 1906 at age twelve and went to work as a capmaker's apprentice for three dollars a week. A year later, he was put on piecework, and his wages increased to twelve dollars a week. He became interested in labour and was active in his union. He describes the 'black bag' practice.

The capmaking trade was very large. People were not unionized; wages were terrible; people had to take work home at night and work at home on Sunday. I remember hearing a speech at the Toronto Labour Council on what we called a 'Black Bag.' Almost everybody took home a black bag with work to do on a Friday night. A couple of kids helped out here and there. It was a terrible thing, wages were horrible. You see each style had a basic rate which the company worked out—not us. Subsequently we got to the point where we said, *'We'll work the thing out.'*

III. STRANGERS

Mrs Jane Walters

Mrs Walters was the daughter of a prominent British family in Welland, Ontario.

The immigrants came just before I left. The Plymouth Cartage Company came from the States to build a big factory, and they brought immigrant labour and built houses for them towards the end of the town. It would be about '12 or '13, I suppose. I don't know what nationality they were, but they were foreign. Oh, there were some from the British Isles, because many of the domestics were British, but this immigrant labour was not British. It changed the town. We didn't know anybody anymore. They couldn't speak English, they looked rather curious with their moustaches, and we had not been accustomed to the kind of houses that were built for them. The story goes that they kept the coal in the bathtubs, but I never believed it because I didn't think they'd be so stupid, because they'd have to go upstairs to get the coal. I think that was somebody's way of describing that they weren't used to our way of life. There was very little trouble with them that I know of, except that the town lost its sort of rural aspect.

Would you say that there was prejudice on the part of the Canadian-born?

No. I can't speak for the labouring class who worked with them. But I don't think there was any more prejudice than people just being aware of the difference. But they were not unkind or unjust.

Mrs Margaret Hand

She was brought up in a well-to-do family in Toronto.

We knew very few foreigners in Toronto compared with the street we live on today, which is practically a League of Nations. We had very few foreign friends. I think we had a kind of built-in suspicion of people who weren't Canadian or British. I don't think it was violent at all, I don't mean that, but we felt awkward. We didn't feel at home with them. You see, none of us had travelled anywhere, we'd never been anywhere. The way kids of today know the world, we didn't know it at all.

There was a kind of prejudice against foreigners. I can remember there were always Italian workmen in Toronto, and the laundryman at the corner was a Chinaman. My father's stiff collars had to be taken to the Chinaman once a week, but I was always told, when I took them in, to leave the door open. I don't know what the Chinaman was expected to do to me! But the Chinese, well they were Chinese, that's all. You didn't associate with them. Of course, it's different now. I remember a Negro family living around the corner from where I lived when I was quite small. We were taught to be polite to them—politeness was part of being brought up in those days, much more so than it is today, I might tell you—but we were never allowed to play with them.

CHAPTER FIVE

JOINING UP

The declaration of war brought a flood of volunteers to recruiting offices in English Canada. The patterns of this feeling for the safety of the empire were deeply etched in the English Canadian consciousness by school curricula, an Anglophilia that pervaded the popular culture, and large numbers of recent immigrants from the British Isles. Not all those who enlisted did so purely to serve the empire. Large numbers of recent immigrants saw enlistment as a means of getting back home to Great Britain free in return for service in a war that soon would be over. Farmers' sons and unemployed workers found a more relaxed regime or a surer wage in the army. As recruiting continued more recalcitrant Canadians 'volunteered' for service in the context of phenomenal social pressure to enlist. War widows and soldiers' sweethearts accosted men in the streets, demanding to know why they were not in uniform. Organized recruiting drives, replete with torchlight parades, resounding patriotic songs, flags, and bunting were designed to arouse fervour in the phlegmatic. No one was allowed to be indifferent. By the time that conscription was imposed, the Canadian army had long since ceased to be a harmonious and enthusiastic fighting unit in the service of the empire.

I.   PATRIOTISM

Bert Remington

His parents came to Montreal from England in 1910 'to give the kids a chance.'
He first worked as a glass-cutter, then as an office boy, then in a 'wholesale
place,' and finally, before he enlisted, at Bell Telephone.

When the war broke out—you cannot *believe* unless you were there. The
country went mad! People were singing on the streets and roads. Everybody
wanted to be a hero, everybody wanted to go to war. Hadn't had a war since the
Boer War in 1899, 1900, which I remember. There was nothing between that in
wars, and everybody was going to be a hero, and I wanted to be a hero too. But I
wasn't big enough. I was only five foot nothing and weighed 85 pounds and was a
boy scout bugler. I remember walking up Park Avenue in Montreal blowing the
bugle, everybody was excited, the war was on. The only way they give it to you
then—there was no radio, no anything—was on the posters stuck on the outside
of shops, in big print telling what was going on. Anyway, I was all excited, and I
went down to the Grenadier Guards' Armories on Esplanade Avenue, Montreal.
I was standing at the door looking longingly and watching these characters going
in and getting sworn in and tested, and I was wishing I was tall enough or big
enough to go. I was old enough, I was nineteen, but I looked fifteen. And the old
drum major—an old campaigner, Egyptian campaigner and a real drunkard it
turned out to be, but a good guy—came and he put his arm around me and he
says, 'Well, I'm glad to see *you're* going with us.' I said, 'Well gee, I wish I
could.' He says, 'Come on, we need buglers.' And I was in, sworn in, tested,
inoculated. In half an hour I'm in the army and I didn't know how it happened.
That night I lay awake all night wondering, 'What am I doing? What have I
done?'
 I went away to Valcartier in civvies, the first little suit I had with long pants.
In those days you didn't go into long pants until you were seventeen, eighteen or
more, you wore shorts with long stockings. And I went away in my first little
shabby blue suit. I paid a dollar down, and it fell off me, I was lousy. In Valcartier
we were lousy, and I was lousy for two years or more after. But nobody would
admit it in Valcartier, till I said, 'Well, I don't care what you guys say, I'm
lousy!' 'You are? So am I!' 'So am I!' And everybody's lousy. We stayed lousy
until I went to the hospital in 1916.

What was the training like?

Oh God, what training? We never had any training! *(laughs)* We went to Valcartier, I went with the advance guard, it was in September. All night on the train,
and we got off at the siding at Valcartier where there was nothing but

'Everybody wanted to be a hero, everybody wanted to go to war.'

field and bush, and we said, 'B-b-but where's the camp?' It was cold, it was frost on the ground, and in this little blue suit I was cold. And they said, 'Well, blow the fall-in.' I said, 'I c-c-c-can't blow anything.' I couldn't talk I was so cold. They said, 'You're going to *make* the camp!' And that was the beginning of Valcartier. They brought tents, and the tents went up like mush rooms, and that was Camp Valcartier in September, 1914.

The training amounted to being equipped, and they gave us the old South African equipment. Some of it was mouldy. All of our equipment was a leather bag and a water bottle and a haversack—and the *Ross rifle*. Don't ever forget the *Ross rifle*! What a bastard! *(laughs)* It was a good target weapon, but for service—uh, uh. It was a political gag with Sam Hughes and the Ross rifle. I'd like to cram it right...! *(laughs)* Anyway, our watchmen would curse Sam Hughes and the Ross rifle and the Canadian government. Germans coming on in mass, and the rifle wouldn't fire, the bolt wouldn't close, the steel wasn't tempered. They'd try to drive it open and they'd blow their brains out.

Robert Swan

He had worked in a bank before the war, and when he joined the army he was quickly promoted to officer's rank because he was the only one able to help the quartermaster. He was again promoted, along with fourteen others after a battle during which most of the officer corps was killed.

There were hardly more than seven million people in the whole of Canada at that time, and yet, without going too heavily into figures, it is interesting to realize that between August 1914 and December 1918, the total number of men enlisted in the Canadian forces exceeded 600,000. And I want to repeat that that's against a population of just over seven million. It simply meant that every man who could stagger under a rifle and carry a pack sooner or later was pulled into the services. Not all of the 600,000 actually left Canada. I haven't at the moment the exact figure for the number who did, but based on a rather faulty memory, I think it was something like 475,000. At any rate, the total casualties during the actual fighting are listed as something better than 230,000, of which 170,000 were non-fatal. And very close to 60,000 men were killed or died accidentally or through illness, one way or another.

Canada in those days was very sparsely populated, but our basic national groupings were either English-speaking or French-speaking. There were certain other small spots where people of other national origins had come to Canada, but the basic mixture was largely as I've already said. We had been living and developing this part of what was then the British Empire. Many of us were old enough to have remembered the South African War, and the educational system was such that we were quite familiar with Great Britain. So that when this war broke out, there wasn't much hesitation throughout most of the country in deciding to give the Old Country all the support we could.

But when it comes to a question of individuals and their reasons or purposes in enlisting, I don't think that patriotism, as such, was entirely the main reason for joining up. I know, in my own case, while I was probably as patriotic as most young men of that time, I was getting restless. I wasn't at all happy in the confinement of working in a bank, and I jumped at the opportunity to get free of some of the restraints that I had been under as a young person growing up and at the opportunity to see something else of the world, and probably, for lack of a better way of expressing it, I searched for a direction.

Now I don't suppose that everybody else was motivated by the same ideas. There was a good deal of patriotism involved and that was particularly true with men of very recent British origin who were going straight home to assist their families and their friends who were already there. But those of us with a fairly Canadian background still had a very close affection for Great Britain and for the British traditions—much more so, I would think, than those that exist today or even existed at the time of the outbreak of the Second War. There was a much closer feeling throughout Canada toward Great Britain.

I don't think any of us realized that so much of the causes of war in general are economic rather than political or patriotic. In later years it was always difficult for me to understand why the Germans ever wanted or desired to make a war on anybody at that time. As far as I was able to understand, they were prosperous. They had been industrious, inventive, and they were breaking into Great Britain's markets all over the world. If you went into a hardware store, for instance, in Canada at that time, you generally bought a German pocket knife, a German razor, a German this, a German that—there was German merchandise all over the world. They were beating the British at their own game. Why they had to fight about it, I don't know!

I doubt very much if one man in a thousand among the Canadians had a really clear and positive grasp of the more deeply seated reasons which brought the war about. There had been a lot of talk about the Germans and their preparations, their effort to create a navy equal to the British navy, and their historical hatred of the French. But I don't think that very many knew. Many men who had joined up here in Canada did so mainly from a patriotic point of view. There was also the fact that when any movement becomes popular a great many men will join it because it seems to be the thing to do, or that it offers an exciting and different prospect than the ordinary humdrum daily civilian existence. There were a number of men that I suppose were shamed into it, if you want to put it that way, particularly in the later stages when the reinforcements became urgently needed. Then they started going around putting pressure on men to enlist, but in the early days they didn't have to put any pressure on —they had more men than they could handle.

What kind of pressure?

The poster was Lord Kitchener pointing at you, 'We need you,' 'Why are you not in the army?' Young girls were going along and they would meet what looked like a pretty good able-bodied man and they'd pin something white on them —called them a coward in other words, because they weren't in the army. 'What are you doing in civilian clothes when all my brothers are in the army?' That sort of thing. That's the kind of pressure. There was pressure through the press and through the communities to persuade the men to enlist.

Robert Franklin

He grew up on a farm in Huron County, Ontario, and enlisted when he turned eighteen.

In 1916 they was wanting men awful badly, and the propaganda was fairly strong, and I'd always played soldier all my life. I'd always wanted to be a soldier. Heavens, I remember the troops coming back from the Boer War. I don't remember the war of course, but I remember the Russo-Japanese war. We used to play soldier, and I always wanted to be the Jap because they were

'They had this terrific propaganda...'

winning. Sure, and my brother was always very anxious to play soldier, and I think he enlisted before I did. He was an officer. In fact, he was taking an officers' course in London the day war was declared in 1914. I would have felt like a poor fool if I hadn't joined the army, as conditions were in those days. We'd just become of age and some of our friends who were a bit older were all in the army already. You were an oddity in the community if you didn't. We had a few I recall who got on the farm so they wouldn't have to enlist. There'd be conscription come along, they wouldn't force them because they were farmers. We had a number that did that deliberately. Some got married and got on a farm. Soon as the war was over they quit the farm.

Jack Burton

He grew up in a small village near Fredericton, New Brunswick, where his father was a foreman in a sawmill. When the war broke out, he was only thirteen, but because of his height he had to carry his birth certificate to appease the military police that stopped him.

Everybody just jumped up and wanted to go to war. They had this terrific propaganda, and there were recruiting officers on every corner. They'd practically grab you by the back of the neck and take you in and put a uniform on you. You know, banners waving and bands playing! It was just like a fever.

Was there a lot of feeling against the Germans?

It was whipped up. All we got was what was fed to us in the newspapers. We didn't have these broadcasts giving you both sides of the picture. If you got a newspaper that was very, very bitter against the Germans, that was the propaganda you got. I can't say right now because it was quite a long ways back, but certainly everyone wanted to get in there and kill all the Germans. That's for sure!

Dean Walker

In the newspapers in those days they used to have notices (this was at the beginning of the war, people were enlisting), and they would say, 'Johnny Jones and So-and-So and So-and-So have enlisted today.' I belonged to a family that was truly English, and every night my father used to read the newspaper. I got so fed up listening to Johnny Jones joining and this other guy joining and so on, I said to another pal of mine, 'I'm going to join the army. Everybody else is going. I don't know what it's all about, but I'm going anyway!' That's how I joined the army.

Ben Wagner

He describes the reaction in Bruce County when war was declared.

The reaction was very quiet. The people who did the most hurrahing were the people who weren't going to be affected in the war. The rest of us just more or less sat tight. Of course, our mothers didn't want us to go. There were three sons in our family and two of us were overseas, so we didn't do too badly ourselves. In the beginning people accepted the war, but it was quite apiece away from us. There wasn't the grimness about it that there was, say, in France or these countries right alongside the war. Of course, there were the usual people, prominent men, who said, 'Oh, it can't last six months, haven't got enough money.' The rural areas of Canada were a little slow to come to realize there was a war on.

Dale and Ellen Simpson

They grew up and married in Toronto and were in their early twenties during the war. Mr Simpson was very reluctant to talk about the war years.

Mr Simpson: You see, the war didn't start in this country. It started over there. We don't remember what was doing over there for a long time.
Mrs Simpson: We didn't know anything about war, I guess. We'd go to bed at night and sleep, and that's more than they could.

Mark Tanner

His family moved from Montreal to Toronto in 1908 when he was ten.

In those days the British Empire was the great fact of life to most young people. We were brought up in the belief that the sun never set on the British Empire. It was the greatest empire the world had ever seen. We were all taught in school by maps showing the far-flung British Empire marked in red on the map. You could look at these maps, and you'd see Canada, Australia, New Zealand, India, other parts of Asia, and large sections of Africa, all in red, showing the magnitude and the power of the British Empire. And it was a power at that time! I think the history that was taught in the school, the ones I attended at any rate, was really

'*...and there were recruiting officers on every corner.*'

British history, it wasn't Canadian history. We were taught of the great victories of the British that fought in Europe and in India, the defeat of Napoleon and the Spanish Armada, the feats of Drake on the sea. We were steeped in the great achievements of past British history. So it's not surprising that when the war broke out, Canadians from all parts of the country rallied to the cause and joined up in the army and the navy and, later on in the war, in the airforce.

Some of my fondest memories are of arriving in London, the capital of the British Empire and the centre of the greatest empire in the world at that time. Everything about London upheld that belief. You would see the multi-coloured uniforms from all parts of the world. You'd see the Arabs from the Middle East with their flowing gowns and their horses and their galloping in Rotten Row, as they called it, in Hyde Park in London; you'd see the Indian rajahs and their colourful uniforms and their horses riding; you'd see the Australians with their hats and their uniforms, and the New Zealanders; you'd see the coloured troops from Africa, and of course, the white troops from Africa with their different uniforms; you'd see the coloured regiments from the Caribbean and again they'd be different uniforms—all tending to the glorification and the development and the building up of patriotism, with the flags and the colour and the bands of a great empire. You thought you were part of it. Patriotism and loyalty undoubtedly played a great part in our lives, in maintaining the spirit of the work at that time.

I think that it might have been different if you had been in the ranks and in the trenches for three or four or five years, as many were, and slogged through the mud and filth and rain and the conditions that existed, that were simply awful. Patriotism and the greatness of the British Empire began to seem not quite as important as it did if you were safe at home. *(laughs)*

Mrs Jane Walters

Her father, of English 'landed gentry' background, owned and published the Conservative newspaper in a small southern Ontario town. Mrs Walters was one of the first women to respond to the call for VADs. Her parents were reluctant to let her go because they had already lost a son.

We were British-Canadians, that speaks for itself. My people were all British, all English. In those days patriotism was rife. You didn't think about the cost to yourself, you just did it when it was needed. Our family did it, and so, I suppose, did the families of the other girls. That's why they had the same spirit. England called. Most of us were British-Canadians: Canadians first, British second. But we never thought of separating them. My father used to have very little to do with our upbringing (mother did it all), but often he used to say to me, 'My dear, be proud you're English, and remember: Honour first.' So that was my picture of an English person—'Honour first.'

We didn't understand the causes of the war. We just knew England was in danger. We couldn't understand it, we hadn't time to think about it. It was only later as we got a little older and read more that we learned about all the underlying causes of war. But even if we had, what would that have mattered? England was in danger, Canadian men were going over, and if Canadian women got a chance to go, they should go and help.

Keith Fallis

The son of a missionary in China, he led a 'secluded existence' until he was twelve. Although not much interested in the church, he was influenced by the non-evangelistic efforts of missions to promote international brotherhood. He came to Toronto in 1910.

I enlisted a few days after I was eighteen years old in January 1917. I must say that, looking back on it, I was completely brainwashed by the society in which I lived. I never questioned the total rightness of our cause. In fact, when I was about fifteen I won my first gold medal in public speaking on the glories of the British Empire. We were encouraged to believe that the British Empire was something very special which had practically been guided by God. We sang 'God of our fathers, known of old,/Lord of our far-flung battle-line.'* We all memorized it and we sang it. In those days they used to have 'One flag, one fleet, one throne' as the frontispiece of the textbook that we used in public school, and also 'We hold a vaster Empire than has been,/ Nigh half the race of man is subject to our King,/ Nigh half the world is his in fee,/ And where he rules all are free' or something like that. We used to have to memorize these things and say them and sing them. We were taught that the British Empire was the white man's burden, and we had gone out with the best of goodwill to try and help the natives, who were backward and stupid and ignorant and so on. Livingstone was a great example of our noble nature. Not emphasizing that Liverpool was built up on slave trade, but just selecting a few noble guys—this proved how good we were. The fact that they had to come out and struggle this way wasn't emphasized at all you see. You didn't prove how bad we were! Anyway, I never questioned that what we were doing was right and that the Germans were all wrong and that we were fighting to make the world safe for democracy.

This attitude was not typical, as I found when I got into the army, of any but a small, idealistic group of students, of people who came from teachers' families or preachers' families. That was one of the first shocks to me. We had a few fellows around who had been over, who had been wounded, and who were doing

---

* First two lines of 'Recessional' by Rudyard Kipling.

some of the training. And they were cynical and scornful—'You'll get over *that* when you get over there'—if you expressed any idealistic feeling about the war.

The average fellow in the army was rather a coarse and to some extent brutal-minded fellow. I went down to Ottawa to Landsdowne Park to train. Of all my fellow soldiers, eight out of ten seemed to me to have no other interest except finding a girl for the night. The coarseness of the sexual jokes and talk and so on was a tremendous shock to me. I came from a sheltered family, and I had the Tennyson idea of bearing the white flower of blameless light, you know, until you got married. I froze up inside to a considerable extent, although I did have many friends. That was a trauma.

Larry Nelson

Why did I enlist? Well, my motives are mixed. I was only just past my twenty-first birthday. The prospect of adventure and travel and so on had a very strong appeal for me. I would say I had other reasons for it too. My reading was almost entirely based on *Boy's Own Annual* and *Chums* and Henty and so on. So I had the belief that Britain always won its wars and that they were always right. This was a feeling that my generation had. I was ten years old before Queen Victoria died, you see. I had a strong feeling for the old regime. Many of your generation look back with disdain at the Victorian period but I don't altogether agree with them.

When the war broke out I was on a canoe trip up to Algonquin Park with my brother and two chums. When we got the news, we came back to Toronto, because we were told by some Americans in a canoe that there was great excitement in Toronto, and troops were leaving for Valcartier Camp, and the British navy had been sunk. So back we came hotfoot, after about ten days up in the park. The four of us said we were going to enlist as soon as we could. Three of us did reasonably soon, but the other one never enlisted at all. But, strange as it may seem, he was the most vociferous one of the lot about enlisting.

I joined the Queen's Own Rifles and was in 'A' Company, which was composed mostly of Queen's Own men. I don't like to be snobbish, but the Queen's Own were mostly recruits from lads like myself. The other companies were a mixed lot. For a year or more, until we actually got to France, we used to be called the 'Baby's Own.' Baby's Own Soap at that time was a very well known soap, so we got nicknamed the 'Baby's Own' because we were still young and wet behind the ears. The truth of the matter was that many of these fellows were like myself—reasonably accustomed to athletics and canoe trips and sailing and rowing and all that. We had athletes in our unit. We were quite a good lot, and perhaps a year or so younger than the others, too.

I think most people joined from a sense of perhaps duty and desire for a change perhaps—you know, occupation, excitement, adventure. I think I would put the emphasis on the fact that most of us were young and saw it as a wonderful opportunity to throw off the shackles of working in an office or a factory or on a farm or what-have-you.

II.   A STEADY JOB

Mark Tanner

He grew up in Montreal, where his father worked as a conductor for the Grand Trunk Railway. His first job was also with the Grand Trunk but by 1914 he was working for a men's clothing manufacturer.

We were heading into another depression in 1914. I can remember I was working on the railroad then, and I'd see the lineups every morning in the freight sheds of the Grand Trunk and the CPR which was right across from where I was working in the Union Station. Men were looking for jobs at one dollar a day, to load freight cars and trucks with goods that were in the freight sheds. The lineups were getting bigger and bigger. There was no unemployment insurance; there was no welfare or relief. I realize now what was happening. Unemployment and the depression were on the way, and the war just came along and swept up these men into the army and later on into the factories and ended the unemployment —and probably prevented any opposition there might have been to the war. They were glad to get into the army at $1.10 a day. It looked very good to them.

Do you think people supported the war for patriotic reasons?

I think the masses supported it for patriotic reasons, but undoubtedly there were some smart men in the top who looked at it from the commercial and financial angle and did see opportunities for profits. Well, they'd support it for that reason, although I'm quite sure most of the big industrialists also were patriotic, although they didn't object to making a little money out of the war. *(laughs)*

Russell Morgan

He tried twice to enlist in Toronto, but was refused both times, so he worked instead on the boats, transporting soldiers and horses.

The army was a job. It was their job, otherwise they had nothing. It was adventure for young fellows because they weren't reckoning on not never coming back. But I know a lot of them went in because there was nothing else for them. There was no hope for them. There was nothing doing. Wintertime closed down, and the jobs were scarce, and I guess the parents was chasing them over trying to get a job. So they joined up in the army, and that was it. I think that was the cause of a lot of it—unemployment.

Sam Beckman

Surprisingly, there was a lot of unemployment in 1913 and 1914. There was a depression as far as employment was concerned, and there were thousands of unemployed people that were happy to join the army. They were dressed properly, they got their meals, their training camps, they enjoyed themselves. They had some purpose in living. So thousands joined the army because of economic circumstances. Very few joined the army from patriotism.

Burt Woods

At the age of eleven he was sent to Canada by an English organization concerned with orphans and street waifs. He worked on a farm for five years before he joined the army.

When the war broke out, I run away from the home I was in, Fagan's Homes. I run away and joined the army, and I gave me age as eighteen. I was between fourteen and fifteen. I didn't wash or anything or shine my shoes or clean anything. I looked just tough, you know, like a regular farm boy. I joined the army and I went in as a sniper.

The average young fella was running away, you know. Things are different now. You see, I was only getting five dollars a year and my keep. When I joined the army I was getting more—$1.10 a day.

John Fisher

His father was a gentleman farmer and builder. Because he didn't like farming, he came to Canada in 1910, at age twenty. He married in 1915 and had a son that year. Although he once attempted to enlist, he was more concerned about job security and spent the war years working for the Imperial Bank.

They made my brother in Detroit Battalion Sergeant-Major of the Eighteenth Battalion, because of his experience in the army and one thing and another. My brother Leonard and I went over to Windsor, we were going to join George's outfit. When we got there, why, he'd left! They'd left two days previously. So then we came back to Toronto and Leonard went and joined the Forty-eighth Highlanders, their Second Battalion, and he went overseas with them. But I never did go any further. I got married and decided I had enough troubles as they were. *(laughs)*

I was actually a member of the Officers' Training Corps at the University of Toronto for some little time. Some boys who went to the University of Toronto and were members of the organization got me talked into it. Most of them were training to go overseas. But not me. I had no intentions of carrying it on. I just had a few pictures of myself in a uniform that I more or less borrowed. I wasn't much of a soldier, never was, and never have been. I would rather bawl somebody out than shoot them, I think, and that has been my idea of getting by.

Were you ever interested in working in a munitions plant?

They were getting quite good money, but I wasn't that interested. I was more interested in saving my job for after. I knew that I was married then, and we started having a family, and I figured that the job at the bank would be there and the munitions job wouldn't.

III. WHY AIN'T YOU IN THE ARMY?

Duncan MacGregor

In the pre-war years, his father was a colonel in the militia in Woodstock, and he himself was a member of the Cadet Corps. In 1915 he enlisted in the Canadian Officers' Training Corps.

In February I was asked by the president of the Sportsmen's Patriotic to sing at Lowes Theatre at Sunday night recruiting meetings. So I donned my COTC sergeant's uniform to go down and sing for them. I had a rather funny experience there one Sunday. Got down in the afternoon and the Queen's Own Band were there. The captain of the band wasn't there in the afternoon and the sarge—a friend of mine—and I had a great time trying to figure out what the heck I was going to sing, because there was no pianist there for my amount of luck. We had to choose something that he could play and something that I knew by heart to stand there and sing it without having to look at any music because I didn't have any. So we chose 'Keep the Home Fires Burning.' By the time we chose the song, half the crowd had moved out, and there were only about 300 in there in the first place. I got out of there so darn disgruntled, sort of peeved at the whole thing, and I felt like going down to the dock and jumping in. But the chauffeur was there to take me down to a job in the east end at a movie theatre. Down there they had a good pianist, and she played the number that I really wanted to sing at Lowes, and I had a darn good rehearsal with her on that.

Oh, Soldier Boy, you look good! Into battle march away
To fight for King and Country in the thickest of the fray.
Came the call for reinforcements as the Redmen marched along,
And to the girl he left behind he signed this parting song.
Fare you well, I must go, little darling,
For this hurting is hard, dear, to bear,
For the boys in the trenches are calling,
I must go, my duty calls me there!
Dry those tears from you eyes, little darling,
You must smile and be brave while I'm gone,
For I'll come back to you
When my fighting days are through
And the war for our liberty is won.

Martin Colby

In them days, it was rather annoying to go out at all because the men in uniform, when you would walk down the street, they'd come and tap you on the shoulder and say, 'Why ain't you in the army?' And I used to have difficulty even when I told them I had bad ears because I'd had scarlet fever. 'Go on, try again. Try again.' I used to say, 'What the hell's the use of trying after they turned me down?' I tried often enough. But, oh Jesus, they used to pressure the life out of you. It was hell. Well, it got so bad that people started to kick about it. But, you know, they used to hold parades in order to work up the patriotism. Ha! Jesus, boy, I'm gonna tell you, a lot of them kids, when they seen them, they wanted to get in there.

George Wilkes

In Toronto at that time there was a Captain Lawson. Saturday night was his big night for recruiting. As a senior recruiting officer, he used to hold up a Union Jack and offer to give any man that would enlist a piece of that Union Jack to take with him to Europe to show what he was fighting for. And, as I recall, there was many a man awakened up a Saturday morning or Sunday morning after having been indulging in alcoholic spirits the night before . . .much to his surprise he awakened to find that he had become enlisted in His Majesty's Services!

As the war progressed, one of my brother's chums, Harry Bowl, he joined the infantry at the age of sixteen and went overseas almost at once. And he returned the following year, having lost his right leg in France. I can recall that, at that time, anyone that didn't join up was referred to as a slacker or a coward. I can recall that Harry Bowl had an artificial leg. The ladies of Toronto should have been doing something else, that is, they should have been involved in war munitions work. They were going around with turkey feather dusters which they loaded with talcum powder, and they used to shower the powder over any person that they thought was a slacker. And my brother's chum, who had already lost one leg at the age of sixteen, he received the same treatment, and so he was covered with flour down near the City Hall. He drew his trousers up to show his artificial leg, and he gave the ladies quite a scolding because he told them he thought they should be doing something more useful.

Ben Wagner

In rural Ontario, by 1915, battalions were recruited by counties, and local men, recommended by the MP and schoolmaster, were chosen to be officers.

Especially in the cities, where there might be four battalions trying to recruit at the same time, they all tried to have something extra, to specialize. One was the Sportsmen's Battalion, and they tried to appeal to the sportsmen. One was something else. And some bright genius down here—I won't give his name, I guess he's dead now, he was a high school principal—had the bright idea of recruiting a *non-alcoholic* battalion. You can imagine just what a joke that was, you see. They were called 'So-and-So's Angels.' At one time some of the magistrates here, if you were up on a petty offence, would give you a choice of ten days or joining the army. Now that wasn't good for the army.

Mrs Elaine Nelson

The war changed her plans to study voice in Europe. Despite her mother's aristocratic attitudes (she was Dutch), she considered herself a 'good Canadian' and helped out in every possible way during the war.

The women went to all sorts of extremes, but people were hysterical sometimes. They had some beloved over there, and they saw someone having a good easy time with a great big cushy job and making a lot of money. They just went after them, tooth and nail. I think there were times when it was really a tragedy that the man wasn't saying what was really wrong with him or what the reason was. I think there were actually several suicides about that because they were so badgered about it. Some women went to terrible extremes about this. But I never did, I thought it was their life and they'd suffer for it quite enough when the boys came home.

I remember one example I always think is so amusing. A chap who had been a neighbour of my husband was a druggist. He sent my husband a powder that he had invented himself, which was supposed to chase away lice. All the soldiers were lousy. He wanted my husband and his brother to try this out, and then write a recommendation for this thing, thinking he's going to make a lot of money, you see. So my husband wrote back and said, 'If you want a recommendation for this powder of yours, you come over here and damn well try it yourself!'

'...it was quite the right thing for the Church to help.'

Mrs Lorna Browning

She taught school in Arden, Ontario until her marriage in 1913. Her husband was too old to enlist in the army.

During the war we helped mostly with recruiting, which I'm ashamed to mention now. But that's the way we felt, that it was quite the right thing for the Church to help. My husband's Sunday School class, they were in their teens, most of them enlisted. We'd invite them to the house to have some music. One of the boys had a drum, some of the other boys played, and we encouraged them to go and be good boys—very good boys. They must have been around eighteen, and we urged them on. I can never forgive myself. Because, of the group that went, the two that I liked the best: the one came home shortly after with arthritis, terribly crippled; he did marry but he never got over it, just was frightfully crippled till he died. The other boy came home and drank terribly and never made anything of his life, never married. He lived with his widowed mother. Finally it got so he drank so much that my sister-in-law, who lived in Tweed, had to take his pension money and all the money and dole it out to him, but he'd drink it all.

I think that something happened there. I think they did what they didn't think was right there. I think we sent them like children into a situation that was terrible. They were good boys, they wanted to be good, but in the situation, I'm sure that most of them did something that disgusted them with themselves so that they never could pick up the pieces.

IV. CONSCRIPTION

Mrs Anna Smokorowsky

The people in Gilbert Plains, Manitoba were very patriotic but almost all were opposed to Conscription, both farmers and townspeople.

There was a lot of dislike for conscription. The farmers didn't like it and the townspeople didn't like it. They felt that it should be volunteer: those that wanted to go should go.

I remember one incident out on the farm, not far from the homestead where we lived. There was a family that had two boys—a father, a sister, and the two boys. This boy was out bindering, like doing the harvest. He was out on the field bindering, and the RCMP came and they took him right off that binder, and left the binder and the horses in the bush there. When the father came, the binder was empty, and he didn't know what happened till a week or a few weeks later. That was bad because the farmers, the older people, felt that they should have their sons to look after this harvest that they were growing. This particular family had a section of land which was like four farms, a lot of land. They were one of the best, because they had a binder, and they had horses, I remember, at that time. So they were very, very mad about that. But the townspeople supported conscription, although I remember this Mrs. Newton saying that she didn't want her boy to go. She said that it was somebody else's war, that it wasn't a war to defend Canada. It was defending some other land that this boy didn't know about.

'There was a lot of flag-waving, of course, and they passed this conscription.'

I don't know what they did with these boys that they picked up. Now this certain boy that they picked up, that I know personally: I don't know what they did with him. They kept him in some kind of a camp, I think. I know there was a big fight that the farmers put up: they wanted these boys on the land; they needed them; it was wrong to pick up these boys because who was going to work the land to feed the army and to feed the war? This was their story of it. I know one boy was released, but oh, the parents put up a hard struggle for it, and they got a lawyer and people fighting for it. There *was* a spirit like that, but it wasn't organized, it was spontaneous. It would come up as the situation came up.

Frank Bell

He enlisted in 1916 when he was fifteen, but just as he was to go overseas his brother insisted that he confess his real age, and he was thrown out of the army.

There was a lot of flag-waving, of course, and they passed this conscription. They used to stop you on the street, and if you couldn't produce the papers, you would be conscripted into the army. I was picked up one night and put in jail overnight because I didn't have my discharge papers with me. By this time I was about seventeen. I was dying to get into the army, but they wouldn't take me. So I was picked up by these civilian police. They weren't the regular police force, they were a special corps that went around at night picking up young men and putting them in the army—press gang is really what they were. However, I was put in a barracks on Peele Street, and the next morning they got up, and all the fellows they had picked up last night, and they handed us all mops, and they told us all to get busy and mop out the barracks. And I told them what they could do with their mop. This fellow had a bayonet on his rifle and he stuck this bayonet up against my belly, and he said, 'Get going on that mop.' So I told him, 'I joined this army voluntarily.' I says, 'I was no God-damned conscript.' I says, 'You want to use that bayonet, you go ahead and use it.' So he backed down. I knew he would. He wasn't going to bayonet me over a simple thing like that. So I didn't mop their floor. In the meantime I had been given permission to phone the powerhouse where I worked, and I phoned the powerhouse, and they sent one of the boys down to my boarding house and got my papers out of my trunk. I had been carrying a birth certificate with me, but they wouldn't believe it.

Mrs Jane Walters

She was a VAD in a military hospital in London, England.

Conscription? That was when we were given the vote in England. My first vote. You see, the vote was taken here, and then all the troops abroad had the vote like they do now. Everyone wanted conscription, naturally. When you had your own there voluntarily, you hated all those others sitting around having a nice time while yours were being killed. You didn't like them. You'd no respect for them. But I never was one of those or approved of going around handing out white feathers. Do you know that some women did? Did you ever know that? They actually went to men on the street whom they knew, or if they didn't know them—strong young working men—and handed them a white feather. Of course, I just nearly died with embarrassment whenever I heard about it. I thought it was the most terrible thing to do. How did they know what reasons those men had?

Ben Wagner

He was a private in the army.

The conscripts were quite good men, there was no differentiation between them. The army clamped down on an attempt to bully them, both in France and in

England, and I think they did a very good job of it, possibly a better job than they did on some other things. There was the usual smart boy who called a fellow a 'conchee,' but they cracked down on that. You could get five days in the clink for telling off one of these conscripts. These men came over, and naturally they were given a very rapid, intense training. A sergeant is a sergeant any place, he's a damn bully anywhere or he wouldn't be a sergeant. They had a rough time. They were bullied in their training, but the day after they got to France, they were just absorbed into the group without much fuss about it. By that time a lot of the soldiers knew that life in France wasn't any bowl of cherries, and if this fella'd come out to share that bowl of cherries, why, he was as good as anybody else.

Albert Dugan

In the First World War, a lot of veterans were terribly neglected. Now you take the fellows who volunteered in the first place. I always felt bitter because they looked down on us draftees. I will say this: when they volunteered they didn't realize that they were going into a spectacle that was very, very dangerous and very hard to continue with. But after the war went on a bit, people realized, with these casualties that were coming home, that this war was a very serious matter. And it was, too. And the boys became a little bit more reluctant to volunteer, and of course, they were drafted, same as I was. I never felt a bit disturbed about being a draftee because when we got into the army and got going training, we felt that we'd fight just as good as the fellows that were volunteering. In fact, we were a better bunch than what they were because they had men 40, 35, and on down to fifteen, where we were all 21 and up-and-going. My brother even told me that himself. He said, 'Your bunch is a far better bunch than what we have because they're all the same, they're up-and-going.' They couldn't use a lot of the fellows that they had because they were too old and couldn't stand the lack of training.

Lorna Browning

When in 1917 the government decided to conscript the boys who hadn't already enlisted, around Arden there were a certain number (most of them young, but a few of them older) who hadn't any quarrel with the German people and felt the war was getting rather sticky and not too pleasant a thing to belong to. So they took to the woods not too far from home, but away from the highway. And they took from our summer cottage and some of the others, blankets and cutlery and dishes, pots and pans, and set up housekeeping with the help of the local farmers and the farmers' wives. They toughed it out till quite a long time after the war, when the government said they could come home and all would be forgiven, no questions asked.

V.   REPRESSION

Mrs Maria Pawel

I remember when they declared war. You know, I didn't know very much. War to us was something horrid. We didn't know what it was all about. So I remember the only thing everybody was shouting was 'War! War! War!' And there was mobilization then, and young men were mobilized. I remember them bravely marching. I worked in a hotel then. It was about a seven-storey building. I could see Scotch bands marching towards the city of Saskatoon and the soldiers are marching behind. I was wondering what it was, and then later on I was wondering, 'What's happening?' So I started meeting some Anglo-Saxon boys that were mobilized and by gosh, that's when I began to think what the war was all about. I had a boyfriend, he was a soldier. He used to take me out quite a bit and when he went away to training he wrote to me. I don't remember the date, it must have been 1915. He went overseas and four days later his head was blown off around Berlin, somewhere in Germany. He was killed. So I remember that and I remember soldiers desperate and I remember . . . I don't know—that's why I'm beginning to hate wars, beginning to find out and reason with myself that there is no reason for it. We're intelligent human beings. Can't we find our ways and means of trying to live with us, ourselves and our neighbours, and our country with other countries' people? When people were coming back from the war (it's not like this today, they hide them now), then you see them on the streets going without legs, without arms—gas. It was a pitiful sight. People never knew. They were taught to be patriotic, and the war came. Whether you liked it or not, you go because it's your duty. Young men didn't realize where they were going.

Were these mostly Anglo-Saxon young men?

Yeah. You see, we come from Austria, and Austria was at war against Britain. So we were aliens. They didn't bother women, but most of the men were round up and put in the concentration camp. My husband was, but he ran away. The concentration camps were mostly in Manitoba and part of Saskatchewan, but they had there all the young men, so-called Austrians, but they weren't Austrians—they were Ukrainians. And they were round up, and they didn't even know what it was all about. My husband says, when he jumped off the train where they were taking him from Winnipeg, close to the Saskatchewan border, he says there was about seven of them jumped the train. He says he doesn't know what happened to the other six, but he says he knew some people that come from old country from his village. He went into there, and they hid him there. He survived that way. He wasn't in concentration camp. No, they were innocent victims.

Paul Sawchuk

He 'became radicalized' in Germany after fleeing from the Ukraine. When he came to Canada, he joined the Social Democratic Party (SDP) and was active in union organizing. The SDP was banned during the war, and many of its members were arrested and placed in internment camps.

There were many Ukrainians in the Socialist Party. In Toronto during the First War, the Socialist Party had about 280 members. Many of them were arrested, and then they were kept and sent to the concentration camp. My brother was one, and he was in that camp for nearly two years.

Why were Ukrainians so radical when they came to Canada?

The main reason is because they were not professional. They didn't know any trade, not like myself. At least this tailoring saved me. I could use it. But they were mostly hard workers, ditch-diggers, you know, just like the Italians now, exactly the same. There was no lawyer, no dentist, now there is a number of them. And they were working such hard jobs for such low wages. There was no union. Now a carpenter makes a fortune, but those days they were not. Therefore they were mostly radicals, and we had to organize the school in order to learn, because in old country they could not finish high school. They hardly could read and write. Therefore we had to organize the school for the Ukrainian language, not for the English, but Ukrainian language. Because it was impossible to organize them without they can read the paper. They issue the paper in order to organize them and bring the workers together. That was the main reason why they were mostly radicals at that time. Actually, it was on a big scale, but during the First War, thousands of them were sent to concentration camps in Manitoba, in Saskatchewan.

They didn't want to enlist?

No, they wouldn't do it. In the First War it was publicly advertised that they should join the army, so the people joined the army in a big scale. But they would not accept those ones that came from part of Austria. There was a quite big number of people that couldn't get their citizen papers, because they were too radical. So there was a difficulty there too.

Do you remember the Winnipeg General Strike?

When the strike broke out, that was exactly the date when they arrested us, exactly. The strike was already on, and our arrest was on a Sunday. I didn't know very much because I just learned after that how the strike was, who was in the strike.

1919 that was the intervention in the Soviet Union. The committee here, English and Ukrainian and others, organized protest. They published leaflets to distribute among the workers, appealing to Canadian people not to go to Siberia, because the Canadian government decided to send the army to Siberia. So, it was on one Sunday we had a meeting, and there was one fella that was organizing the pamphlets' printing. They used to call it 'subversive activity.' So we used to organize at night, but the main thing that was a question was how to print, because all printing shops were under the rule that they had no right to print such things. But one fella, a young English fella, was working at the Telegram Printing shop on King Street. So he illegally printed thousands and thousands of those leaflets, and then distributed them at night-time to various houses. So it was quite interesting. The government was surprised how they got printed. They were looking in every printing shop in Toronto, except that one. *(laughs)*

Because of this, we were arrested, and eleven of us were charged in court. We were at a meeting on Sunday, and it happened it was in May. They used to always open Centre Island; there was music, all kinds of entertainment, so lots of people go. So I got a new suit and a new tie, a hat, everything, and went to the meeting in the morning at eleven o'clock. After that, the detectives came. There were five of them. We had a trial. The trial was that we distribute subversive literature. So two fellas got two years in Kingston Penitentiary and myself and five others got one year in Burwash. They took us on a train after the trial, with others that were arrested already and also sentenced. So we went to Burwash to work. It was very hard, very poor food, and there was a dissatisfaction among those people.

What other things did the socialist group do?

During the First World War they were issuing a newspaper. They also held educational party meetings and lectures at night. That was the Socialist Party's doing. Also interesting was that they were interested to organize the unions. Some of them have been officially members of the executive, for instance myself. I was in the Amalgamated Clothing Workers Union. The centre was in New York, but at the same time, the local branch here in Toronto was working, and there were quite numbers of members of the Socialist Party who were also members of the National Executive. So that was quite interesting.

Mrs Jessie Cartwright

Her family emigrated to Canada from England in 1911. Her parents were active in the Salvation Army and were stationed in a number of places, including Winnipeg, a mining community in British Columbia, and small towns in Ontario.

When we were in British Columbia, in Fernie, there was a lot of German people there. And they were pro-German, and they thought, 'Well, we'd better watch,' because it was a mining place and a lot of things could happen. So they *interned* them. They had internment camps. Now these camps were very nice and they had plenty to eat and clothes to wear and they didn't work at all. They wouldn't let them work in the mines, you see, because they were afraid of what they might do. So that was quite interesting from the point of view of how they were being taken care of. They really enjoyed themselves. They were quite musical, and they'd have these stringed instruments, and they'd be sitting there playing these instruments and singing, you know, to us having a good time. And all we could think of, 'Well, here they are having a good time, and our poor fellows are over there. We don't know whether they're being blown to pieces.'

Were they really pro-German?

Yes, they made it very clear that they were, and this is why they were under guard. There were quite a few nationalities in that place. There was Italians and Polish people and Ukrainians. But they didn't seem to be in the picture. It was these Germans.

CHAPTER SIX

ORDERS

Canadian soldiers responded to the regime of army discipline with a curious ambiguity. They possessed both an intense pride in their superior qualities as soldiers and a reputation for disorderliness that preceded them throughout the rest camps of Europe and the British Isles. The soldier found himself within a hierarchical structure based on absolute obedience to orders that issued from on high. NCOs were provided to bully the refractory or recalcitrant and harsh penalities were provided for disobedience. Officer and soldier found themselves in a new kind of relationship for which their social experience had little prepared them. Persistent grudges and volatile tensions between them found many startling and sometimes grisly outlets. The inchoate and largely undirected riots for which Canadians became famous were the forerunners of new kinds of social conflict ushered in by the war.

Andrew Douglas

In 1910, at the age of eighteen, he emigrated to Canada from Scotland, because his father thought 'England was too small for him.' He worked at Eaton's for two years, then for the Salvation Army, and then for Tamblyn's Drugstore. He joined the army 'a half hour after the war broke out,' and fought 'out of loyalty to Great Britain.'

You had to take orders especially when you went to the front line. If you deserted before you got up there, you were shot and no questions asked. Lots of times we didn't do what our officers told us, but they didn't know it. Our army wasn't like the British army and that. They were all disciplined and that. You couldn't do anything halfway in the German army or any other army, but ours was a volunteers' army, same as the Australians. Now we got away with a lot of stuff that those armies couldn't get away with. But I'll tell you a thing: the Canadian army was the only army that didn't lose an inch of ground that they didn't capture back, and it was the only army in the world in the war that didn't lose a gun—not one gun!! Now you can look that up in the archives and find that.

I'll tell you the difference in the First and Second World Wars. In the First World War you said, 'What can I do?' In the Second World War they said, 'What is there in it for me?' That's the difference. That's when the world changed, between wars. When you got over there you never kicked or anything. You was there to do a job. If you were going to be killed, well that's alright. It didn't matter. You never even thought of being killed—*never*! I've seen lots of men killed around me, lots and lots of them. It never entered your head that *you* were going to get it.

Peter Watson

The Canadians wouldn't follow discipline. Discipline's okay, but . . . ! It was just like in the Boer War. When they used to be marching there, the Boers used to put up a bunch of brush, and they were so well camouflaged that you'd just think that it was a clump of brush. Well, the British troops would march right up into it. Pretty soon somebody'd start shooting at them in this clump of bush. Well, the Canadians got wise to it, and they wouldn't wait for an order. The first clump of bush appeared, they'd shoot into the clump of bush. The same thing was in France. The Canadians would follow the discipline, but if they seen that it was better not to follow it, they wouldn't follow it.

Canadians, you see, were pretty well all of British descent. They were British, Irish, and Scots born, but they had been over in this country so long that they had learned to make decisions for themselves. The battle in Canada is just as hard today as it was then, but it was really harder for them. My father worked in the bush all winter when he was fifteen years of age, and he got 50 cents a day. Tough work. He used to cut 200 logs a day. I remember my father saying, when we were young, he went in to see a man about cutting marsh hay. That was all that hay that growed out in the bush, you see. And this fellow had a marsh. My father went in to make arrangements to cut it, and the fellow was only offering him half of what he should've got. So my father said he wouldn't do it. He turned around and walked out. But he got thinking of his five children at home, and he didn't have a bit of flour to make food or anything else with. So he went back and took it, and then shouldered 50 pounds of flour and carried that nine miles on his shoulders back in. But *there's* an instance where it proved the *toughness* of life in there.

Alfred Nevin

We had discipline in our house. It was accepted. Father said, 'You do it,' you did it. Now around the farm there was always things to do, which was a very good way to be brought up. You know, you don't have to think of things to do. Father wasn't a slave-driver, and we had fishing or we went to the fair, and whatnot. But there was always certain duties that I had to do every day, and the only way I could get out of it was to be really sick. Or if you wanted to go to a certain thing, why, father would make arrangements. But you just couldn't say, 'I don't feel like it today.' You just had to do it. That's a very useful thing—you have to have discipline to live. The army reinforced that in a way.

Ben Wagner

A farm boy.

I think the farm boys were possibly the best of the bunch. First of all, they were used to a bit of outdoor life. And they were under orders from their father. To me, the hardest man to handle was the chap who had been more or less a bum in the city of Toronto, who was used to whining, 'I don't like that, and the YMCA wasn't any good' and so on. We had a number of those, and they were a headache. Farm boy and city boy—I don't think there was a great deal of difference, except I think the farm boy fell into line more quickly than the city boy. For one thing, he'd gone away from home a volunteer, he hadn't volunteered with his pal next door.

Christopher Arnold

There were lots of them that did things. I won't mention what they did, but some of them did things in order to get out of the army, and maimed themselves for life possibly, just to get out of it once they got in there. There was one man I can tell you about. He joined up as a working man. He was an engineer and he joined an engineering battalion. He came to the Twenty-eighth Battalion while I was there. He didn't want to go into the line to fight. They used to tie him behind what they called the horse wagon, to take him into line, but he never would fight. I didn't come in contact with him much while he was in the regiment because he was always in the clink, as we call it, because he wouldn't fight. They kept transferring him; he was court-martialed; they transferred him from one battalion to another; but he never deserted from the front line. If you desert from the front line, you're shot. But he never went in the line. He always had some excuse.

Robert Swan

He enlisted as a private, but was quickly promoted to officer because his experience working in a bank was useful to the quartermaster. He later received a commission on the field and became a company commander.

The reaction of different men after they did enlist was greatly varied. I think the majority of men found it fairly easy to adjust to some of the less desirable and less comfortable factors of military life. But there were some men who evidently did enlist for very patriotic reasons, who hated the darned life from the very day they came into it. They were never happy. I think they had more courage than probably lots of others in that they stuck it out when they were so desperately unhappy. They couldn't adjust themselves to the rough conditions that they had to face. It wasn't that they were ninnies or anything like that, but they shrank from mud and dirt and too close contact with large bodies of other unwashed men. That's what they had to face. And then the types of food that were available to them were not what they'd been accustomed to, and they disliked some of it very badly, but they hadn't very much choice. In later months after they actually got into real action, combat action, some of these men were desperately frightened, and yet they had the guts to carry on and never show it. I think in that case they were probably deserving of more credit than has been given to them.

There's a difference, quite a radical difference, between fear and fright. A man can experience fear, and any man who saw any amount of actual combat service knows all about it, but it never reached the point where he couldn't control his fear and carry on in any way that appeared to be necessary at the time. But when a man gets frightened, he panics, and it takes two forms: either he freezes solid so he's incapable of moving at all, or his one and only instinct is to turn and run, to get away from what's causing the intense fear, when his self control is broken. It's pretty pathetic when that happens.

Through experience, as the war progressed, why, those of us that had some responsibility of one form or another, either as non-commissioned officers or as commissioned officers, learned to detect the beginnings of this sort of thing in some of the men before it actually broke loose. There were different ways of dealing with it. Either you could relieve a man from duty temporarily and consign him to some other area where he would have time to gather himself together again. Or, it wasn't entirely common, but there were cases where the quickest way to control a man who was getting jittery was to go and slap his face good and hard and make him so damn mad that he'd forget that he was frightened. In some cases that worked and he'd thank you for it later on. But that was all part of what was going to happen later on and hadn't anything to do with the early days of enlistment.

In the early days we were very green; our officers were just as green as we were. Nobody knew what we were up against, and the higher up in the army you got, the more you were working on the basis of the South African War. Some of the equipment that we got in the early stages very definitely dated back to 1900, 1901. When we actually got into action, a great deal of what was given to us as instruction during the training period had to be completely forgotten or readjusted to face existing conditions. War never follows the rulebook completely. I think one of the reasons for the success of the Canadians was the fact that when they found that some of the rules and regulations just didn't work, they had the ability to reconstruct them as much as necessary, without breaking them, to fit the situation.

Burt Woods

Was there any conflict between the officers and the ranks?

No, not at all. Anything would happen behind the lines, you see. We couldn't divulge that. It made a man of me, that's one good thing it did. I thought the discipline was right, I thought it was good. You can't run an army on say-say. It's action all the time, you gotta obey. One thing I always learnt to my men who was under me: obey your orders whether your officer or sergeant is giving you the wrong order; you obey whether it is right or wrong. That's one thing I used to drill in. Your superior was never wrong. If he did something he shouldn't have done, you didn't go against it. You always obeyed orders as they were given to you by the command, because your superior was always ahead of you and superior to you. That was drilled into me, and I used to drill it into the men what was under me.

Robert Franklin

From a prosperous farming family in Ontario, he was a private in the army.

There was discipline alright. You had to follow by it, there was no doubt about that or boy, you were in trouble! You had to be kinda tough to obey all orders without any comeback and to do the things at the time you were supposed to do them. I managed to keep out of any real trouble. I used to get awful mad within myself though. I wanted to tell some of these NCOs off, that were pretty bossy fellas. If I met one or two of those fellas today, I'd like to tell them what I thought of them in those days. I still hold the grudge. *(laughs)* NCOs are like any other kinds of men. There's some awful bulldozers among them and some fine fellas among them. But those who love to throw their weight around and deliberately abuse other people for no reason on earth—oh yes, there were quite a few of those fellas around.

Michael Sheehan

Sergeants are very important. The backbone of the army is the sergeant. They're a very big man in the army. You'd think that the captain and the colonels and the majors and everything else were big, but the sergeant is the man. He's the backbone of the whole thing. The men know him, call him by his first name, or 'Hullo Sarge!' Curse the army, curse the commander, curse everybody to the sergeant, and then he'll get out and drill you. Ah, they're wonderful, wonderful men, those sergeants!

Eric Rosen

I was at brigade headquarters, and we had one sergeant—now he was a sergeant, but he didn't get paid for it, he just had stripes for what we called protection. He was very pompous and nobody liked him. We couldn't stand him, but we'd have to, of course, till we got to England. We were on our way home, war was over. I'll never forget it, it was a real joy to me. Two of us were sitting in the orderly room, we were on duty, and Sergeant Bailey came in and, as usual, looked at himself in the mirror and that. It was cold and he said, 'Orderly!' And we didn't pay any attention. 'Orderly!' Didn't pay any attention. He says, 'Who's on duty?' We said, 'We are.' He said, 'Get a bucket of coal for this stove.' We said, 'If you want a bucket of coal, you get it yourself.' Boy, he hit the roof! We said, 'Go ahead, do what you like! The war's over, we're on our way home. We've put up with enough from you.' Oh, that was a real satisfaction. *(laughs)*

Charles Riddell

He was born in the Parry Sound district. He quit school when he was ten to help on the farm, and then worked in lumber camps in northern Ontario. He enlisted in 1915 because he 'didn't want to be conscripted.'

I was the mounted orderly for the officer. They had called out on the parade for people that had been used to horses. I was used to horses on the farm, and a guy nailed me!*(laughs)* I was in the horse line most of the time, on parades, you see. I'd get the horse ready and I'd have to walk with the colonel and the majors and sergeant-majors. I didn't like that! I'da sooner been back with the boys. Every time they'd stop for a rest, he'd get off and I'd have to look after the horse.

You know, we couldn't shave our top lip when we was in the army. I had a moustache and I had it waxed out. I was out over the weekend. I come in Monday morning, and they were going on a route march. So I got the horse ready and I took him up and we had to line up—A, B, C, D Companies. My pal next to me was a Scotchman. The officers come in, and my officer didn't know me. I'd had my moustache off. And he come down and was talking to the Scotchman. He says, 'Where's Riddell?' He didn't even know his horse! My pal says, 'There he is right there.' He come over to me and says, 'What have you been doing, Riddell?' 'Oh,' I says, 'not much.' So he got on the horse, and I went and fell in, in front of the rank. I was right beside a sergeant-major. Oh, he had it in for me! He never said a word. He says, 'Where's your rifle?' I says, 'I don't carry a rifle. I can't carry a rifle and look after a horse.' 'Well,' he says, 'here's mine.' He made me carry his rifle. That made me mad, my gosh! We were away all day. When we come back, I give him his rifle. I never used it because I laid it down all the time. So I hand him back his rifle. He says, 'You be ready for office tomorrow morning.' So I had to go up before the colonel for shaving my moustache off.

If I'd been wise, I'da just got the barber to clip it and not shave it. I'da been alright then. I'da got about ten days in the clink, but my officer said he needed me and the colonel let me off. I let it grow back. When we got overseas, we whacked them off, and they never said nothing. The orderlies had to have a weekly shave, so we kept shaved. But if that sergeant-major had ever . . . ! He was too cold-footed to go to France with us. He stayed back in England. If he'da went to France, he wouldn't have went far because the first time that he went over the top, he'da got it, because I'da give it to him. He didn't like me and I didn't like him. He'da never come back.

Allan MacTavish

He became a lawyer, in deference to his father's unfulfilled dream, and hesitated to enlist for fear of hurting his parents—he was supposed to be a lawyer,

not a soldier. Pressured by recruiting 'propaganda' and his own feeling that he
wasn't doing enough, he obtained a commission in the artillery early in 1916.
The war had a great impact on his life and changed his outlook.

We weren't in danger like men that were in the infantry, but nobody could say
that when they got up in the morning they were going to go to bed at night. You
got a concept of the things that were worthwhile. There was no jealousy, no
meanness. When we lived together in a mess, there was nobody trying to get the
better of you. Now there might be the odd one, but if there was, he was treated
with contempt. It was like living in a society where there was very little difference in meaningful relations. You did have army ranks because you had to have
that for the purpose of command and control, but it didn't make any difference.
Now other people's experience might have been different than mine. I know one
man was telling me about being in the field artillery, and the major got killed and
they all said 'Hurrah!' They disliked him very much. Our major wasn't a lovable
fellow, but we kinda laughed at him because he was a chap that let other people
do the work and he got along with as little responsibility and work as he could.
You didn't admire him, but at the same time he was alright.

Were you an officer yourself?

Oh yes, I had command of a section, which was a small command. I was a
lieutenant, what they call Number One in charge of a section. We had a captain
who was a character if ever there was one. You saw funny men, and you laughed
about them. He was kind of a contemptible character, but at the same time I lived
with him and got along alright. But he would steal like nobody's business. He'd
never get under shellfire if he could help it, but he would go under shellfire if
there was an opportunity to steal something. And he was a lawyer! After he got
home his inclination to steal was still there, and he finally got struck off the roll.
Of course, the men held him in contempt. Quite rightly so, because they knew
his propensities.

Ben Wagner

It was the big thing of the war that you met people not only from all over Canada
and occasionally from the British Isles, but you met them from all ranks of life,
and they all looked the same. We were in Whitley Camp and right alongside us
was a battalion from French Canada. We didn't speak much French and they
didn't speak much English, but they were the finest sports you ever saw. Any
kind of spare time you had, they were out with a baseball bat or something like
that. And they were a dandy crowd, jovial, friendly. I got an entirely different
opinion of the French Canadians because of being with these people. You met
people from Nova Scotia, or from Prince Edward Island, clean through to

British Columbia. Very often you didn't take any notice of the fact unless they happened to mention it. And you never knew if the fella alongside you was a Catholic or a Protestant, or—which is almost as serious—a Liberal or a Tory. You just took him for granted, and he took you for granted, and that was all there was to it. The phrase was 'a good man on the line.' That was a fella who knew his job and did it. There was no dissension that way. It also gave you perhaps an insight into Canada that we wouldn't have got otherwise. You heard them talk about sheep ranching in Alberta, or timber cutting in B.C. We all knew enough about these things to sort of understand what they were talking about, but it was always interesting. I think there was a great deal of tolerance in that. And you know, the first three months after I came home, I was homesick because I was living in a room by myself in Toronto. I was homesick because you didn't have the people around you all the time. You get used to this, to always being in a crowd.

'You get used to this, to always being in a crowd.'

Richard Mills

He taught school in a Mennonite community in Saskatchewan before the war. Members of the community tried to dissuade him from enlisting, but he was adamant. He found army life 'just wonderful' after teaching.

We had more and more contact with the English officers, and they were arrogant. If they had one star on their shoulder, they thought they were the Lord Almighty. I remember one time, not so long after we were in France, I was sent back to Le Havre and while there, there was a little pipsqueak of an officer with one star on his shoulder, just a kid out of school. He says, 'You, sir, you,' he says, 'pick up my luggage and follow me.' I was a corporal and I could defy him, but I knew I shouldn't defy him, so I picked up his luggage, followed him where he wanted to go, and stopped and put it down. 'Here's a bob! Here's a bob!' I just turned on my heels! I didn't say a word. I didn't take a bob from that little pipsqueak. There was a lot of that in the army.

Was the Canadian army less hierarchical than the British army?

Yes, and it got more so as the war went on. In the final days of the war, there wasn't a junior officer that hadn't come through the ranks. At the start though, in the infantry, there was bank clerks, lawyers, the mayor's son, and they got commissioned right off. They had no background at all. One of the reasons the Canadian Corps was so effective at the end of the war was that all the junior officers had raised through the ranks.

Mark Tanner

He joined the airforce, trained in Toronto, and was given a position in the Royal Flying Corps.

In the Britain of that period of the First World War, there was a very definite class distinction, a class barrier that I think has gone, and I think it's a very good thing that it has gone. To be an officer you were considered in the upper group, you were something special. I don't think that the British people or the Canadians would ever tolerate such a condition again, but it did exist at that time. I can remember having a letter from a friend of mine that I'd gone to school with. He was a bit older than I was, and he'd been in the army in the infantry and had served in France and was back home in London on leave. He wrote me a letter and said, could I meet him in London and we could have dinner together? So I went to the commander (this was a naval station and the co was a commander) and said, could I have a day off to go down to London, to the centre of the city, and have dinner with my friend? He said, 'Well, you can't be seen in public with a private. You can have the day off, but you'll have to get a room in a hotel and go up and talk to him there. *(laughs)* You can't have dinner with him in public or meet him on the street in public.' It was not completely a class barrier. It was partly based upon the belief that officers mustn't fraternize with the men, and they must have absolute authority, and they couldn't do that if they were socially mixing with the men. I was only eighteen, and I couldn't understand what it was all about. *(laughs)* I did see him in London. I think we just talked in the lobby of a hotel and had dinner in a restaurant. That was breaking the rules and the regulations at that time. However, that wouldn't apply today.

Mrs Jane Walters

It was difficult as a VAD getting used to the English sisters. That was very hard. The discipline in a British military hospital was something! We had our meals in a vast room, part of the original building. You went down steps into it, and it was long, and towards the other end you went up steps, and there's where the lord and lady of the manor would sit in the olden days. You remember the saying 'below the salt?' You went down steps and all the tables here were for the nursing sisters and the VADs. The matron and all the senior nursing sisters and the heads of the hospital would be up there. The matron only came to second dinner, and when she would come, the VAD who was sitting at the end of that table, the nearest to the door through which she would come, would get up and go to the door and hold the door open. When the matron would come in, you'd have to give her a little bow.

We didn't grumble—the hierarchy didn't affect us. Some of the nursing sisters in charge of each ward were very strict. Some of them I couldn't bear. One of them was so rude to me one day that I just turned round and sauced her back. I said, 'I haven't come 3,000 miles to work voluntarily to be spoken to like that by anybody.' Of course she reported me to the matron and I was up on the carpet. So I was changed from that ward.

My experience as a VAD certainly broadened me. You met people from all over the world. You did things you never thought you were going to do. And you had stern discipline, and you had hardship—terrible things to look at, to see, and to do, and you had to just grit your teeth and do it. It was a wonderful character builder.

Robert Swan

He served as a company commander.

There was a camp in north Wales, Rhyl, and there were a lot of these Canadians had started out from the camp (at the end of the war) to go to Liverpool and go aboard ships, and then the ships were diverted to take home a lot of American soldiers from France, who hadn't hardly landed and got their feet wet. When these Canadians found it out they got mad, because they were right on the verge of going home, and they were stuck at this camp at north Rhyl. The worst of it was that they had been paid off at the camps before they left, and they'd blown their pay because they expected to be on the ship and to be fed anyway, and all their records had been sent forward to Canada. There they were without any pay, and without any money, and stuck in this camp at Rhyl, and no idea as to when they were going to get home. They got *mad*, and they started to make a fuss. When the authorities didn't pay any attention to them, they wrecked the damn camp from one end to the other. They just burnt the damn thing right down. They rioted. Then they found some ships in a helluva hurry and brought them home.

We had a riot after we'd landed in England. We had a dirty riot in Folkestone the first pay night. The whole of the second division was on the loose with money in their pockets. Folkestone isn't a very big place, and they got in there, and they got jammed one way and another, and of course, part of the trouble was that they were all clamouring for service and food and other things at the same time. It got kind of nasty. Somebody with more beer in them than was good for them took a crack at some civilian, and then they started an efficient ship-shop down on the waterfront. Before they got through with it, they began to just tear the place to pieces. And everybody was running to see what was happening and then getting into it. They had to block off the whole of the city and send in two cavalry regiments, and then they'd go to work with the horses. They'd go in where these boys were gathered together rowing and fighting one another, and cut out ten or fifteen or 20 of them, and drive them ahead of them, and put them on a bus, and get them out of town. They broke it up that way. But they rioted all night. There was a lot of damage.

They had a little riot in the camp at Sandlings, because the canteen was being run by a British crowd and they were overcharging our men for very poor quality food. Our boys kicked about it four or five times, and they didn't get anywhere. They complained and complained and complained. So they said, 'To hell with this, we'll fix that.' So they went in one night and burnt the place out, and drove the civilians right out of the camp. They didn't hurt them. They just took them by the back of the neck and took them to the gate and kicked them out onto the road, and said, 'Now get going and don't come back.' Oh, there was a commotion about it! There were all kinds of staff came down from London, war office people, this man, that man, so forth and so on. But we got a new canteen, and then we got some service. It wasn't that we objected to it. It was just the fact that somebody was getting rich on us and we didn't like it. After we kicked about it and nobody did anything, well then the boys did something themselves.

There was a very nasty riot in France. I don't think it was ever made public, at least I've never heard of it being mentioned in any history or anything. When the Aussies came up from the Dardanelles in the spring of 1916, why, the proposal was that they were going to come right in alongside the Canadians. They thought that being colonials and being more or less similar in background one way and another, they'd get along pretty well, and we'd all be together. The idea was that they were to take over our provisional headquarters in Bayeux, and we were to move just a little north, and then the troops would be brought in battalion by battalion and filter into the areas and take their proper places. Well, the very first night when the advance parties from the Aussies got in there and our men were still there, they met and they got along pretty good for awhile. Then somebody with a big mouth on the Australian side said they'd come up to finish the job the Canadians couldn't finish. So the next fellow turned around and said, 'Why didn't you finish where you were before you came?' Because the Dardanelles were a fiasco and a disaster. And that started the riot. Unfortunately, in those days, the sergeants always carried what they called sidearms, they carried their bayonets on their belt. They never carried their rifle, but whenever they were out walking, part of their dress was their bayonet. Well, these bayonets kept coming out, and they began to carve each other up. And before they got through with it, it was a real humdinger, and they never did publish anything about it. Kept it dark as far as that was concerned. There were some men killed. How many nobody knows. There were a lot of others that were badly hurt. They finally had to bring in other troops to stop it. Then they found out that there was no way of putting the Aussies and the Canadians together. So they always kept a couple of British divisions between them.

Robert Franklin

I was in a riot down in Seaford. There wasn't any particular good reason at all. Everybody wanted to get home, they were impatient, of course, and generally cantankerous. I remember a gang of them got into one of the canteens with all kinds of beer. They stole the beer and went running away in all directions, getting half tight. The first thing you knew, they put a match and burnt the place down. I remember coming back to my hut, where there'd be about 70 men, and about 20 pails of water for fire protection. When I got back there, the pails were all full, but they were all full of beer! *(laughs)*

Wally Ross

A sergeant, he was on guard duty the night of the Seaford riot.

How did it start?

Well, it's just one of those things we don't know. Spontaneously. You don't really know those things now. I don't see what the reason was, why the fellows got so restless. It wouldn't bother me. But you know how it is sitting around there, nothing to do. Has to be a certain amount of discipline, and then they kept promising, you see, some will be going, and it didn't happen. There are always a few who want everything to happen. You have it today—they call them militants today. The bloody war was through, and we waited to get home. To heck with them! We didn't want to be bothered with button shining, divine services on Sunday morning. We were through with that. We wanted to be free!

Richard Mills

He served as a corporal.

We were in Seaford, Sussex. We were in south camp—it was all machine gun, and the north camp was all Canadian engineers. The morrow the armistice was signed, our commander of the Officers' Training Corps called the usual parade for seven in the morning, and he said, 'The armistice was signed. We'll carry on the training in the usual manner, and if anyone breaks training, back to France with your units!' So we carried on our lectures and training. Everybody else in the whole camp—well, discipline broke up. They got tight. In fact, they were all just roary-eyed, I shouldn't say all but there was just no parade whatsoever, and the town was swarming with soldiers, and a lot of them were tight. In about three days all their money was spent, they'd all drifted back. Colonel Moorehouse was a camp commandant, and he called a muster parade. He waited about three days until the money was all gone and the men sobered up, and then he called a muster parade. I don't know how many thousands were in that. There were about 20 deep in a line square. At the centre of this was a kitchen table and kitchen chair. In due course, we were all called to attention—'Break ranks.' So we broke ranks. There was this pompous-looking fellow with a red hat and red tabs and all his aides dancing around him. They helped him up to the chair and up the chair to the kitchen table. He had a bullhorn, and he spoke this way *(gestures)*, and he spoke that way, and he spoke that way, and he spoke that way. And the gist of the story was that 'Anyone breaks discipline, I'll impose full military law. Get back and carry on under regular discipline there.' And I believed him. To me, a man like that with red tabs, *(he pauses)*—well, you mean what you say! In that message he said, 'This is only an armistice. We may see the worst fighting yet in France.' Anyway, in about a week's time everything was settled, and they asked who wants to have leave. They wanted us to go away, to disperse.

Anyway, that story about the camp commandant and his muster parade: about fifteen years ago a friend of mine invited me to the Arts and Letters Club on Elm Street—you know the place there, where you sit on long benches on either side. And the man that sat across from me was a little (well I thought he was little) white-haired, pink-cheeked fellow, introduced to me as Mr Moorehouse. It meant nothing to me. I got talking to him. And then he said, 'I live in Oakville, I'm a retired architect.' Retired architect... Colonel Moorehouse at Camp Seaford was an architect, I'd been told. Now this can't be the same man, this man with the bristles on him, I thought. I said, 'Mr Moorehouse, did you ever serve in the armed forces?' 'Did I ever serve in the armed forces! I served 24 years, and five of them in the Great World War!' And I said, 'Well Colonel, I had the honour to serve under you.' 'Well, where was that?' So I told him that I was in the officers' training class at that time, and then I told him the story I told you about the muster parade. I said, 'Do you remember it?' 'Do I remember it?! I was never more scared in my life!' Here's a man in power putting on a great show. You know, that's just true in life. People in the high spots, you know, they maybe aren't sure of this and this, and they're wondering all the time, will it work or won't it work?

CHAPTER SEVEN

AT THE FRONT

An entire generation of young Canadians experienced well-organized recruiting drives in which their government exploited every aspect of the English Canadian psyche. Enlistment to save the British Empire brought hundreds of thousands to boot camp organized by a permanent staff who had learned the martial arts from textbooks and service in few campaigns more dangerous than the annual militia muster. The deference to authority that they tried to impress on their recruits was no preparation for the stark horrors that they would encounter in the trenches of France and Flanders. Soaked by rain, bespattered by mud, crawling with lice, the recruit inhabited a world which reeked of omnipresent death. Numbed by altering intervals of deafening artillery barrages and long periods of quiet punctured only by sniper fire, he saw his glorious crusade transformed into a struggle for survival where doing one's duty was often the surest way of losing. Distinctions between ally and enemy broke down in the heat of battle and the long boredom of stalemate. No one who experienced it would ever be quite the same again.

Keith Fallis

There's one memory that stands out in my mind very clearly. I was in the group that were mostly young fellows in their twenties. We were in the Signals, it was engineers then. We were held in England until we were nineteen, because they had come to the conclusion that it wasn't good to send eighteen-year olds out to the trenches. Too many were breaking down nervously and so on. So we were given all kinds of special training. One day we were taken out to be taught bayonet-fighting. They had straw men there, you see. After you had done a certain amount of training about how to hold your rifle, then you had to practise taking a run and a jab at this straw man. 'In, out, and on guard' is what the sergeant would shout. The two places that you tried to slam your bayonet in are his throat and his stomach. I think more than half of us just couldn't eat our supper that evening. From that time on, I always had this kind of ambivalence: 'I'm glad that I'm in the Signals, at least I'm only doing the telephoning,' but knowing that that was not a moral position. If the war is justified, then you have to accept all your responsibilities, you see. But I never went over to Siegfried Sassoon's position that, because of the nature of it, you have to repudiate it. But I think that because of that experience and also going over to the front and seeing men killed for the first time, and horses shot to pieces, I froze up. I just wouldn't think about it. I just hung on to this: the best we could hope was that this war would make the world safe for democracy; and it's a helluva business, and the sooner we get it over with, the better.

Basically I sort of froze up. I didn't want to discuss moral questions or religious questions. I did sometimes feel after my experience in battle, how could anyone believe in God as having an influence in human life and have this sort of thing happen? But I never went on to discuss it. I just froze up intellectually.

Mark Tanner

We were sent out to the Isle of Shapiay, Eastchurch, where we had our training. I'm astonished, when I think of the way they train pilots today, at the quick training they gave us. They used to turn out pilots with as little as two and a half or three hours flying time with your instructor, not solo. After two or three hours, the instructor would step out and say, 'Well, you go alone now.' Quite a feat! When each one of us would start off on our solo flight, spectators on the ground would all be watching, expecting the poor bloke to crash. Getting off is hard enough, but getting back on the ground again is the real difficult thing. Sometimes they wrecked the machine. They didn't break themselves—it wasn't that hazardous, but it was an experience. They used to talk in the squadron that the average life of a pilot on the front line in France was ten hours' flying time, and I think that's accurate. The casualties were quite severe.

'One day we were taken out to be taught bayonet-fighting....'

Michael Sheehan

I'll never forget our first sight of the Germans. We had those beautiful Ross rifles. They were absolutely the slickest rifles you could find anywhere, but no good for war. The Germans were coming, we could see them coming across down there. So we opened up with these Ross rifles, and I bet we didn't fire more than a dozen shots before it seized. It got hot. (It was made so beautifully.) They had absolutely seized, everything just as tight as could be. We stood on the bolt to try to open the breech, nothing doing! The rifles were absolutely useless, and here the Germans were, coming down the road down below us, about a couple of hundred feet. We had barbed wire about as high as a table—it wouldn't stop anything. And we looked down at this great big column of men, about a thousand of them marching down there, just keeping step, the officer ahead and a couple of them behind. You wouldn't believe it! They could have walked up that hill, and we didn't have anything. We didn't even have a revolver. We couldn't have done a thing. They could have just walked up and then walked right through for the next fifty miles. We were the last line, you see. We don't know yet why, but they turned around, about turned, and marched right back.

Bill Boyd

What was your attitude towards the Germans?

Not particularly hatred. It seemed to be that they didn't want to be there any more than we did. But it seemed to be that somebody else was manipulating the strings behind the line, and we were just put there to work out a game. It wasn't really hatred. Only sometimes you did hate, when you see your chums and your friends get shot. It would be pretty hard on you that way, and you could say you'd hate for awhile, but not necessarily hate that you wanted to kill. But you had to kill or be killed, if you wanted to survive. Sometimes you'd think of all the killing, how unnecessary it was, when you could live in peace with each other till somebody stirred up a lot of hatred and then get you into this fighting that you had no part of really. They seemed to be playing a game of this.

Sometimes at that time there, I felt, well, it's so unnecessary. A bunch of men, say a hundred and fifty yards or a hundred yards away—you could talk to them and you could hear them talking, hear them working, and here you was, you got to make an attack. And you had to kill them or get killed. And you would sometimes wonder what it was all about.

Tom Held

The front line troops never used the word 'Hun.' The name we gave was Jerry or Heine or Fritz. First of all, the word 'Hun' was used back home by the newspapers. Hun was a popular word, but front line troops didn't use it. After all, we felt that poor old Jerry was having just as tough a time as us.

The following is an excerpt from an account written by Tom Held shortly after the war. In it he details a Canadian attack on German lines a few days after the successful assault of September 27 on Canal du Nord.

I wouldn't call this attack a blunder, but I want to emphasize the fact that not all attacks are as successful as September 27.

After a couple of days' rest, we were told that we were going to take over the front line again, and that we were going into a quiet part of the line. Guns were cleaned in the daylight, petrol tins were filled with water, and each sergeant drew his issue of rum for his crew. About four o'clock in the afternoon, after an hour's wait, Old Don Battery—that's our battery—were permitted to unharness our packs again and to make tea. This often happens in the army: wind up and take it easy. Then a couple of more hours waiting and off we go, limbers following along the road. (The limbers—the name of the vehicle carrying machine guns as far as they dare go—were drawn by Texas mules, and since a mule cost a lot of money, you couldn't risk losing a mule; so they didn't go up where the shells were landing too frequently.) About an hour of this ends our easy marching, for the limbers are unloaded, and we march on, across fields and along ditches, carrying guns. It's a dark night, and I lose all sense of direction, but I puts the blind faith in the guides.

Rumour says that we're going into a quiet front. As we get near the vicinity of the star shells, conversation dies down. 'Put that cigarette out,''Stop that mess tin rattling,' and so on. The Germans were at least half a mile away, but some of our boys were a little bit uneasy. I'm beginning to wonder if the guide knows his job, and others show a similar curiosity. 'How long does this march keep up?' 'How about a little rest?' Finally we halt on the brink of a freshly dug trench. The troops we are relieving are expecting us, and they're starting to march off almost before we have dropped our ammunition. 'What's it like here, chum?' I ask. 'Oh, it's pretty quiet. No shells much, but you've got to keep your head down in the daytime, because those machine guns are pretty careless.' 'Well, that's alright,' I thought, 'I'm willing to do that.'

The trench was narrow and about five feet deep, just a fresh trench that had been dug, you see. This was almost open warfare—no dugouts. There were little funkholes scooped out along the side of the bank, large enough to shelter all parts of me, except my seat. Everyone goes to sleep, except those on the guard. My turn comes from midnight to two o'clock in the morning, when Charlie takes over from me. I sit down for a sleep in a funkhole, and although the rain begins to pour, only my feet become wet. About an hour of this and then the water in the bottom of the trench is running into my funkhole. 'Why don't they dig this funkhole a little deeper?' is my grumbling remark. Sitting down in water not being very conducive to sleep, I try to sleep in a standing position and wish it were morning.

About four o'clock in the morning, everybody is awake and blessing the weather, the army, and everything in general. Well, along comes the sergeant with *rum*! This looks suspicious. Why do they give us rum if we are merely going to hold the line? The last time we were given rum, we were sent over the top. 'Well, probably it's on account of the rain,' was my thought. I was in a generous mood and gave half my share of the rum to the sergeant. There were two nose caps for each of us, a double issue—something very unusual. I now feel warm again to my very toes, so warm in fact that the odd crumb begins to liven up the recesses of my shirt. (Aside: You know what crumb is? *Lice*. They used to enjoy living wherever there were any creases in the undershirts.)

Well, about four o'clock in the morning, the racket begins. Our guns set off a noisy clamour as if there was a war on! Fritz's star shells' sputtering dazzle the sky and display the road just in front of us, with its fine row of elms, still largely unharmed, on each side. 'Stand to! Get ready to advance!' comes the order. This is a shock. Why didn't I drink all the rum I had? Here we are, going over the top again. Charlie and I are barely awake, but we climb into our equipment, wearily lift up our belt boxes, and clamber out of the trench. We had no inkling, but—*c'est la guerre!* That's the war, you see. We wait for the barrage to lift, and then we're off. No orders are given in this affair, except to advance—how far we don't know. Each gun crew is warned to keep together. It's nearly daylight as we stumble across the road and down the field. Haven't quite reached the German front line yet. Our guns are firing rapidly, but nothing in comparison to September 27. There's no opposition as yet.

Our gun crew straggles out into a long line, with the sergeant leading. We meet barbed wire. There is a path somewhere through it, but we can't find it. So we just try to wade across anywhere. The wire is too low to crawl under and too high to easily step over. I manage fine because I have long legs, but Charlie's legs are too short. The seat of his pants is ruined in no time. It's quite a balancing feat to carry three boxes of 250 rounds each and step over a barbed wire two-and-a-half feet high. By holding the wire for each other, we manage better. There seems to be no end to the wire, but finally we get through after what I would say was twenty or thirty yards of it. The rest of the crew are still okay, and on we go down the slope of the field. No shells or machine gun bullets have landed near our gun crew … horseshoes, alright! (You know, we *were* lucky.)

Halfway down the field, we meet a few walking wounded in a hurry to get back. Then suddenly the fog lifts (the morning mist, you know), and it is now broad daylight—too light, in fact. Here and there are little German funkholes, vacant, about three feet deep, two feet wide, and about six feet long. The Germans didn't have time to dig an elaborate system of trenches when they were retreating. There seems to be no continuous system of trenches, merely machine gun emplacements. The walking wounded are now more noticeable and seem in such a hurry to get back. Occasionally the odd Fritizie prisoner is seen on his way back, usually unattended. (We didn't have to march them back; they were glad to get out of the war.) Sometimes four of them would be carrying a stretcher. They can be trusted to do that. They're quite willing to get to the rear.

Everything is still going smoothly with our gun crew. We're strung out on a line, with Sergeant Jake Miller in front and the other five trailing behind. Suddenly, the dirt flies up in little puffs around our feet, and little noises such as a cat makes when angry, only in very rapid succession. This sss, sss, sss, is very close. Immediately the chap in front of me falls down with a bullet through his knee, and the chap behind me has got one through his ankle. Both of them rolled hurriedly into a shell hole for protection, and the rest of us looked them over, and they told us, 'Keep going, don't bother with us. We can wait on each other.' We stick their rifles in the ground, bayonet first, and tie a white cloth at the butt of the rifle as a signal that here are wounded. And we decide if we can't help them, might as well keep going. So they assure us that they can dress each other's wounds, and they'll wait in the shell hole until some stretcher-bearers come along that way.

We were in plain view of the enemy on the railway embankment way up ahead, and he evidently sees us. The thought that he is deliberately aiming at our particular group with an attempt to kill was an *alarming* fact, and we somewhat resented it. Machine gun fire from the enemy ceases, or else they are firing somewhere else, and since the dirt ceases to fly up, and those personal, little, rapid whistles are absent, we decide to go on. Sergeant Jake Miller now carries the machine gun; Charlie, my chum, the tripod; while the rest of us that are left, Gallagher and I, are left to carry the ammunition. We are now down to four men, instead of six. Well, we all hurry down the slope and drop into some small funkholes at the bottom of the slope for a rest. Gallagher and I crouch down in the same funkhole, our heads just below the surface of the ground, while the machine gun bullets are firing at us. In a few minutes, enemy machine gun fire lessens, and the sergeant decides to go on. So he says, 'Now look. I'll carry the tripod. Charlie, you carry the gun.' And he says to me, 'You follow right behind with some ammunition. And we'll make a run for it.' Halfway up the next slope, we meet another burst of machine gun bullets. They seem to be just skimming the ground. It's foolish, therefore, to lie down, in my opinion, but we dropped flat. The sergeant crouches behind an anthill, and I barricade my head with all those three boxes of ammunition, hoping that that will help. It's strange the thoughts that go through your head, you know. I thought to myself, 'Well, three belt boxes might help.' So we lie there until the machine gun pays attention to somebody else. There's no shell hole handy to tumble into, so we were right there on the ground. As soon as the strafe lets up, we stumble on in a hurry. There is just twenty rods ahead to reach the sunken road, which is our objective. (And I think that I did that in twenty seconds flat . . .well, less than that—ten seconds!) The last few steps are raced in real marathon form, when we slide down into the sunken road with a big sigh of relief.

The road is a long sunken road with a high bank towards the enemy—that's lucky—and a fairly low bank on the opposite side, so that we were fairly safe from attack, from shellfire. It was already lined with our troops, a mixed lot of infantry battalions and machine gunners. One battalion, the Fourth, has gone on further, but they were held up on the flat open field. A few wounded managed to get back, but they were just pinned down, as we say, for the rest of the day. After a few minutes, Charlie comes along. I was worrying about him, you see. He wasn't as fast a runner as I was, and he was supposed to be coming along with the gun. But he comes along, slides down, and we are now ready for any counter-attacks. It's now about nine or ten o'clock.

A German airplane furnishes a little diversion, and none of ours were in sight. The plane sails calmly up and down, just over our route, so low that captured German machine guns fire at it. The plane is kind enough not to fire in return, but in a few minutes, shells begin to land near the road, either just in front of us or a little too far. Only one ever lands in the road, due to the fact of the high bank on the side towards the enemy. We thank the German plane for being the cause of this sudden attention from German artillery.

Corporal Jimmy Bryden, one of the coolest men I've ever met, discovers thirty or forty Germans hiding down in a dugout, and promptly brings them up. Immediately all the troops make a wild dash for the souvenirs, tearing off buttons, badges, and belts to the resultant discomfiture of Fritz. Love letters from sweethearts or cherished photographs are pulled from the pockets amid the appeal of Heine. He doesn't mind handing us his field glasses, his revolver, his belt, buttons, and so on, but he doesn't like to hand out his love letters. Can you blame him? Jimmy Bryden obtains so many revolvers that he gives me one. It is a large one with a detachable wooden butt—a Luger which can be fastened so as to convert the revolver into a rifle. The whole affair is so heavy that we just can't lug it around, and we sell it to a military police chap behind the line later on for thirty francs. He got a bargain.

We employ our morning eating bully beef and digging into the side of the bank next to the elevator. I remember during the morning I thought to myself, 'I wonder if I'll still be alive when noon comes.' And when noon came, I said, 'My word, I'm still alive. What's the matter? What are you worried about?' I fear the results if a shell should land right in the road, so I desire a little funkhole as a source of comfort.

About ten thirty in the morning, Bunny Burgess (I don't know why he was called Bunny) who was a runner carrying messages from the front to the rear and back again, came hurrying up to reach our road. Just as he got on the brim of the sunken road, he was flattened with a whizzbang. A German whizzbang shell bursts right beside him and sends him flat. He waves his hat to show that he's still alive, and we carry him a little bit down the road. We look him over carefully and we can't find any serious wound in his neck or his body or his legs, just a little piece of shrapnel. Several small pieces of shell hit him but apparently no vital spot. At any rate, we bandage him up and tell him he's lucky. We take four German prisoners, and we assign them the job of carrying him out. Rather reluctnatly they start off, because the shelling is still going on, and the shells don't know the difference between Germans and Canadians! We hear that Bunny Burgess gets back to the rear alright, but that he died of some wound in hospital.

We have very few casualties in that sunken road. But out in front, the Fourth Infantry Battalion—they were called the 'Mad Fourth'—they weren't satisfied with reaching the sunken road; they wanted to reach the enemy trenches. They were pinned right down in the flat field for the whole day, and they simply couldn't move forward or come back. When nightfall came, those that could came back, but they lost heavily.

Now, we were actually in what's called a salient, in a very exposed position. Because of the enemy resistance, the troops on the right and on the left weren't able to come up equal to us. In the afternoon I saw what I thought was a very foolish thing, it's something I've never forgotten. The Eleventh Phoenix Division tried to bring the line forward on our left, in order to relieve us. And I watched these English soldiers coming along in little groups of four or five across a level field, in broad daylight in the late afternoon, just in order to straighten up the line—see, we were being fired at from three directions—and they never made it. Under heavy shellfire and machine gun fire you'd see them drop to the ground, and finally there was no movement.

So the reason I know that that was a failure was because that night, under cover of darkness, we were told to make a strategic withdrawal back several hundred yards, which we did. Now histories will tell you that was one of the costliest battles of the last hundred days. If we had had a tank or two, things would have gone better. The purpose of this act was to keep the enemy on the run, but he just decided that he'd put up a little resistance, and he did.

Harold Wheeler

Born in England in 1883, he came to Canada in the 1890s and worked as a junior inspector for the Imperial Bank of Canada before his enlistment. He was taken prisoner in the second battle of Ypres.

On one occasion the men were ordered to dismiss. The Germans called it 'Dismiss Victory.' So they dismissed. But one English sergeant-major was very indifferent to the German command. He turned round very slowly to go back into the barracks. He was a big man, and the German private was very wild, very mad about it. The private drawed his bayonet and slapped him on his back, with the flat of his bayonet. And the German said to me, 'What are you going to do about it?' What on earth could I do about it? But then he hit me with his bayonet, so I wrote a letter in English to the commandant of the camp. I said it was a *dastardly* and *cowardly* thing that this German private did to a British noncommissioned officer, to hit him with the flat of his bayonet on the back of his head. I demanded that this man be punished.

There was a Belgian in the camp who could speak German and he translated it into good German. I wrote the letter to the commandant of the camp, telling him that it was a violation of the Geneva Convention. I didn't know what the heck the Geneva Convention was, but I guess it was something which would reward these people their dues. And I presented it to the commandant of the camp, and he was *mad*. He was *furious*. And he gave that man three days in prison. So the men were satisfied. The Germans had great respect for the Geneva Convention.

Michael Sheehan

It was the United States that really turned the tide. The Americans used to say, '*We* won the war,' and in a way they were right. They're the same way as if there are two fighters in the ring. They fight away there for perhaps ten rounds and then one of them leaves. He says, 'Oh, I have to go and get a drink.' So he puts another man in, a fresh man, against the fella that's already tired, that's out on his feet, and this new man knocks the other fella out. Well, he won the battle. You understand me? That's what the United States did. We couldn't have done without them. They were a tremendous force, absolutely irresistible. They had money and men—everything. They were a tremendous nation. But to hear them say they won the war just made us see red—that's ridiculous—because we fought over there without them. In fact, it was the submarining of the Lusitania that brought them into the war.

Patrick Malone

We had an awful time in England with them Yankees, you know. They are no good. They'd have never went into the war if the Lusitania hadn't been sank. Now when they went over to England in 1917, the war was just about over. And there was a joke that went around, like this: One of the fellows went into a hotel to have a glass of beer. He said to the waitress, he says, 'This beer is stale.' She says, 'No wonder! It's been waiting over here for you for three years.' *(laughs)*

Robert Swan

After a certain length of time we became fatalists, because there wasn't any rhyme or reason. You could ask why a man, So-and-So, was killed, and why you weren't killed, or why this was done, or why that was done. There wasn't any answer to it—*never*! Couldn't find an answer. So you just had to accept it and roll with the punches and say, 'Well, I'm here today and I'll make the best of it and get as much out of it as I can, and keep out of trouble.' But if you stopped to try and reason it out and make any sense out of it, it was just impossible. We'd no explanation for many of the things that happened.

There was another factor which I think had a bearing on the whole situation. Here you had a very large number of young men at the very height of their physical condition and under rigid training. So they were honed down and tuned down, as fit as they ever would be, and with all the natural instincts of a young man. Yet we were facing the fact that, 'Well, we're here today, but we might be gone tomorrow. So if we're going to have any life at all, we'll take it when we can get it.' And if they were inclined in that way, and there were very large numbers what were, without any doubt, they went to the women. I think that they had much more reason, there was much more excuse for them doing it than there is in the modern attitude toward sex as it is today. These boys just didn't know whether they were going to have any of that, or whether they weren't, or how long they were going to have it. And being, as I say, in the prime of physical condition, with all the human natural urges that result, you can't blame them if they took what they could get while the going was good. I don't say that every man did that, because there were many, many who didn't. But it was a very general experience, particularly after a long trip in the trenches or something like that. I expressed it in two pieces of verse that I wrote about this thing here.

If you think it crude to be rough and rude,
This tale is not for you.
There's nothing nice about rats and mice
From any point of view.

Yes, the rats do roam and make their home
In the fields where the dead men lie.
Yes, the lice do bite all day and night
And never quit till you die.

Here the human moles from their stinking holes
Crawl up through the muck and slime
To hide all day, then work all night
Till there is no sense to time.

The great shells roar through the leaden skies
As their targets crouch in the drains,
Then burst with a roar and the shrapnel flies,
And it rains and rains and rains.

On a dirty night when your nerves draw tight
And you rouse to the gas alarms,
In a dank shell hole you'd sell your soul
For a night in a woman's arms.

When the grey green mass of chlorine gas
Drifts down from the eastern sky,
You choke and spit till your lungs are split
And you hear your best friends die.

In the stinking stench of a rotten trench
Mid the swarms of filthy flies,
Some men got caught so their bodies rot,
And the maggots eat their eyes.

Here tattered bums from city slums
With pampered sons of the rich,
All lie with God on that sodden sod,
And you can't tell which is which.

In that sea of mud you can feel your blood
Go cold as you shake with fright,
And among the dead you raise your head
To stand to your post to fight.

So a few survive and are still alive
When at last relief breaks through,
And the press reports all quiet,
As they bury the lads they knew.

Theirs was the fate from German hate,
Its greed and mistaken pride.
In far-off days, a soldier prays,
'Forget not why they died.'

Trench Fever

Discussions in the trenches often coupled pleasant wenches
With attempts to learn the language of the land.
Life could be very merry with a sleeping dictionary
To pass the time and get to understand.

They could talk among their pals of dodging loving gals
Who had gently tried to trap them into marriage.
They were good at fast romance, but shuddered at the chance
Of being nailed to push a baby carriage.

To improve the army diet, they would snatch a hen and fry it
With potatoes which they also got for free.
There was bully beef and cheese which could be flogged with ease
For more tasteful liquid products than their tea.

When they tangled with a limey, he was quick to holler 'Blimey!'
As they bashed his blinkin' head against a wall.
Why would any bloomin' gent foster further discontent
By more gentle ways to quell a free-for-all?

When a message from on high urged them forth to do or die,
There was little they could do except to cuss,
And among themselves to wonder how to dodge this latest blunder,
While the senders held a five-mile start on us.

For the language of the forces never came from college courses,
Nor resulted from intensive foreign studies.
It was fractured, it was bent, it was borrowed, it was lent,
But they never brought themselves to swallow butties.

In times of sudden stress, it was anybody's guess
How the wicked always managed to survive,
While their more deserving brothers, along with all the others,
Scratched and scrambled just to stay alive.

When fighting chores were done, they manufactured fun,
Avoiding ways to harm their precious skin.
Without damage to the nation they would take a short vacation,
And risk a call to answer for their sins.

So before you turn aside, remember this with pride:
In the game of war they played the hands they drew.
You will never understand how they loved their native land,
But they proved it as they lived and died for you.

You know, the first baths we had, they didn't have any special bathing facilities, nor did they have any new replacement underwear or anything. But they had built these shacks out of any old boards they could get. There were cracks through the boards, and you could feel the wind coming through like nobody's business. You went into a dressing room section, and they had nails in the wall, big spikes, and you took off your stuff and hung it up on that. And then you went to a hole in the wall, and you threw in your underwear and your socks, and went into the bath house. The bath house had tubs made out of beer barrels cut in two—they were good and big, you see. There were ten tubs in this one that I'm thinking of. You worked in gangs of twenty men, two men to a tub. You were given a piece of yellow soap, like laundry soap, and you got two buckets of cold water and one bucket of hot water. The hot water was heated on an old boiler that they had out in the yard, which they fired with anything that would burn. The bath attendants filled the tubs, and the two men stood in a tub, washed each other with the soap, and sloshed themselves off. You were given three minutes, and then you had to get out. Then you went to another door where you got a towel to dry yourself. You went up to another wicket and you got a suit of underwear and a pair of socks. It was the old army game of one man, one shirt, and you never knew when you got them what size they were. You might be six feet tall and get a suit of underwear for a midget, and some other guy would get one where they had to roll the sleeves right up to his elbows. There was a lot of horse-trading in the dressing room, trying to get something that would halfway fit you. And this was all reconditioned underwear that somebody else had had, but it had been disinfected and smelled of creosote. But at least it was clean!

That's the kind of bath you got once in a dog's age when you came out. Otherwise, if the weather was halfway decent, and if you were out in the camp somewhere, all around that place there, there were shell holes that had been filled full of water. By that time, the mud would have settled, and the water would be clean—it would be rainwater. If you could get some sort of biscuit tin or something to scoop it out without disturbing the mud, you could get yourself enough fresh water to strip off and wash yourself right out there in the open. At least you could get some kind of relief in that way. But if it was raining cats and dogs, which it did most of the time, that wasn't pleasant or possible. But you took any kind of means you could to keep yourself clean.

Later on of course, they built real bath houses with shower heads in the roof, and then you'd go there. Then they got new clothing. The army began to bring in clothing frequently, so that when you turned in this dirty, filthy underwear that you were wearing, you never got that back at all. I don't know what they did with it.

The early days there, for the first winter, oh boy, I want to tell you, primitive living alright. They were packed into a lot of dugouts, six or seven or eight men all pushed in together as tight as they could go, and wet right straight through. We never took off our shoes or our clothes, we just slept in them. But we'd take any sandbags that were halfway dry and pull them over our feet and tie them one on top of the other, four or five on each leg. Your body heat and that of the other men would more or less heat the place, provided it wasn't too drafty. And in the morning when you woke up, why the outside sandbag would be soaking wet, and as you peeled them off, by the time you got the last one off, your legs were dry. But they were all puckered—parboiled, you know—and when you went out and you hit the cold air, and put your feet into some cold water—boy, it was just like getting an electric shock. When it hit you, you'd feel it right clean to the back of your neck, until you got yourself adjusted again. When you were in the mud, at least it was soft, it wasn't so bad. Of course, your feet were soaking wet the whole time. But when you had to walk or march along some of those Belgian roads that were cobblestones, your feet were so soft and tender that it was just pure punishment every step you took. Once you got out to your camp and got a chance to dry out and get cleaned up, and at least had a dry shelter for a day or two, you could get more or less comfortable. But then, as soon as you left there and started back up into the forward area again, you went plunk right head first into the rain and the muck again. That was worse than the fighting. Of course, a lot of the time there wasn't any fighting. The Germans couldn't move any more than we could.

Ben Wagner

The drinking was perhaps a sore point in the early days with the Canadian army. The army camps in Canada, in the days of our wonderful militia, had always been dry. I don't know why, but they had. But they went to England, and on Salisbury Plain, they found that all these little villages had pubs. And although there was no place they could drink in the camp, they went to these villages. And they got obnoxious, they got too much to drink, you see. The usual city bloke from down around Jarvis Street got too much to drink and became obnoxious. So the army commander, who was an Englishman, opened what they called 'wet' canteens. Now they could only get beer, they couldn't get hard liquor. But the wet canteens served two purposes. They kept a man at home where he could more or less be kept under cover (I've seen a man lugged off to the clink lots of times on a fella's shoulders) it kept them from annoying the English people who were very friendly to us Canadians. And ten percent went to a fund that was used to buy things for the soldiers. So although there was an outcry from the WCTU (Women's Christian Temperance Union) across Canada about this whole thing of the wet canteens, it was a very good thing.

In the camps we had what we called the 'wet' canteen and the 'dry' canteen. In the dry canteen you got 'coffee'—quotation marks around the coffee —biscuits and things which you had to pay for. Very rarely did you get anything free. Now *that* was one of our bitter points. At the YMCA you got nothing free; at the Salvation Army, if you didn't have the money for the coffee, you got the coffee just the same. Its coffee was a little bit worse than the YMCA's, but not too much, because the English don't know how to make coffee anyway.

As for the diseases, there was regular inspection that kept them under control. It wasn't like in civilian life where a boy might become almost rotted with VD without ever going to a doctor. There you had regular inspection. Whenever you went sick, it was on your daily orders: 'So-and-so: diphtheria, So-and-So: VD.' It was always public. I might say that perhaps 5% of the battalion had had VD. But they were immediately put in hospital and under treatment, so that there wasn't the bad effects of it. It was checked.

Eric Rosen

Every unit had its padré. The RCs, of course, would always have an RC padré and their church service on a Sunday—that would be all it would amount to—and the same with the denominational churches. Mostly the padrés were Anglican, as far as I know. Unfortunately, in our unit we didn't have a very good padré because he too used to drink, and that was a very poor example to us. I had gone to the Baptist Church, and we were under pretty evangelical preaching, but when we got over there, there seemed to be just the formal Sunday morning church parade which you had to go to.

Myself, I always had a hatred of anyone who would ridicule the Bible. One of my best friends (I don't know why we chummed up like that) was bad like that, to my mind. One night we were all in bed on the floor, and he was opposite me, and he said something about Bible-thumpers, so I heaved my boot at him.

Another thing that used to annoy me: we had one man in particular, who was a very boisterous fellow. I seen him stand outside and shake his fist to the heavens when it was raining and say—he used to refer to God as 'Huey'—'Send it down, Huey!' and it used to make me cringe. He'd get out there and shake his fist. He was one of our runners and one night, he and another runner were out. We were in a rough spot, and they were being shelled. When they came in, the chap that was with him says, 'Boy, he didn't shake his fist tonight, he got down on his knees and prayed. We were really in a spot,' he said, 'He didn't shake his fist.' That shows you what it'll do to some people.

I often used to talk to my brothers about it. I can't understand myself. It used to annoy me no end, but I dodged church parade or anything if I could, and I wasn't any better than a lot of the fellas. But that used to really get me when anybody said anything like that.

Another thing: prostitution was very, very easy, particularly in France. When we were out on leave, it was on every hand. It was nothing to walk down the streets of a town, and the little boys would be out there touting for their sisters. Little boys would take men to where there sisters were. Possibly as young fellas we didn't have too strong views on those things, even though we were instructed from the time we entered the army very, very strongly against this sort of thing—not so much from the angle of the moral aspect of it, as the danger of infection. Some of the lectures they gave us—I can see them now- —were terrible, awful! We'd come away from them, and they would be saying they'd never look at a girl again, but that lasted for about five minutes. It was unfortunate that there was so many that did become infected. In France it was easy. It was licensed, I guess, so it was easy. And of course, in England, where we go on leave, there was always somebody, particularly if you went into the pubs. Myself, I found it rather difficult, because everything of that sort of thing was hush-hush in our family life. I'll say this: there were some—men who were old enough to be our fathers—who led us younger guys into things that they had no business doing. To me, as a father now, I see how wrong it was.

Robert Swan

His 'Love Poem.'

Dear Maizy,

If I last another week, my leave comes up, and I will be on my way to London to see you again. If you enjoy the birds, the bees, and the flowers, take a good look at them before I get there. After that, you will not see anything but the ceiling for the next six days. Hold everything and hope for the best.

XXXX Arthur

Mrs Jane Walters

Patients had a habit of falling in love with you. They were so glad to get back home and have young girls around who weren't too hard to look at and who were kind, who helped them. I remember there was one Roumanian soldier, and he thought he was in love with me. I kinda thought I was in love with him too. He was very attractive. You know, a girl who has ideals—and we had ideals in those days, I hope you have now—to be thrown in with men like that, all kinds from all over the world, it took some doing to keep level, not have your head turned. But you had your heart hurt very often.

Mrs Anita Phillips

She nursed in hospitals in England and France.

We had a doctor on our ward, Dr Robertson, I think it was. He'd been there for quite a long time, and I had been there for a long time too. And he came in one morning, and he said, 'Have we got Nursing Sister White here?' White was my name. We all looked so amazed at him. I said, 'Why, of course. What's the matter?' He says 'Well, you tell your boyfriends that are flying over this place to stop dropping bombs on my head.' *(laughs)* They had little things that they put weights on, and they put a note inside it, and they dropped them. He happened to be passing, and it dropped right on his head. *(laughs)* The notes told me where they had been, and when they'd be back, and hope you'd be at a little dance, or something like that. Just nice notes.

Did that happen often?

Quite often, yes. Not the dropping of the bombs! But friends coming to the hospital, you know.

Larry Nelson

I joined the Nineteenth Battalion. I'll never forget this: a chap one night was rather inebriated, and he was the life of the party. Someone asked him where he got the money for his celebration. He happened to be a batman, and his officer had given him clothing to be washed, and he gave him five francs to pick it up. On the way to get the laundry, he happened to see a sign: Champagne, five francs. He thought the five francs would do him more good than the laundry for his officer, so he bought the bottle.

During the course of that evening, one of the chaps in the Nineteenth was reading a *Jack Canuck*, and it just happened to be that there was a lonely soldier's letter in *Jack Canuck*. This chap stumped this fellow (who happened to turn out to be a very, very good friend of mine) to write a lonely soldier's letter. This he did, and this was around about the end of June. His letter went something like this: 'I am a lonely soldier. I've been in France for umpteen months. I have never received a letter, a newspaper, or even a box. Would some kind soul please remedy this situation for me?' This letter appeared in the *Jack Canuck* around about the middle of September, just when the people of Canada were thinking about boxes for the soldiers in France. You have no idea the amount of mail this chap received, it was just fantastic!

Was that a common practice to write lonely letters?

No, it wasn't at the time. I think it was just one of those incidents. People would hardly believe what this chap received, and I saw with my own eyes. He had parcels from India, parcels from Australia, he had them from every nook and corner. The strange thing—he had so many letters that he couldn't attempt to open and read them all. But a real coincidence was: one day he put his hand in the bag, and he pulled out a letter. He opened it up, and it was supposed to have been from a fourteen-year old boy in Barrie, Ontario. My friend says, 'Boy, any kid fourteen years that would write a soldier in France certainly deserves a reply!' The correspondence kept on all during the battles of the war, and when it was all over, he finally got a letter and a picture. It turned out she was a young lady twenty years of age, and it was quite a thrill.

CHAPTER EIGHT

AT WORK

The demand of a war economy for large numbers of articles produced in a uniform pattern accelerated the rationalization and streamlining of work methods. The power of craft knowledge, which had played such a prominent role in the primacy of the skilled worker in the workplace, gave way to processes where production was strictly controlled by foremen and managers. The influx of large numbers of new workers, who lacked the broader cultural patterns of working class solidarity, further eroded the control workers had traditionally exerted over the shop floor. These developments contributed to the evolution of new patterns of relationship between employer and employee. The new struggles that emerged as a result were based on broader sensibilities than paternalistic control and craft pride.

I.   MUNITIONS

Mrs Elaine Nelson

Until the middle of the war, 'no one worked in factories.' The women were all involved in 'pretty work,' such as knitting for the Red Cross. Then 'all of a sudden,' masses of women entered the munitions industry.

Someone asked me one time—it was either the YMCA or YWCA— if I would join a team that was going to serve in the canteen in the big munitions factory, which was the Fairbanks-Morse, which was on the corner of King and Lansdowne. Well, it was about two hours' journey for me by streetcar, and we were on an all-night shift, but I went, and found it very, very difficult to stay awake. There were certain hours of the night that were very, very hard to stay awake.

The people would come in perhaps off and on all week. There was always a rush before and after the time when they were going to work. For instance, in our case, we were working the night shift from eleven to seven. If they came in at eleven, they were cold, they'd been on the streetcar, they wanted a bowl of soup. Then when the machine broke down, they'd come in again, and then when they were through, before they'd go home, they'd want to have a bowl of soup because it was still slightly dark and miserable, and they could have that and go home and go right to sleep and have a bit of rest, before they woke up for something to eat.

Was it common for that service to be offered in munitions?

No, I don't think so. I think probably Fairbanks-Morse decided they were going to have as many conveniences for their workers as possible, and probably offered it to the 'Y' and said, 'We'll give you this room and equip it for you.' It was just a huge, long factory room. It could have been forty feet long. There were tables and chairs and the big counter and coffee urn and that kind of thing, and ways of heating the soup up. It was all Campbell's soup—can't *bear* the smell of it to this day. (I wasn't used to canned soup at any time anyway. Ugh! Terrible stuff.)

We were all very annoyed because the supervisor—I imagine she was the only paid person—was determined that we were going to give very skimpy ladles of soup to the workers who came in. We felt it was *not* fair. They had to go from their factory building across a long area in the cold or the heat or the rain or storm to get to the building where this canteen was. And they were cold, and they were tired, or they were hot and tired and hungry. And I felt that they needed that good generous bowl of soup, and I ladled it out regardless, until finally we really came to a thorough understanding. I told her that I thought that they were getting that soup either for nothing—it was canned soup—or at cost certainly; that the factory supplied the great big room completely equipped for them to work; that all their workers were volunteers, and that it behooved them to be very generous to these people who were making the shells with which we were going to help win the war. And I resigned promptly.

What was your reaction to seeing big industry for the first time?

I didn't see it until I started to work. I just arrived at the canteen and never got anywhere else. Then, when I asked if I could get a job there, then my first experience was when they said, 'We'll allot you the first set of the howitzer shells.' The foreman met me at the door, and he just beckoned to me. The reason why he couldn't say anything was because you couldn't have heard him! And I just had to follow him. I went through all these avenues and avenues of clanking, grinding, crashing machines. Some of them were so close together that in order to get to their machines they'd built a kind of a stile—several steps up, and then you walked across, and then you went down again. On the line that I was on, some of the people had to get to their work that way.

Well, the foreman just led me in behind this machine, and I stood by the wall and watched. He demonstrated how to do *one* shell, and then he stood aside and pointed to me. And so I very gingerly walked up to the machine and did what he had done. Then he stood there and said, 'Again!' and I did another one. Then he just waved me goodbye and off he went. I was *panic-stricken*. But I got used to it, so used to it that pretty soon I was looking around me seeing what my fellow workers were like.

You couldn't talk to anybody—that was another thing! When you got up to the rest rooms and the cafeteria it was bedlam there, because no one had been able to talk all day or for the eight hours. So you were just jabbering for all you were worth, *(laughs)* jabbering and eating because you were hungry, you were cold, or you were hot, one or the other. The canteen was a godsend for those people , that and that restroom. We had to punch a clock when we went in, in the morning. The offices and that, and the little cupboards that we kept our clothes in—I always forget their name—but those were all in the one building. Then when we got dressed, we had to go across this big yard to the other—oh, it was literally a *hell-hole*! It was terrible.

What was the process like?

I imagine the shells came out of the blasting furnaces first, and then they would have to be put out into the yards to cool. And then gradually they were brought in and they were put on this conveyor belt. I was near the end with my back to the wall. Those things came along there, and there was a woman in front of me and on the side opposite to me, she did the first cut and I did the first cut. We pushed a

'You had to quickly knock off these jagged long pieces before they got as far as your face....'

lever and that lifted the shells up onto this conveyor belt and then a man—I don't know how he got there, I don't know what he did—but I just remember that he did something that lowered it into our machines. When the shell came, I pushed this lever and the belt caused a knife to go just against the shell, and then it would start to peel. The shell was turning all the time. I pushed that lever against it. It would turn, and you had to *quickly* knock off these jagged long pieces before they got as far as your face, because they would just swing around, back and forth. You just knocked them off, and they fell behind the machinery. I imagine that every once in awhile they had to go and clear all the jagged stuff out. Then the next machine to me did the next cut and so on until it got to the end of the row. Then it was just like a beautiful piece of polished steel. Then it had to go some other place for other things. Oh yes, and right over there where this thing was—it looked like a great big chisel—was this little tap. Just before you put your machine on, you turned that little tap so it was pouring chemicals over that thing. And then you started. It poured all the time, and as these jagged pieces came out, it splashed this stuff. And that's what got all over us. It was really a miserable thing. There was a duckboard around our feet. It was right across this pan. I guess they were made of iron or something, because they would be about, oh, five, six inches deep, and it was full of that stuff. Now there must have been something that caused the suction for that to come up through the little tap when we turned it on. But we were standing over this wet, and our feet were wet, and the duckboards were slimy. There were little spaces in between so that all this stuff could go back in there. It was quite an endurance test, let me tell you.

I worked there almost a year and then I worked three months, perhaps four months, as a government inspector of these caps for the shrapnel shells. It was still a long journey for me and it was worrying me too much. I just had nightmares that I passed a shell or somebody else with me had passed a shell that had been imperfect and might kill our own boys. There were terrible accidents from the American shells in the First World War and in the Second too. But that was just a game. People were kibitzing, talking and laughing. That's why I couldn't stand that inspector's job. I couldn't stand it because some of the girls in that group —and some were my friends—were laughing and talking too much and not watching exactly what they were doing, and that worried me. I wanted to get out of it.

Were there many injuries?

The machinery was all open. The one thing they were terrified of was the belts and our hair, so we had to cover our hair. I used to wear a red bandana because the caps that they had—yellow caps with a frill on them—were ghastly things. We used to call them 'mop caps,' and they were made out of the same thing as our uniform. You looked so terrible. I wore a bandana, and I was called 'Gypsy.' *(laughs)*

I don't remember any great tragedy but there could have been, your clothes getting caught or something getting caught. Certainly these jagged little things—I used to get a little panicky sometimes if I didn't break it. After it got a certain length it could just slash you. If it wouldn't break off you were literally

'You looked so terrible.'

fighting for your life almost. But gradually you became expert at doing that. Also you learned right from the very beginning that there was no fooling, there weren't any second chances with machinery like that. Oh, and on the other side of the wall where my back was, there were great big blasting furnaces that these shells came out of, so if ever there'd been a fire, there was absolutely *nothing* would have saved us. *Nothing* could have saved us.

This business of being well: if I hadn't been as healthy as I was, I'm sure I would have had pneumonia for sure. Because you had to go wringing wet like that across this long courtyard before you got to the place where you could change all your clothes. It was bitterly cold. Your feet were frozen and the rest of you was just roasting because all the machinery was hot. You could smell this heat coming from behind you but you couldn't feel it. You could smell the hot molten metal and when we were on the way out there was one great big doorway where you could look and see. They'd open the furnace and it would just look like hell. *(laughs)*

Why did you decide to go into munitions instead of working with the Red Cross?

Because anybody can do those other things—the older people could do that. It took young vigorous people of a good will to do that kind of work, you know. Things were bad for the war, for us, and we just felt we had to get our shoulder to the wheel and get down to business. When you're young, you do what everybody's doing. As soon as a few girls go in, then they all want to go in. It was the thing to do. But then when you got in you were interested, just as I happened to be. There was a kind of *esprit de corps*. Everybody wanted to be there; you were in the swim of things; everything was war, war, war. I think a lot of the girls—there's always some that are miserable and stupid and badly behaved —but on the whole they were a wonderful bunch, and I see so many of them to this day. It enriched my life really.

There was everybody, every single class, from the squire's lady to Judy O'Grady and some a few shades lower than Judy. I thought it was fascinating. You get in the canteen or up in that big restroom there and hear them talking. It was very, very interesting. And there's every kind: wonderful, brave women who were saving every nickel they could so they'd have enough money to buy a home when their husband came back; and some flighty, silly little fools that were running around with other men. You'd just see every kind.

I used to get a little cynical because I used to kind of feel that some of the good men had rotten wives and vice versa. I can just think of some of the experiences. One girl, pretty, little empty-headed thing, ran around with some fellow. I couldn't see any reason at all why he wasn't in the war. She apparently had a very devoted husband, and he eventually was killed. She put on the fanciest widow weeds you could imagine and continued to go around with this fellow, but he didn't marry her. And I just thought it served the darn girl right. He just thought, 'Well, if you can try that on your husband you can just try that on me too, girlie.' I was very glad.

In meeting these people that we had never had any opportunity to meet before, and finding they were just the same as we were, but they just hadn't had the chances that we'd had for education and that kind of thing, we began to realize that we were all sisters under the skins. Wars do bring every class together and I think we need to do a little bit more of that without war if we can.

Another thing too: there's nothing that draws people together more than mutual trouble. When you read the newspapers and you see columns of deaths, of boys being killed, you read those names and you say, 'Oh, So-and-So's gone,' and then somebody's husband's gone, and somebody's fiancé's gone. And things went so much against us so often, so long that we just felt we *had* to. The boys are doing that for us, what are we doing for them? You just rolled up your sleeves and you didn't care how tired you were or anything else. It's a terrible thing that it takes a war and a national tragedy to pull things together.

When I first started I just wore the underclothes that I would wear ordinarily. In those days girls who had money wore what you call *crepe de Chine*. They were real silk underwear. Of course they just rotted in a week. When they got wet with the chemicals they just rotted. Of course they were stained hopelessly, so I smartened up pretty quickly about that. And incidentally anyway, they weren't warm enough. So I had my brother's longjohns—he was six feet tall —and I had to roll them up to here and turn them back on the sleeves, and I was darn glad to have all that extra warmth.

I was amazed because the people who had never had anything much were the ones who were most careless with their clothes. I was simply astounded to see this one woman who had been our cleaning woman. Every week she would come and she'd perhaps pay $25.00 for a blouse. Well, that was an outrageous price to pay in those days. And she'd put that on, a beautiful blouse all beaded and everything. And the style was pearl grey or beige or white kid boots, and she would buy those and she'd wear them right into the machinery because she wanted everybody to see them. She'd leave the smock open a little bit so you could see this beautiful blouse. Of course the shoes were ruined the first day she was there and so was the blouse. But then the people who were used to good clothes looked after them, and the ones who weren't used to it just spent money like water.

They'd never had much money before and they would probably have had to pay a neighbour or someone to look after their children. But they wanted to get this extra money so they'd have a lot when their husband came back. And then, incidentally, they had never had much so they did treat themselves to some things, and they deserved it—but not the extravagances. The cleaning woman wanted to wear the kind of clothes that I would have worn. You could hardly blame her, she had never had them in her life. But she didn't have sense enough to look after them. Well, I would have been tickled to death if she had had all those things—she deserved them because she was a hard-working woman. But she thought that if you were rich, you waste, and rich people don't waste. The reason they're rich is because they have never wasted.

Mrs Miriam McLeish

She grew up in Beaverton, Ontario. Her mother died when she was thirteen, and she became responsible for her six brothers and sisters. Her father was a foreman on the CNR. During the war she worked at the arsenal in Lindsay, weighting shells.

I had a very hard job. It had to be that you run a machine of weights into the shell, and the weight had to be just exact. Quite a few of them didn't have the patience. Well, my father brought us up that when we went on a job, we did it and did it the best we could. So the foreman was very glad. He came about four or five times a day to make sure that the weights in the shells were right. It was interesting work but very hard on your nerves.

Were you afraid it was going to blow up?

Well, it did blow up. There was a machine went on fire. This friend from Beaverton was on the machine that blew up, and I run to her and we had to go down on our hands and knees and crawl out of the place. So we had a little experience of what it was to be right in a war shooting up.

II. HARVEST

Mrs Anna Smokorowsky

Do you remember if farmers in Gilbert Plains (Manitoba) were very much affected by losing their sons to the war?

Yes, the older people noticed it much. Those that had a few acres wouldn't notice it, but those that had more land did. They had machinery like a binder, they had the most modern way of working the land. Anything went wrong with the binder, he was stuck. He was handicapped with that. He'd have to quit and go into the village and pick up somebody to come and fix his binder. But when the sons were there, they understood the binder. I guess when they buy a binder, the fella that sells it to them puts it together in their presence, where they know these different parts and whatever goes wrong with it. So they did notice the difference.

But then during the war too, they were encouraged to grow more grain, to raise more hogs, to raise cattle for meat. The government encouraged them and called on them to support them by growing these things. I remember that there was an upsurge of wheat and everything to support the war.

Scott Brooks

His father was an editor in a publishing company in Toronto, and his mother was one of the first women to graduate from the University of Toronto. His sister was a VAD.

They had what they called 'Soldiers of the Soil.' So in 1917 and 1918 I went farming. And we were given medals for being 'Soldiers of the Soil.' I was very fortunate. Some of the fellas had awful experiences, but I got a wonderful man somehow, and I was just one of the family. Mind you, you worked, but I really enjoyed the whole thing, and I still, every once in awhile, think back to those two years I spent from about May till September. I enjoyed them, and I think it gave you a different slant on things to see these people. You know, city people don't know anything about people living on a farm. They knew about a bunch of fields up there that had some crops in them, but that was about all they knew. We did a big milk business. We had a lot of milk cows, and one of my jobs was driving the milk out, about six o'clock in the morning, to the Metropolitan Railway and putting them on the stand there. Then the car came down and picked them all up. So that was one of my important jobs, to get the milk out in time. It was awful early.

A tremendous number of boys went. We got leave of absence from the school. I think we got out three weeks earlier or something like that. You see, there used to be a lot of transient labour. Well, the transient labour kind of disappeared. So they went to the schools, and lads who were in fourth and fifth form—some were in the third if they were big enough—went farming. You were told where to go, more or less. But some of the farmers were good people and good men and thoughtful men, and others didn't care where you slept or if they worked your heart out. I was one of the fortunate ones—there were a lot of fortunate ones—but a lot of them were treated very miserably. I mean, stuck in a little room up in an attic with an old fallen-down bed or something. Some of them, you know, they were just skivvies, they were just slaves to them. This fellow would drive me himself out to Yonge Street so I could come home for Sunday, and then I'd say I'd meet the such-and-such train, and he'd be out to get me with the team, with the horses. So he was terrific, and I think I paid him for it.

I was paid about three bucks a week or something like that. *(laughs)* I wouldn't like to say exactly, but I know it was just a pittance. But he was really very, very good to me. I didn't want for anything. As I say, my experiences were terrific, others had ones that were awful.

What did you do?

I farmed. We got up in the morning at dawn and milked the cows, and then we got a bit of breakfast. And then at about seven o'clock I'd start to drive the milk out while he was doing some work around the farm. Then, when we'd come back, we'd have our real breakfast. Then we'd go out, and there was hay to cut and ploughing, and of course milking about fourteen cows twice a day was a lot of work. We had a spring there and we put the milk cans in it to keep it cold. How sanitary it was I don't know! But now all the milk is just dumped into one of these great big vats, and a truck comes along and just pumps the vat dry, sterilizes and cleans it out, and he drives on to the next farm. He only goes about twice a week, but it's kept in perfect condition. But all the farmers just took the cans out and dumped them on a wooden platform and left. Left them right out in the sun and everything else. And then the railroad came down and got them. The Metropolitan it was called then, but it doesn't run now. They came down and picked up the cans and took them into the city. Then when you took yours out, there were empties left for you.

Do you remember any of the problems farmers faced then?

I don't know whether they were faced with any. What I mean by that is that things were good. I mean, no matter what they grew or what they did, they could get rid of it at, not prices of today, but at prices which they thought were good, and in those days they were. I mean it's like any other business. Maybe 60% of them do pretty well at it and the other 40% couldn't make a go of it even if they tried! This is my war medal. *(He brings out his medal. It has a beaver on the top and grain in the centre.)* I found this the other night. 'Soldiers of the Soil, Canada Food Boy.' All the people who worked on the farms got those. I keep it in my treasures. The only medal I got from the war. As I say, too young for the first, too old for the second.

Mrs Brenda Parsons

Born in 1885, she grew up in Newfoundland, at that time a British colony. Her father was a lawyer, and like many girls of her class, she finished her education in England, and 'came out' when she returned. She married in 1909 and came to Toronto with her husband, a bank employee. Shortly afterward, he took up farming.

We had the Indians for the picking of the fruit in the summer. We had a small house down in the valley which we called the 'Indian House,' because the Indians lived there, and they did the picking. There'd be about twenty, I suppose. They came from an Indian Reserve down near Peterborough; I forget the name of the reserve. They were very good pickers. They'd carry a wooden thing over their arm, a box-thing that had nine boxes for berries. And they'd fill those, and then they'd bring them into whoever was packing them. I think they used to get, at one time, a cent a box for the strawberries. *(laughs)* We had what we called packing houses. We had two or three on different parts of the farm, nearest wherever the berries were.

Then during the First World War we couldn't get the Indians to pick, the men had gone to war. We had the National Service Girls come out. We had our little house cleaned and everything, and they lived in the little house. And these were just girls, and they came out every summer. We had to have them after that until the war was over. Some people called them farmerettes. They had quarters where we got them, where we'd have to write here in Toronto, where they were called the National Service Girls.

They were all single, and they were about sixteen and eighteen and some older. There would be about twenty. They lived in the Indian House. The 'mother,' as we used to call her, looked after them down there. I think that she used to look after their meals for them down there. She was somebody that we'd get here in Toronto who would answer an ad. My husband would go to some service that would provide somebody to come out. I had so little to do with anything like that. *(laughs)*

They worked for us perhaps a month. Our first picking of strawberries—our biggest picking of strawberries—was always the first Monday in July, because after the weekend they'd have ripened, don't you know, and we always had our biggest picking. And then, from that on until the strawberries were over, and then raspberries came in, and then the cherries and all of the different other fruits—blackberries and thimbleberries. Yes, it was quite an experience.

Did the girls get the same pay as the Indians?

Yes, then I think it went up. I think they were paid two cents a box. *(laughs)* It seems perfectly ridiculous now when you . . .*(laughs)*

We got eight cents a box, I think, seven and eight cents a box. If we got more than that we thought we'd be doing well.

The girls couldn't start to pick berries or do anything like that until the dew was off. So that it would be after nine o'clock in the morning when they'd start. And they'd go through till lunch-time. Then at twelve they'd stop. And I think they had about an hour off for lunch, and then they'd go on and pick up till four o'clock or perhaps later or whatever. It really all depended upon what had to be done. The evenings were perhaps the worst part for them because there was really nothing 'round the farms, don't you see. They could go into Port Credit or perhaps up to Oakville if they had any means of getting there, but not very often.

'...they were called the National Service Girls.'

I think they used to play cards, and I think that when they were down in their 'little house,' as we called it, they used to play games down there.

Did men friends come and visit them?

No, I don't think so. I don't remember any. If they did it was unbeknownst to us. *(laughs)*

Mrs Elaine Nelson

She came from an upper-class Toronto family. When the war broke out, she was on the verge of a singing career, but instead she poured all her energies into the war at home. She joined the Red Cross, served in a canteen in a munitions plant, worked in munitions factories, sang at hospitals and army camps, and responded to the advertisements for farmerettes.

We were farmerettes, but we didn't live in one of the camps. We went down to a farm at Niagara-on-the-Lake and picked peaches. It was a Baptist minister's farm. It was very nice, but they were funny. They were supposed to give us our food and our lodging. When we arrived, they said, 'Well, the government doesn't allow us enough for the food, and we won't be able to feed you as well as we would like.' My friend was just terrified, and she wouldn't open her mouth, and I finally said, 'Well, you know, we're going to work very hard for you, to help you. And if you think you can't feed us, it's no use staying. Now we can just sit down for a little while on the veranda while you make up your mind.' Very nice and friendly, you know, but they knew I meant it. We were the best they'd had. But we got plenty to eat, don't worry. The only trouble was that every breakfast, before we had our breakfast, he got the Bible out, and he read the Bible. Then he got down on his knees, and we all had to get down on our knees, and he prayed for half an hour for everything from the King of England to the kitchen sink. It was terrible. *(laughs)* However, in his own way, he was sincere.

We decided to become farmerettes when we read in the paper that there was a big crop and they needed people to come, and there were no men. So this friend and I said that we would go. We volunteered. Masses of young people went out and brought that all in.

They had beautiful peaches. They were very, very well packed; my friend packed them and I picked them. They had to send them to the middleman. And that middleman used to send them back a cheque, sometimes for next-to-nothing, and say that so many had gone bad, and other ones hadn't been sold, and just so many were sold. They failed that year with that great big crop. It was a terrible thing. I've damned the middleman ever since.

III. WOMEN AT WORK

Morty Stein

Born in England in 1894, he came to Canada when he was twelve. He immediately went to work as a capmaker's apprentice, and a year later he started doing piecework. He became active in his union at the age of seventeen and was chairman of the union when he was nineteen.

During the war women went into industry. Women were taking jobs that men usually did. In fact, down at CPR/CNR they had women truckers.

Did people find it hard to accept that women were working?

Well, people had two thoughts on it. Unions' thoughts were: these women are going to take our jobs. The ordinary man who had a brain to study it said, 'Well, what's the difference? They need money as well as we do.' Nobody liked women working, they were afraid for their own job. It got to the point where the minimum wage for women in those days was about eight or nine or ten dollars a week. They wouldn't hire women, they'd hire men, because they could pay them anything they wanted. If they could hire a woman for, say, $8.00, they could hire a man for $6.00.

Mrs Adrienne Stone

During the war she was a VAD with the St John's Ambulance in Toronto.

Everybody worked at two things. If you were at the university, you'd work during your holidays. And there was either the voluntary nursing service, which I went into, or farm work, or munitions, or any other thing that happened. But you were all needed. Actually, I really think that was the time when women—*all* women—began to work, because it became the accepted thing to do. (I'm not sure if I'm right historically on some of these things.)

There were all kinds of articles telling you how to behave when you went to work. One of them said that, if a child was crying on the street and your streetcar was coming, get the streetcar, because you were due on your job; another woman would comfort the baby. That's a true story! The idea was: cultivate the attitude that your job was what you're doing. I don't think it was the same after the war because everybody, by that time, was taking it for granted. The only difference, as I remember it, was that you married *or* worked. It was a choice, and a free choice, with no stigma attached either one way or the other.

You couldn't do both?

You married or worked. It wasn't a matter of 'couldn't,' you *wouldn't*! In other words, it was a job.

Mrs Roberta White

In 1909 at the age of eleven, she was taken out of school in Toronto to look after her younger brothers because her mother was ill, and she never returned. She worked in a bookbinding firm.

I was doing the paging, which was a machine for numbering cheques and that sort of thing. It was nerve-wracking, really hard. You couldn't make mistakes, you know. You had to concentrate so as not to put a wrong number or a blurred number. It was really awful. Anyway, my health gave out—my eyes, the doctor said—which I don't think was so unusual, but it was strange to me. I was very ill, nausea, and this sort of thing. Indeed, the poor lady told me afterwards she thought I was pregnant! And I was only engaged. The doctor told my mother that the nerves of the eyes affect the nerves of the stomach, and that's what my problem was. I was concentrating too hard on my job, so I had to quit. The doctor said I was to stop this work and do housework. Well, housework wasn't all that wonderful in those days, and I was quite sure I wouldn't be very wonderful at it. My mother wasn't that kind of housekeeper—you know, we were clean, but we weren't fussy. So my husband said, (he wasn't my husband then, of course), 'Well, why don't you marry me and do my housework?' So I said, 'Oh, no! Oh, it's bad luck to put the date of a wedding ahead'—which was the reason I thought you didn't put the date of a wedding ahead! So I went to housework for a while, and I learned a lot. I learned a very great deal. Besides, my mother hadn't taught me much, you know.

I hired out as a maid, and I worked for a lady that lived up on Ellerday, which is off Danforth. She thought I was dreadful, which I was, of course. Here I was, a girl planning to get married, getting on for eighteen, and I couldn't peel a potato. I was a real mess. Poor woman, she had a terrible time with me. But she taught me a lot—I wasn't stupid, you know, just untrained. Then in December of that year I went to a Miss Burgess down at Scarborough beach. This would be 1916. She was a maiden lady, and she taught me a lot too. She really was wonderful. She was economical, which my people had never been.

I stayed right in with Miss Burgess. She had tried to clean the snow off her sidewalk, and she had fallen with the handle of the shovel around her arm and had broken it. So I worked for her until I was married in June. I think I got about $20 a month. I know I was quite satisified.

Was there any difference in prestige between work in the bookbinding places and domestic work?

I don't think so, because I was only in factory work anyway. It wasn't as though it was office work, for instance. If I had had an opportunity to complete my education, or get some sort of an education, why, I suppose I might have thought housework was a come-down. The only thing: I just didn't know anything about it and I didn't want to do it, but I had to, because my eyes had petered out. I'm afraid I'm not very conscious of class anyway.

Did people at that time look down on domestic work?

I think they did, up to a point, you know. But I think it was really more in the old country than here. A lady's maid and butlers and cooks were important, not chambermaids or housemaids or kitchen maids—they were lower in the pecking order.

Mrs Edna Dupont

A graduate of the University of Toronto, Mrs Dupont was an occupational therapist during the war, and later became a teacher.

There weren't many openings for women in those days. When I first started to teach on the Toronto staff I was paid $600 a year and had a degree and so forth. A young man with the same school at the same time, who had just an ordinary certificate, was paid $1200. It irritated me but it was the accepted practice. The medical officer thought it was quite justifiable because that man would have a family. I said, 'Well, you have no guarantee that he has a family. He's paid that whether he has one or not.' I think a woman has a right to support a family just the same as a man. All the way through the women were handicapped. They were paid less, they were given less opportunity for advancement. You would use your brains and do a grand piece of work, and the head of the department, being a man, always took the credit, and the men, being the heads of the departments, always had the financing to determine just which interests would be looked after, where the budget would be applied.

Now I'm afraid I was a suffragette. In my high school days, in matriculation form, I was writing letters to Mrs Pankhurst in England, and to be sure I was fair, I was writing to the anti-suffragette association. I believed in women having the vote. And it irritated me in the First World War when they gave the vote to the wives of soldiers, and here people born in this country, paying taxes and so on didn't have the vote.

What were the anti-suffragettes saying at the time?

Oh, they were nonsensical. You see, all through my professional life I was up against that: that the men had to be the main officials, had to have a larger salary, had to have the say about everything. I tried to get the arguments on both sides so as to be fair, but I'm afraid that they were strongly weighted in favour of the suffragettes.

Did the women organize together at all?

Well, no. You see, at the time we were so busy with the war work, we let such things as that go by. Other things were much more necessary. I've been a suffragette all my life, but not a violent one.

Donald McAffrey

The suffragette time was before the war. That subsided a bit during the war. Women had other things to do. They worked on the farms here, and they worked in the factories. Very gradually almost all our factories who could do it here in this country were transformed into munitions factories. And women went into these factories and worked and they did it even more than in Britain. Now that was really what got the women the vote.

Now, this is a little bit of history: in 1916, I think, Emmeline Pankhurst came over from England. She went out to Winnipeg and got the women there organized. Now Nellie McClung lived in Winnipeg at that time. The women there organized, and Nellie became a public speaker, went all around Manitoba speaking in favour of the suffrage. One of our friends was a child in Winnipeg at that time and lived right across from Nellie. Her father hated everything that

Nellie stood for. He said, 'If that damn woman would stay at home and look after her unruly brats instead of gadding about the province talking unutterable nonsense, she might amount to something.' That's what a good many men at that time thought. I admit I didn't. The women in Winnipeg didn't resort to chaining themselves to fences and breaking windows and all the rest of it. They felt that ridicule was more deadly than violence. So they formed a mock parliament, and Nellie took the place of Sir Roblin, the premier. And they put on this mock parliament in the downtown theatre in Winnipeg and they discussed whether men should be allowed to vote. Wouldn't that upset them? *(laughs)* They set up a howl of laughter. Everybody in Winnipeg was there. The newspapers took it up and gave it a full account. Well, Roblin was dead set against anything as unprecedented as women's suffrage. Well, his government went out, and the women got the vote in Winnipeg in 1916. As far as I know, that was the first time in the English-speaking world, and it was done by ridicule.

Nellie was a famous author. *Sowing Seeds in Danny* was a very homey, sort of humorous type of book. She was quite a woman, you know.

What about the women you knew at that time? Did they think it was important to get the vote? Were they conscious of that kind of thing?

I don't think they were. I think most of the women I knew were perfectly contented with their lot.

IV.   THE SHOP FLOOR

Bruce Cole

Practically all of Tip Top was turned over to making uniforms. Making uniforms and that was the forerunner of the present way of producing garments. It was done in sections. Each machine ran a circle line and then they handed over the garment to the next person, who put it on the machine and would do another piece, and so on. Uniforms are uniforms.

Do you think this changed the clothing industry?

I think it did. Before, once upon a time, a man's suit would be made by a tailor sitting cross-legged on the bench, and he would make the entire thing. He would *build* the garment. Well, that was many years ago. Today it isn't done that way, not in mass production anyway. It's done in what they call section work. And I believe that the making of military uniforms was the forerunner of making garments that way. I understand in ladies' garments, dresses are sewn the same way: one machine sews one seam, say a longitudinal seam, and then it'll go on to the next machine and it'll sew another kind of seam.

Mrs Jill Halpenny

Her mother was persuaded to come to Canada from England because of better conditions. She believed 'the streets were paved with gold.' (Her father was dead). Life was difficult at first, in Toronto, and they lived in the basement of their first home until they could afford to build the first floor.

I was sewing at Eaton's, making blouses. Summer we worked on winter coats, and winter we worked on summer clothes. There was a big room with rows and rows of sewing machines, power machines. I was tucking blouses and sometimes making the sleeves. You never finished a garment up. Some days you'd be working on sleeves; another time you'd be working on the tucking machine, putting tucks in them; some would be working on collars. I remember my number yet: '1888!' They'd throw a bundle over to you. 'Get that through. They're waiting for it in the store.' We had to work hard. We worked piecework, and if we made five or six dollars a week, that was good. We didn't dare complain. We just rushed it through. We had a lady overseer. Nobody else bothered us. But if you weren't satisfactory, you were let out. I don't remember any being let out, only when it came a slack time, and then they would call you in again when they had more work. If you got a better job, well, you took the better job.
    You were kept busy. There was no coffee-break or anything like that. We worked from eight o'clock till six, with an hour for lunch. At lunch, we sat where we worked, on benches, and we ate our lunch off them. We had to take our own tea, and it wasn't bags like it is now—it was loose. We took that with us and got some sugar and just had them scalded. Oh, we had to sit right by our own machines. That's all we had—no lunchroom.

Frank Lloyd

An unskilled labourer, he came to Toronto from England out of a sense of adventure and was always able to find a job.

Fellas didn't get much in those days. That caused a lot of distress. It was not through a man's inability to *do* the jobs, but very often they'd say, 'Nothing doing' on Monday. You'd got what you call a steady job then. Now, if you go looking for work, you might go ahead and get a job that would last you two days, and then they'd call you back and you'd lose it. You see, it was a very, very funny situation.
    I came back to Toronto after the war and I got a job at more money, after making all that money—you know, anything from $7 to $12.50. In two or three days the superintendent came and took me off this little boy's job and put me on running this machine. About two days, he said, 'You're doing three times as

much work as the man that worked before you.' And I said, 'How about giving me some more money?' 'Oh,' he said, 'I can't give you more money right away.' I said, 'I'm giving you the work right away quick.' 'Well,' he says, 'I'll try. I'll try a little bit later.' So in about four months' time—good God! I was paying my rent out of my bloody bank account—I went up to him and I said, 'You know, Jim, I'm running a pretty big establishment.' (I was in a new apartment, you know. I think I was paying about $40.00 a month.)

That was a lot?

Oh jeez, I'll tell you it was! So, I had a very, very nice apartment down East Toronto for awhile, $23, and then when I bought my car, $5 for the garage. So anyway, I asked him for more money. He said, 'I just can't give it to you. We're going to move.' So just after we moved, he give me five cents. So then I started on keeping track of my production. From then on—(*snaps his fingers rhythmically, indicating that he got more money.*) Then they gave me two helpers. Then they fired him, and the new superintendent came in. The first thing he did was ask for the wage slips—wage list. One of the boys out at the office came down. He said, 'Hey, Frank, you're in trouble.' 'Why?' He said, 'The man saw you on the top of the list and said you're getting as much as your two helpers. That's too much.' So then they took the two helpers away. This new man came down and told me what to do *next*. This is something *new* for me to be told what to do *next*. So anyway, I did it. In about an hour the production boss come along to me and he said to me, 'When are you doing so-and-so, Frank?' 'I don't know. Go ask that guy upstairs.' 'What do you mean?' 'Well,' I says, 'he told me to do these. I was going to do those—what you're asking for. Now I'm production stock.' So the guy came downstairs and he says, 'You do pretty well what you like down here, don't you?' I says, 'What do you mean?' 'Well,' he says, 'I mean, maybe I shouldn't have said it that way. Nobody ever tells you what to do here, do they?' 'No,' I says, 'you're the first person that's ever told me what to do here. Since I was here about three weeks, I keep in cahoots with the stock-keeper. Therefore we *never* go out-of-stock.' He says, 'Carry on.' Then he says, 'I owe you an apology.' 'You don't owe me any apology at all,' I said. 'Yes, when I came here,' he said, 'I said you were getting too much money. It wasn't reasonable. I find you're not getting enough.' Then he give another five cents, and he said, as he was leaving, 'There's more where that came from.' So you see, these are very peculiar situations. Many a man in my position then would have walked out! I was a top money man then, you see.

Shortly after he came, he went out the front door, and five guys went in the men's room, you see. He went 'round the building and come through the back door and right into the men's room, and there's five of them in there smoking. 'Out!' He fired four of them. The fifth guy, just a boy, said, 'What about me?' He said, 'You go back to your work.' 'No,' he said, 'if you fired them for smoking, I was smoking. I'm going too.' I met that guy years later in a very good job; I admired him very, very much.

But, you know, I got along with that stinker—wonderful man! Maybe I like strict people better than the easy because I think the easy guys get taken advantage of. But now they've got the strong unions, *everybody* gets taken advantage of.

I was right deep down inside me honest, not only honest to myself, but honest to the person I was working for, no matter how much he had me across the barrel—and a lot of them did.

In what way?

I would say the overall run of manufacturers, years and years ago, had no respect for anybody or anything but profits.

They had you over the barrel, but at the same time you were trying to be as good a production worker as possible for them. Isn't that contradictory?

It isn't. I don't say it's contradictory. It's very, very stupid and very, very hard to understand. But one day, just to give you an idea: the general manager of the work that I was doing came down and said to me, 'Frank, what's wrong down here?' 'What do you mean, "What's wrong?"' He said, 'There's something *wrong* down here and you know it.' He was a university man, an electrical engineer, and I just thought the world of him. And him and I got along just like that. I said, 'There's no contentment down here.' 'What do you mean, "There's no contentment"?' 'Well,' I said, 'when I worked at this firm about a week, they sent a time-study man down and timed me on my work. And soon as he timed me for about an hour—took the time for *every* move I made—one of the old hands came to me, and he said, 'You know you're crazy? If you don't give them a screwing when they are timing you like that, you're in trouble.' Well, this was so foreign to my way of thinking! Seven years after that, I had the pleasure of telling that manager those very same words. And I said to him, 'I'm very sorry to say to you that I find this is true. I'll work when I'm being studied exactly the same as I do when I'm not being watched. I'm working for myself, and I'm a son-of-a-bitch to work for!' These are the words I said. This man would come down and study me, and after, I'd find I have to work a lot harder to make the same amount of money that I was making before. He not only has knocked off 10% for undetected loafing, but he's possibly made one or two mistakes in the favour of the firm. This is the only way where I say the unions came in, and they were very well justified. But personally I never got *any* benefit, and I'm very proud to say that. Mind you, I think I should have had a certain amount of defence —protection—against that practice. It was under a certain system—I just forget what the system was—but this was very, very common in the United States. Of course, when you're working for United States firms over here, which many,

many people do, they're testing you here, and they've already tested people over in the States, so they know the complete story of what can be done on that job. And very often the Canadian worker is being expected to do with more or less obsolete machinery where they've been doing it with the most modern machinery. I don't think I'll get any contradiction on that from anywhere. That's being in the game.

Wally Ross

He found it difficult to settle down after the war. He had been an accountant but wanted to work with his hands instead, and got a job in a Toronto factory. He left the factory and went back to accounting as a more lucrative profession once he decided to get married.

This place was on King and Dufferin. It was called the Russell Motor Company originally, then the Russell Gear and Machine Company, and then Acme Gear and Machine Company. Here's what I wrote about the Inspection Department, or the members of the Inspection Department. I just made notes when I went along. This is dated 5th February, 1920. It sounds awful!

> The Inspection Department is the place where they see
> If the things made here with the gauges agree.
> Mr Williams, you know, is ne'er at a loss
> To keep us all busy—you see, he's the boss.
>
> Round, round the tables, Mr Turgeon doth go
> Instructing the young ladies in things they don't know.
> Tom piles up the scales with bushings and pins
> And to put down the numbers on cards he begins.
>
> All over the works, a truck Wally pushes
> And down after chain links daily he rushes.
> The diameter of bolts is tested by Scotty
> And the snap of his gauges will soon drive us potty.
>
> Harry, also, for bolts shows a lust
> While he spits tobacco juice in a box of sawdust.
> To Alice and Nina come many a tappet.
> If one is found good, they gaze wond'ringly at it.
>
> Mable and Ivy inspect wiggly chains,
> And o'er other things they worry their brains.

Of hinges and porcelains we've got quite a supply,
But Ethel and Beatrice sure do make them fly.

Gramophone parts, why, there's boxes galore,
Which Nina and Margaret send to the store.
You'd think Alma and Peggy had once worked at Knox's
To see them pack spark plugs in pretty blue boxes.

So from morning to evening we work right along.
Oft midst the noise comes the strain of a song.
Saturday comes and we're all full of hope
To see what we'll get in our pay envelope.

Now excuse my endeavour to put into rhyme
The things that we do to fill in the time.

Richard Mills

I think I certainly matured awfully fast in the war. I don't think it did me one iota
of harm in health or attitude at all. I learned an awful lot in the war of working
with people and organizations, and how to get things done, and getting along
with people. People who suffered in the war were, of course, the wounded,
casualties, and the maimed and sick who lost their health. They suffered, but I
don't think I suffered one bit. That's why I thought these high school boys
coming into our engineering class at University of Toronto were so immature. I
thought their ideas . . . well, they were ideas, but unworkable ideas. But if an idea
is unworkable, why even consider it, y'know?

I remember one job I had. I was plant superintendent for the City of Toronto
in the old area around here, for the Bell Telephone. I'd taken a certain number of
men off a certain job because we'd improved the organization, and in fact we
didn't need these two men. The union fellows stepped in—we weren't going to
put them somewhere else, no! 'The men who used to work in here are going to
stay in here.' Well, I talked to them, told them all the reasons for it. 'These men
have a right to stay where they are. They don't want to be moved.' So I went to
our personnel officer, told him my story. I thought I'd talk it over with him. He
says, 'But they shouldn't think that way.' Well, that's the idealist approach. You
don't go through life how you *should* think, you deal with people how they *do*
think, and work from there.

Brian Wilson

From a poor farming family near Owen Sound, Mr Wilson worked for a music company from the early 1900s until the Depression.

People changed a lot after the war. The people would do anything to go down on the other fellow, to gain a point for themselves. I noticed that in particular, they'd try to get ahead themselves. But of course, they didn't get ahead of me at all.

Why was that, competition for jobs?

Well, I think so. We brought some over from the States. You see, we were connected with Thomas A. Edison. He was in the States and I used to go to New York twice a year, once in June and once in February—the Dealers' Convention and the Jobbers' Convention. And we brought a couple of fellows over from there. They were that type, down on anybody to gain a point for themselves.

What made the difference?

I don't know.

But you didn't notice it before the war?

No, we were helping everybody.

Richard Mills

He was studying engineering at the University of Toronto. During the summer of the Winnipeg General Strike, he was working for an engineering firm based in Winnipeg. He was the time-keeper on a work train.

Were a lot of the people working with you on construction foreigners?

Oh, I'd say all were foreigners. The first summer we had a foreman, he was a Scotsman from Winnipeg, but the gang were all—well, there were Ukrainians and what-not, a few French-Canadians. But there was no English-speaking people in the gang at all. The cook—we had a lot of cooks—he and his wife were Cockney Englishmen. They were rough people, smelly, gambling people. *(His voice trails off.)*

Was the pay good?

Oh, at the time it was good, oh boy! People thought I was making a packet—$150 a month, $175. 'How'd you get a job like that?' That was big money in those days.

Were there many Ukrainians working there?

Yup. Some of them were certainly communistically inclined. Russia, you see, had just had the big revolution over there.

I'll tell you of another incident down there. We were building a pipeline, and the sewers were up in a town called LeCoul. Where we were working was about seven miles from LeCoul. We had a tent camp out on the bald prairies. We had a gang of about, I'd say, 40 or 50 people. During the night we had one of those twisters there, took the tents all down and ripped them, the rain poured down and we were soaking wet. In the morning we had a disgruntled bunch of men. We were soaking wet and the food was all scattered over the prairies. The men were all talking in Russian: 'Mister, I'm going to quit.' They'd signed a contract that they'd stay until the job was finished, but it wasn't worth the paper it was written on. It's got to have a starting time and finishing time for the contract to be a worthwhile paper. I didn't know that, and I had all the contracts. So we talked to them, and over half of them said they'd stay on and help get things organized. About fifteen said no, they were going to quit. I took out these contracts and said, 'Here's your contract. You said you'd stay until the job was finished.' But 'Oh no, we're gonna go.' So off they went across the prairie. I hooked up the horse and buggy. I passed them on the way going in and stopped and said, 'I'm going to the magistrate to tell him. You can't do this.' So on I went. I got to LeCoul and I asked who the magistrate was. They said, 'He's a shoemaker.' (He was a peg-leg—there wasn't a boot on it—just one peg-leg.) I told him my story about these fellows that signed the contracts, and that they were walking into town to take the train. 'Well,' he says, 'I'll get those sons-of-bitches, I'll get them. You bring them in here and I'll take them to court.' There was an empty schoolroom where we were to have the court, you see. In the meantime, he says, 'How much money have they got?' I says, 'I paid them all last night, and the least payment should be around $35.' So the first fellow comes up, and 'Are you gonna go back to the job?' And it's no. 'Here's your contract. Says you'll stay.' 'I won't go back to the job.' 'Take him to jail.' They had a little cage about eight feet square and there were steel chains all around. They were going to put him in there, but the guy says, 'No! I'll go back to work, I'll pay a fine.' '$35 or I'll put you in jail.' 'I'll go to jail,' he says. As he was going into the cage there, he says, 'I'll pay my fine.' So he fined them all $35, and then they went and took the train and went on their way. The next summer I had one of these same fellows on the gang that I was on. And of course he told them of what I had done, fined them all for quitting their jobs. I didn't have a man that quit that summer.

I'm kind of ashamed of what I did because it's illegal. But he was against them from the start: 'Oh, they're Russians, are they? We'll fine them, you betcha! How much money have they got there?' It was awful as far as the application of the law, it was terrible.

You mentioned that some of them were communists?

Well, there was one or two that I could talk with and wanted to talk with me. They said that it was a better system. They said, 'Here we only make a little money. You big boss, you get big money.' As a matter of fact, some of them were making more money than I was. It was all piecework, this particular job. He wouldn't believe me. He says, 'You're making big money.' So they had that on their minds: 'Everyone who was a boss has a big salary and a lot of money,' and 'We're depressed people here.' It was just an exaggerated opinion of the whole situation there.

Stanley Weekes

Originally from Poland, he came to Canada in 1913, and like many Jewish tailors, wound up working at Tip Top Tailors in Toronto. There was no union, and the tailors made eight dollars per week. He recalls going on strike only once.

Where did they get the strikebreakers from?

There was a lot of people there, young people was coming from every part of the world. That time they advertised for their own people to work. They didn't tell them they're strikebreakers. They were green, everybody was green. It didn't matter, they just took them into the factory. But when they worked there two or three days, we started to picket the shop. Then they called the police to protect those strikebreakers.

The whole shop went on strike, it was more than 60. You see, we didn't go on strike. He locked us out because we asked for a raise. He kept us outside till springtime. Six months before, we got a little bit of a raise. I'll tell you. Those days they made a suit for $14. This was the price, not more, not less. So the wages weren't as big. If you make $12 or $13 a week, that was a lot of money that time, because other places you couldn't make that. We asked for a raise, and this was the time before Good Friday. At the beginning Mr Dunkelman didn't want to give the raise, but we stood out a day, then he settled with us and told the foreman, 'Give them $2 more.' But the time before Christmas was slack. He reminds himself, and he comes and he calls me over, and he says, 'You remember last time you didn't want to go out in the busy time. I don't need you now,' he says, 'Go out. Go on strike.' So we went on strike. It wasn't a strike, he locked us out, but some of us he took back six months later. He didn't close the shop, but he couldn't get along with the strikebreakers because they were not mechanics, you see. They didn't have training, so they couldn't get out the production. So he picked out of the sixty about half of us and he called us back to work. We didn't care if he gave the raises so long as we got the job back.

Paul Sawchuk

I work for awhile in Lowndes Company, then I change to Eaton's. Work in Eaton's for a few years, then I change to go to another shop, called Haberling.

Now, in that Haberling shop we start to talk about organizing union. That was 1915. It was very hard to get people together because everyone was afraid. Because if the boss find out that you are organizing, he can fire you. So we had to be very careful that we don't talk about union in the shop, but we always talk outside, and also go from house to house to convince them that it is better to organize the union. But it took time, nearly two years, until they were able to get together workers and decided to send the organizer right to the boss and tell him the people wants the union. That was about 1917. The organizer of the union went to the boss and tell him what the people wish and so on. It was a question of union, not so much of wages, but it's the first thing to get the union in. We were all surprised: boss agree. He even propose 44 hours a week instead of 48 hours a week. And that was the first union that organized 40 hours a week.

It's interesting also to say that in Eaton's we were trying to get a union too, but it was impossible because as soon as the Haberling shop accept the union and raise the wages, Eaton's did also, and it was hard to organize the people there.

The trouble was in the craft union. There was discussion, you know, exactly how to get around that craft union. Because, for instance, if the cutters go out on strike, the others are out. Now, for instance, if the tailors go out, then the cutters would have nothing to do. When the cutters are working, then the others do. So therefore, it was quite a struggle to get it instead of craft.

What was the background of most of the other people working in the tailor shops? Did a lot of Ukrainians work there?

Oh, yes. Majority of people were Jewish, because they are very good tailors, because in old country they were already experienced—not like today, for instance. Today you just learn one part of this, then you go, but those days, that was really good tailors' shops that were working.

How were people trained?

Usually they brought those that doesn't understand the tailoring, doesn't know anything about the tailoring. But it was during the wartime, the First War. The foreman knows already who can teach those young people that came to the shop. When he sees that I know tailoring, he put another fella with me to teach them. Especially during the First War, when the uniforms was needed right away. So it was very busy. You work overtime too, even in order to deliver uniforms.

Barry Richardson

We moved from Montreal to Toronto in 1920. I was eighteen. I spent some time looking for work. If you were not a veteran, it was very difficult to get employment.

Did you look for work for a long time?

No, the most I was ever out of work in my life was three days, because I'd take anything. That's why I pushed a bicycle around the city of Toronto making money delivering telegrams. When they were paying $12.50 a week, I made $35 a week delivering telegrams, working overtime. You're supposed to be in to work at eight o'clock in the morning. If you noticed, some of the older men that were pushing telegrams were always there before you. So gradually you get down about six o'clock in the morning. The rate was three cents a message. But if you got down at that hour, you would get 50 messages for the Union Station, 50 messages for the CPR building, 50 messages for another bank, and then when the staff started to come in, you'd go for your breakfast. The ordinary route would be twelve messages, but you've already made a day's pay by getting in that much earlier. Then everybody goes to eat between twelve and one, so you don't eat between twelve and one. Therefore you pick up extra messages. And if you wanted to work nights—and most them didn't want to work nights—you could get more. They would always give you them in the west end of the city or the east end after the local offices were closed. If you stayed from twelve to two, you got an extra $2. Your messages for night work were 25 cents a piece. Of course, you'd only get two or three at a time, and generally you would get a tip at night where you wouldn't in the daytime.

Did you get along with the employer there?

Got along alright, but I left there on account of a strike in about 1920. I was working for the CNR Telegraph office at the corner of Wellington Street and the CPR boys were just up Yonge Street. Now the CPR boys were given uniforms. The CNR boys were not given uniforms. Then they decided to give them uniforms and, instead of three cents a message, only two-and-a-half cents a message. We didn't think that was just right, so we called it a strike. But we just walked out of the office. It was a beautiful day, the circus was in town, and we decided, 'To hell with the telegraph office!' and we went to the circus. Altogether ten of us walked out. When we came back, they didn't want us any more.

Frank Bell

He worked in Montreal during the war years because he was too young to enlist and there were no jobs in his hometown, Lancaster. He boarded in Griffintown, one of the poor sections of the city. 'Farm people lived like kings compared to Griffintown,' he remembers. He describes how the men working in the coalyards supplemented their meagre wages.

When I first went to work in Montreal I got a boarding house in Griffintown. Now I didn't know one section from the other, but Griffintown was the Irish section. There were two Irish sections. There was Point St Charles and there was Griffintown. Now the poorer Irish lived in Griffintown and the better-off Irish lived in Point St Charles. It was pretty hard to tell the difference sometimes, but there was apparently a difference in the rent. A little better housing in Point St Charles, but in Point St Charles you got all the smells from the slaughterhouse which you didn't get in Griffintown. But anyway, I went and lived in Griffintown. It was supposed to be a very, very tough section, but of course I didn't find it tough. The police used to patrol the area in pairs, because it wasn't considered safe for them to patrol the area singly. I guess it depends upon who you were. There was a lot of poverty, a lot of stealing. For instance, I boarded at this one place and I had to share a room with the landlady's son and he had just got out of jail. What had happened was, he was working in a coalyard and they used to deliver the coal in two-wheeled carts because Montreal was very steep. If the horse couldn't get up the hill with this two-wheeled cart, they would turn the horse around and back the horse up the hill. And then when they got to where they were delivering the coal, they could just trip this cart and spill the whole load of coal. They didn't have to shovel it. Well, the boys in the yard made a deal with the 'checker,' you see, that he would signal some guy going out that his load wasn't checked. It was on the free list, so it wasn't checked out. He would go out and sell his load, and then he would 'divvy' up with the rest of the boys. So everyday they would sell a few loads and divvy up, and this was the way they made their wages up. Now you may think this was stealing, but the boys didn't regard this as stealing.

I don't know what the profits of the coal company were, but things were tough. We used to have a cigarette called the Derdry cigarette. Now it was put up in a package of six cigarettes and it sold for five cents. Now in Griffintown these little corner stores would open a pack of Derdry cigarettes, and they would sell these drivers one cigarette for one cent, and this way they got six cents for the whole pack. This way the driver could have a smoke when he couldn't afford the whole pack. I don't know what their wages were, but they couldn't have been very high when you had to buy your cigarettes one at a time.

People had various ways of making a living. I remember this one old fellow. He had a pushcart, and he used to go around behind the horses, picking up the leavings and cleaning up the street. They called him a street sweeper. The horses made a lot of mess those days. The boys on the coal carts would pass him, and every time they passed him, they'd reach back, and they'd push off a hunk of coal. And of course in sweeping up, he'd pick up this coal, and by the time the winter come, he'd have his winter supply of coal. And this was the way they helped each other.

Sam Beckman

Born in 1886 in the Ukraine, he participated in the revolutionary events in Russia in 1905, and was deeply affected by the anti-Jewish pogroms. He came to Canada in 1908 and was active in the Socialist Party and union organizing.

Many socialists were street-corner speakers, preaching socialism on street corners, and I especially enjoyed speaking on one street corner on Dundas and Spadina. All the Jews were so much upset because of an old man singer, a *mishimit*—he was a Christian missionary. Even non-religious socialists were negative; we disliked a Jew being a *Yeshiva bücher* in the young days, coming here, joining the missionaries, then using it as a job to try to convert the Jews in the Jewish neighbourhood to Christianity. So I always enjoyed taking the next corner with about a couple of dozen of our socialists and speaking on a box while he had three, four people listening. I enjoyed standing there on a box and talking, preaching, telling them to be good trade unionists, fighting for shorter hours and better wages, against exploitation of the sweat shops, and also calling them to join the ranks of the socialist movement because we'll never have any freedom or economical security unless we bring socialism. And I used to say, 'Why, this fellow over there is promising you pie-in-the-sky. We promise you something now!' We had a wonderful time with that missionary, but the poor fellow was so disgusted because we were capturing every passerby. So the street corners were our means for years. We had dozens of our fellow activists in the *Arbeiterring*, in the trade union movement, in the socialist movement.

CHAPTER NINE

AT HOME

The war prevaded the domestic front. Women in families where husbands remained at home coped with scarcities and shortages of an unprecedented nature. Anxious and committed women threw themselves into service work with a feverish intensity, rolling bandages, knitting socks, and volunteering as nurses. A grateful government bestowed generous benefits on the wives and dependents of soldiers overseas. However, such stipends did not totally replace the absent 'man about the house'; rather they presented to women the necessity for a relatively autonomous existence which did not vanish after soldiers returned home. For many it was a time haunted by the possibility of a dreaded telegram or telephone call. The loyalty, tenacity, and ability that they demonstrated on the home front over the war years won for them a recognition from patriarchal governments that over half a century of women suffrage reformers had not.

Dr Martha Davidson

She was in her mid-twenties when war was declared. She had been a home economist prior to the war, and then worked for Farmers' Magazine in Toronto. She was active in the Women's Institutes all her life.

When the war started, I can remember that I had no idea whatsoever what it meant. A lot of people, including many of the volunteers, didn't think it was going to be much of a war. They hoped they'd get over before it was cleared up. As for myself, I wasn't much concerned with what went on in the rest of the world. We just began to think of what you could do, how you could knit socks and all that sort of thing. And, of course, the Women's Institutes went right into that like every other organization did, and did an amazing job in providing material things.

That movement started in Ontario and then went from here to England, and they are way stronger in England. I mean, their membership's far larger because their population is more dense. The reason that it got started was this: there was a woman in Hamilton, a Mrs Hoodless, quite a socialite and a very gifted and brilliant woman interested in education for women. Her oldest baby died when he was two years old, and the doctors told her that it was the result of contaminated milk. She felt so dreadful; she said her baby had died because of her ignorance. She hadn't known how to take care of him, she felt. So she started a campaign for clean milk in Hamilton, and then she talked about these family things. She was a very attractive, very charming woman. There were very few women going around doing any public speaking. Of course, she wasn't on anything that anyone could foresee as having to do with the suffrage movement, so there was no prejudice there. A lot of people thought she'd be better to be at home, of course, but she was very interesting. The farmers had an organization—we called it the Farmers' Institutes, it wasn't exactly that—and they had an annual convention at the Agricultural College at Guelph. They liked to bring their wives with them, and they'd like some entertainment that their wives would be interested in. A young man from Stoney Creek (his name was Erlind Lee) had the idea of having this woman come and speak, which she did. She told the men that they knew far more about feeding their livestock than their wives knew about feeding their children and that if they had an organization to help them with this, how much more important it was that the women have an organization which could bring them education along their lines. Well, it so impressed this Erlind Lee that he asked her if she'd come out and speak at Stoney Creek the night that the Farmers' Institute had their Ladies' Night. She did, and as a result of that, the women thought they wanted to form an organization. Erlind Lee and his wife went around the countryside, all over the township, drumming up people to come to this meeting. There were 100 women and one man, Erlind Lee, at the meeting. There they set up the first Women's Institute, and it was for the betterment of home and country.

What did the women in the Institutes do during the war?

One of the things was Britain was very low on food, you remember. The submarines were putting down the ships, more than they would let be known. But they were afraid of being starved out. So some women from Ontario (one from Ontario and one from B.C. who was originally from Ontario) went over to England. The government set them organizing Women's Institutes to concentrate on food preservation, and they taught canning all over Britain. That was new. Here, one of the things they did was to set up three, or maybe there were five, stations—canning centres. They made quite a lot of jam to be sent overseas. We spoke about knitting socks. Well, they sent a lot of blankets and bedding and all sorts of materials. Soldiers' housewives *(she pauses)* . . . Well, a housewife was just a little needle-case thing to help them with their mending.

Another thing that the Institutes did: the great majority of them at that time were farm women. Of course, you couldn't get farm labour, so these women took on men's work on the farm that they had never done in their lives. Some of them, of course, knew how to do it and had done these things and got back into it, but for some of them it was a new experience.

Did these women who did the heavy work on the farms continue to do it after the war or did they go back to work inside the home?

No, they went back as fast as the son would come home, or other men were released.

Mrs Adrienne Stone

I was a St John's Ambulance VAD. The courses were given in home nursing and first aid, and you took them during the winter and were trained. Then you volunteered or signed up for voluntary service in the hospitals. I think that it's pretty true that the volunteers were a necessity. There were not enough nurses and enough trained people to do the job, so they taught what we needed to know to volunteers, and we did the work in the hospital.

I worked at Davisville Hospital, which was an orthopedic hospital —convalescent. The men were brought back from overseas, say after the first operation, either because they were permanently crippled or because further surgery was needed, and they would have to be in the hospital for longer periods of time. When we first went on, we did things like making the beds and cleaning, not floor cleaning, but cleaning things around the wards. Then, if you were staying and were good enough, they moved you onto something, say a diet kitchen on the floors, or onto a ward where you did small things for the patients. Then, after that, there were dressings in the dressing room, and in that case you might put on top bandages and go on the wards with either the doctors or the nurses to do the dressings. You'd put on top bandages and hand things and wring out compresses, so that they could accomplish more than they could without that help.

Did you get along with the nurses pretty well?

Most of them. There were a few who sort of resented and were resentful of the fact, thinking, I suppose, that volunteers were taking their jobs. But actually, when you think about it, what we did was what ward aides and nursing assistants do now. There were no such people then.

The shifts volunteered. For volunteers, it was four hours for the first shift, and then you moved up to eight as you got a little more responsible job. So it was a full eight-hour day. We worked pretty hard.

We were under the direct jurisdiction of a VAD officer. She posted us to our post and was responsible for us, for instance, carrying around a tape measure to see that our skirts weren't more than eight inches from the ground! *(laughs)* *Eight* inches was the thing they had to be. But she did do the general administration, and the regulating, and the placing of the volunteers. But while you worked, you were under the direct control of the nurse in charge of your ward. In kitchens we worked more or less under the orderly sergeant, I think you call it.

We got regular lunch hours at regular times, and volunteers lunched in sergeants' mess. Nurses lunched in the officers' mess. See, nurses were commissioned officers during the First War. I was very lucky because I was working with one of the nurses on dressings at the time, and she managed that I went to lunch with her—but that was just because she was a nice person. There was a mess for the men who were outpatients. It was army, definitely army, with army rankings. You accepted it, but you didn't feel it. It was not a burden.

Mrs Penny Plante

She went to the University of Toronto in 1909. The war 'came as quite a shock,' and her class was decimated. Like some women in her class, she joined the army as a nurse and was in uniform for four years. Most women university students hadn't planned to work after graduation, but the war effort 'spurred them on.'

I went into occupational therapy. I had wanted to go overseas as an ambulance driver, but somehow I could not. I was in uniform four years. It was one of the broadening influences of my life.

They started to do some research. They found that men going from hospital to their homes could not adjust to the haphazard routine, and they had nothing to do and very few people to talk to, in comparison to a hospital. It was particularly hard on mental cases. So we started a service (I had charge of that), and we would visit the man in his home and see what the possibilities were, and then try to interest him either in studies or in craftwork. One day we would be teaching matriculation studies in the morning, and in the afternoon we'd be teaching basketweaving. It was a very broadening influence.

We worked from different hospitals. When we started the research in the home training, it was from headquarters down on Spadina, and then eventually we had an office at the Christie Street Hospital.

There were many interesting things that occurred. Those four years were invaluable. They changed your whole outlook. You were faced with a challenge. You saw what other people were going through, and you had to use your ingenuity to help them. At first, it was a very difficult job to have occupational therapy in the hospitals. Doctors and nurses were a little bit afraid. When we went into a hospital, the nurses looked on us as something objectionable. We had to win our way.

It is hard to say how many were involved, they were spread right across Canada. I had a staff of five or six, something like that, and we went out into the homes from the workshop in the hospital. Outpatients would come sometimes for supplies. But a mental case sent home from the hospital with nothing to do and no one to speak to him—perhaps his mother and his wife would be busy doing the housework—it's pretty hard.

You had to gain acceptance, not only in the hospital, but in some of the homes. And then the men were rather difficult to deal with. For instance, there was a man with TB they could not keep in one of the hospitals; he just got up and walked out. Finally they decided they'd let him stay home providing the home followed certain regulations. Now they had several children, several cats, several dogs, and they had no bathtub and facilities like that. It was a little difficult to keep that family in order, you might say. I could only interest the man in basketry, because it was something very large and showy. One day when I was there, the mother bathed the oldest boy (about ten or twelve) in the tub, and then she put the next child in, and then the next, and finally the baby (about two). She said, '*Now* you can tell them at headquarters you've *seen* the children bathed.'

Mrs Elaine Nelson

I wanted to help do my share, and I joined the Red Cross and helped roll bandages and knit socks. My first ones were big enough to fit an elephant, and after that, I became vey proficient—*so* proficient that I knit a pair of socks a day without any trouble.

We rolled bandages, and we distributed wool for knitting, and we would go and deliver it to older people that could do it. There were a thousand-and-one things. We made pneumonia jackets and all sorts of things.

You see, *everybody* felt they had to do something. You just couldn't sit there. There was such a thing as just doing nothing but going to afternoon teas and dances and parties, which we had done. That was *out*! In the first place, all our beaux were overseas.

'...I knit a pair of socks a day without any trouble.'

The women involved in the Red Cross were mostly wives and mothers of the soldiers, I would say. There were all different classes. I can remember in one of the Red Cross groups I was in, there were some women who had known how to knit long before any of the other ones. There was no reason for anybody to knit then, you see. If you wanted anything, you had somebody else knit it for you. But these women came, and they were able to help.

Mr and Mrs McAffrey

Mr McAffrey: There was a phrase, 'Doing your bit.' Well, that was pretty well the keynote of feeling all through that First World War. Everybody was extremely patriotic, and everybody wanted to 'do his bit.'

Mrs McAffrey: That was the stock phrase. I don't know who started that. It came out in some speech or other, and everybody took it up. You must 'do your bit.' And we all felt the same way. If there's anything we could do to help, we must do it.

Mr McAffrey: Women, of course, all took to knitting. Every woman was knitting socks and so on for the troops overseas. And there were Bairnsfather cartoons. Now he was an Englishman, but he was drawing very humorous cartoons. I remember one that showed a soldier holding up a pair of socks, and the caption was:

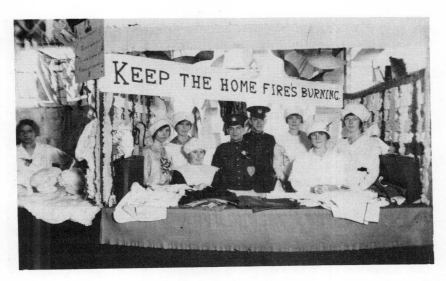

KEEP THE HOME FIRES BURNING

'...*everybody wanted to "do his bit."*'

Your parcel of socks received. Some fit!
I wear one for a helmet and one for a mitt.
I'll see you after I've done my bit,
In the meantime, where did you learn to knit?

(*laughs*) Well, there was some pretty weird knitting done, I suppose, but also some very competent knitting.

Mrs McAffrey: The whole country was in flames about the war. You couldn't talk about anything else. So many of the boys I knew went over, and so many of them were killed. It was a very trying time for us women who stayed home.

I didn't do any volunteer work because I had to keep my job in the newspaper office. We needed the money. I learned to knit. I knitted vigorously for all the rest of the war, and I have been knitting ever since. There were Red Cross depots all over. All the towns had big Red Cross organizations, and the churches had Red Cross organizations. Everything was organized for a state of war all over Canada, even out in the West. Quebec wasn't quite the same. We used to resent Quebec, because French Canadians didn't think they should fight Britain's wars. They forgot that they were Canadians, you see. I didn't think they were any better than the English boys, and I didn't see any reason why their lives shouldn't be risked as well as the English boys'.

Everything was subservient to the war. The paper I worked on, the *Woodstock Sentinel Review*, was full of it. The people were all talking about nothing else. But I don't think it made any difference to working conditions. Except, of course, there were reservists in the *Sentinel Review* office, and they were called up. They had to go, and a lot of others went. The mechanical staff was depleted, but eventually there were some Americans who came over and went into our office and filled up some of the positions.

Dr Martha Davidson

Do you think that the experiences of women during the war changed people's attitudes towards women or women's attitudes towards themselves?

I don't know, and I don't know whether the war would be responsible or would figure in it. You see, these women in the West responded to things that were wrong in their own surroundings. You've heard of the time they went to ask Roblin for votes for women? Well, they made themselves busy, and very properly too, with anyone around them who seemed to be oppressed. Now there were a lot of girls coming in from other countries, didn't know our language and that. Sometimes the women they worked for—they all had to go at housework first—didn't treat them well, and they'd take advantage of them. Like the case of one woman who persuaded the girl that worked for her to take her old fur coat instead of wages in money. The girl didn't want to at all, but the woman somehow or other got it arranged. The girl came to some one of these women. There was Nellie McClung and there were three or four of them that were all working together. I think their central organization was the WCTU. They decided this wasn't fair and the woman must give her wages. So one of the women said, 'Leave it to me.' She had a cousin on the police force, so she called him and told him, 'Will you come over?' this night on his way home. When he arrived, she had her hat on, and she said, 'Just first, will you come with me? I've got to make a call at a certain place.' And he went along with her. Of course, they had been after this woman before, that she must give the girl her wages. When the woman opened the door, here was a woman with a policeman in uniform, so she said, 'Now never mind. It's all settled. I'm going to give the girl her money.'

Some of the married women must have hated to go back to their work in the home after the war. That was another problem. The war meant that families of children grew up with the father away and the mother not at home, and running wild. I think it possibly may have turned a number of them into being irresponsible, wanting to get into gangs and that sort of thing. You see, there was no such thing as daycare. I believe Toronto was one of the first places to pioneer for mothers' pensions, as they called them then, mothers' allowances. Peter Bryce was a minister up at Earlscourt and in his congregation so man of the men left. The women went into munitions, and the children suffered, not just by running wild and misbehaving, but by neglect, irregular meals and that. So he felt that the thing that must be done was to give mothers a pension to allow them to stay at home. And that was the first of the mothers' allowances. I remember Peter

'Peter Bryce was a minister up at Earlscourt and in his congregation so many of the men left.'

Bryce and Dr Helen MacMurchie debating so hard for that. I've been with them on sessions when they'd go into the legislature to argue it, and that was what got the mothers' allowances started. They had them started before the war ended, I think, and it was a great rejoicing. I think it was $10 a month. They weren't trying to use it to support the children. They were using it for the mother. This $10 was for the mother to put her on a little more of an equal basis with her sisters who continued to go out to work.

Frank Bell

This woman I boarded with in Griffintown, in Montreal, had two young girls. They were younger than I was, so I always regarded them as children. Her husband was overseas for four years, and she certainly never went out anywhere. They led a pretty lonely life. She wasn't even allowed to have a telephone. She got $20 a month from her husband's pay and she got $20 a month from the Patriotic Fund. But this was a gift; it was charity, it wasn't from the government. This was administered by a group of rich men's wives, and if they found that a wife was running around, or that she was living beyond her means (they thought), or something, they would cut her off. One of the ways she could live beyond her means was to put in a telephone, because obviously no soldier's wife could afford a telephone. Now I wanted a telephone in the house, because all the girls used to have to call me up at work. And I was very popular because, with all the men in the army, any sixteen- or seventeen-year old boy had so many girlfriends he didn't know what to do with them all. So girls I didn't know at all would call me up at work and talk to me and kid me along in the hope that I would make a date with them and take them to the show, because, as I say, girls just didn't go to the show alone. Generally they wanted an escort. It didn't really feel right if they weren't escorted. So a soldier's wife had a very tough time of it. Anyway, I wanted to put in a phone, and I offered to pay half of it if she'd put in a phone in the house. She wouldn't do it. She said, 'No. If I put in a phone they'd disqualify me. I'd lose something.' So you see how it is.

Mrs Ethel Cameron

A lot of girls married before the war, and I don't think it was such a smart idea, because so many of them were left pregnant. They were left with a little one coming and . . .well, it was just too hard for them, it was too hard of a life. I think that's what changed a lot of the girls, because maybe a lot of their marriages were not too good. I always said I was not going to be left going to have a child and my husband going overseas. I was going to wait for that, because I thought it was much better. I'd seen too much of it, and I didn't like it.

'It's kind of hard on a woman to be left all alone....'

Did the girls get bitter because they were lonely?

Maybe they didn't get bitter, but maybe they were lonely, and maybe they felt they were not having much pleasure in life, that they were being denied when the boys were away. It's kind of hard on a woman to be left all alone, especially if she has a young baby to look after. What could her life be? Really a very, very lonely life, and you had to be a very strong person to do what was right.

Mrs Doris Rosenburg

She came from Roumania when she was eleven and went to work immediately. She eloped with her husband, a presser in the garment industry, and lived in Toronto. During the war years, life was very difficult.

It was very rugged, because—you know, inflation—everything became expensive, eggs $1 a dozen. You couldn't get an orange for no money. I remember that Eaton's put up a sale on oranges. By that time I had my first baby, and I was carrying a second one, and I wanted an orange. I went to that sale of oranges. People were climbing one on top of the other to get at the oranges. You had tables piled with oranges. I took one look and I passed right out. *(laughs)* They had to take me to the hospital. That's how rough it was to get anything that you wanted. Only those that weren't afraid of black-marketing and things like that, they really came out on top—rich. But those that were afraid, and I was one of those that were afraid, we didn't have anything. It was hard.

I remember one time, you know, Eaton's made a sale on eggs, and it was just before Easter and the Passover, and you know everybody needs eggs. I went down to get some eggs. It was terrible! You couldn't get near the crate of eggs, and the people were crowding around and lying over the thing. I did a crazy thing, you know. I got mad because I couldn't get near the eggs. This one woman was lying over the crate. She wouldn't let anybody in near. I took my hand, put it on her head, and just shoved her head right into the eggs. *(laughs)* The manager took one look, and he started to laugh and run, he ran away so fast. I don't know where I got that nerve.

It was awfully hard getting eggs. I went down to St Lawrence Market, went around the chicken coops. Whenever I saw a chicken lay an egg, I stuck my hand in and took out the egg and went over to the dealer and paid him for it. And that's the way I gathered up enough eggs to last me for a week. I would get it cheaper, and also other things from the farmers; we got it more reasonable than going to the stores.

There was rationing. That's why a lot of people went into black market. You wanted their things, you had to pay three times as much for it. But I don't ever remember having a ration book. No, I never had a ration book, because every time I made do with what I had. My family wasn't big. By the time the war finished, I had three children. You managed, you tried to do the best with what you had. Sometimes when I think back, what did I accomplish in those years? Raised a family, that's it. I raised ten children, you know.

Mrs Adrienne Stone

It is important to remember there was no radio and there was no television. Nowadays we're so used to hearing everything in the world that happens within perhaps an hour of the moment that it happens. And we don't realize that the only way then was the newspaper and rumour. Rumour was terribly, terribly strong. It would put the place almost into an hysteria over a weekend. Say that the troops had left, that they were probably on the ocean, and rumour would come that there was a Canadian troop ship down in mid-Atlantic. Well, if that had happened over a weekend, everybody was just unnerved by the end of the week! There were the 'Extras.' I can remember them calling 'Extra' late in the evening if something had happened that they had gotten news of. The other thing was that if you were particularly interested in something, you went down to the newspapers, and they put bulletins out as they came in. So you'd go and stand in front of them. From Saturday night until Monday morning, if you wanted to know what was happening, you had to go down to one of the newspapers and read the bulletin board. It meant that everything was less definite. I think it meant quite an hysteria and much less knowledge of what was really happening.

The casualty lists came through quickly. There was the telegram, of course, and the notices of deaths or woundings. And then there's your personal communications. But general knowledge that so-and-so happened one hour ago in a remote part on the earth was just an unheard-of thing. I think that had a lot to do with the atmosphere of the time. It's hard to think of, to go back. You probably can't imagine it.

Mrs Margaret Hand

Did the men talk about the war in their letters?

Very, very little. The letters were short. 'What's going on at home? I've just come back from leave. It was marvellous.' You got very, very little information. Of course, all their letters were censored. We got many letters just blotted out.

Which parts, criticism?

It wouldn't be so much criticism as location. It would be suggestions of where they were and what was happening. They'd be giving away military secrets.

Were you surprised that they didn't write more about the actual fighting?

No, I don't think we were really. We were just glad to hear from them that they were alright. They'd probably say they'd been on leave, maybe they'd seen a certain show, and they'd be telling us about that, and they'd be thanking us for parcels. That was one thing: there was always the acknowledgement of parcels, and 'How well the socks fit,' and 'I couldn't have got along without that onion.' We sent all kinds of things overseas—onions wrapped in waxpaper to keep them from spoiling the rest of the parcel, bully beef, any kind of canned stuff that we could get, cakes, fruit cakes, and so on.

Wally Ross

He enlisted when the war broke out, and spent the war building railways in France.

You liked to get letters. We were on the move quite a bit, so sometimes it would be awhile before our mail would catch up to us. We had what they called a 'field card' that you'd just fill in and then shoot off if you knew you weren't going to be able to write for some time, you were on the move. They were little green cards, I forget what was on them. You daren't give out any information, just tell them you're quite well and you'd write them later. They were just to let your family know, to save you writing a letter.

My younger brother was on signal duty out on the line. We got awfully lousy when we were in the army. *(laughs)* They crawl all over you; the lice drop all over the place, you were just lousy with them; they were in the ground. So he was busy writing, and one apparently dropped down. It was crawling along, and he let it crawl on this letter. Then he got the candle and poured the hot wax over it and sealed it there. He sent it away to my mother. *(laughs)* And she kept that thing. Oh, she thought it was a big joke.

Oh, those lice, I'll tell you . . .and rats! Boy, the beggars were that long. I remember one time when we were more or less on rest. It'd been quite a battlefield at one time. We used to go to the gunning place, and they left behind sticks of cordite, what they use for the guns—it looks like wild macaroni—so we used to get bundles of that. We'd light the end of that and stick it down a rat hole and put a bag on it. And it'd go 'poof!' Then you'd see the rats come out, drive them right out. We had a little fox terrier bitch. Oh, she was a marvel! She'd just take off, and as fast as she—now I'm *not* exaggerating—she'd just grab a rat, she'd twist it like that, and in no time at all she'd kill half a dozen. Just one shake and off she'd go. When she saw these bundles of cordite she'd follow you all over the place. *(laughs)* It was fun for her. Then the beggars, oh jeez, I remember them! It just depends where you were. Those were the things—oh, you can laugh about them now, but sometimes it was disagreeable.

When you wrote home, did you mention in detail what you were doing?

No, they'd censor it, you see. I recall I put something in a letter to one of my brothers. They said that they'd cut a piece of it out, I don't know why. It'd been done because we'd been warned that we must not give any clue to our location. I might have done that unconsciously. They were very particular about it.

Did you give disagreeable details in your letters?

No, you didn't. You'd just say it was all right, you didn't grumble at all. As I say, you were younger, and you didn't take these things too serious. You thought, 'It's not worth talking about.' Now, as you get older, you wonder how the dickens you put up with it.

We got papers from London. They were delivered to us on the line. But we didn't get much news. I think the outside world knew more about the war than we did. We were not informed of any detail, we just had a general idea. Half the time you didn't know where the heck you were. We used to get the *Daily Mail* from London. By the time we got it, it was stale news anyway, days and days old. But it was nice to read about all that was happening around us that we didn't know about.

Mrs Jessie Cartwright

In Windsor they had small flags with stars on them. They were a white flag with a red border and red stars. Almost every home had one of these flags in the window. One star, that meant they had one person overseas, two stars . . . and so on. This was a sight really, to go past the streets and see all these little flags hanging in the windows. I never did know whether they had it in any other place. I don't know who started it. But it just sent chills through you when you saw a telegraph boy coming along the street, because you felt, 'Well, this is bad news.' Of course, he stopped at our place. That was a terrible shock to us.

Mr and Mrs McAffrey

Mr McAffrey: The telegram notifying you that your son, your husband was a casualty, that was an experience.

Mrs McAffrey: We were afraid to hear the telephone ring. You see, my three brothers were all over, and the oldest one was killed in May '17. He was married, so the telegram went to his wife in Simcoe, and she had to telephone my mother. And then the other one—we got the news over the telephone because the telegraph people phoned us. But it was a dreadful period. We absolutely were petrified every time the telephone rang.

Mr McAffrey: Then the long lists of casualties in the papers, long, long lists. It was a terrible thing. Now, her brother was wounded at the Somme. They made the French and British attack on the Somme. There were 60,000 casualties in that one brief attack—60,000—terrible. And her brother was one of them.

'...the oldest one was killed in May '17.'

Mrs McAffrey: It wasn't just dreadful, it was scandalous, because they let them be slaughtered just as if human lives didn't mean a thing.

Who were 'they'? Who made the decisions that were going to let that happen? I always heard that the Canadians were a great army in the First World War.

Mr McAffrey: They were, but so were others too. But it was so stupid. Now, my brother was in the airforce, and he described one experience he had. He was at that time an observer, not a pilot. They saw a cavalry regiment lined up below the hill, so they just circled to see what was going to happen. That cavalry regiment was given the order to charge. Up they came, galloping to the hill, and then the machine guns set loose on them. He said they just went down as if a scythe had cut them off. Now, that's the sort of thing that went on. The generals would sit back with their bottle of scotch, miles behind the front, and pin pins in the map, instead of getting up and seeing what their troops were doing. They put them through hell at Passchendaele, for instance, in mud and blood. Terrible.

Of course, *then* these things just weren't said. They talked more about German atrocities and this sort of thing, though, as a matter of fact, the German troops behaved just as well as any. There were things they did, but I could tell you stories of what some of the Canadians did. A chap I knew, his brother was shot. He was asked to take half a dozen German prisoners back, and he started off with them, but he never got to where he was supposed to get. He returned. What happened to the German prisoners nobody ever knew.

Russell Morgan

He came to Canada when he was in his early twenties. He tried twice to enlist but was not accepted, so he worked on the boats, transporting men and horses from Toronto to the camp at Niagara.

Were there any Germans in Toronto at that time?

Oh yeah. I remember one we had on the boat. He used to work with us. He was a German, I knew. He could speak English good. He said he was an interpreter somewhere or other. He told me for the second time I met him. I didn't trust him. 'What are you doing here? There must be all kinds of jobs for you.' But anyway, he didn't stay too long. I don't know how long afterwards, I was going over to Lewiston on the American side, and I seen this guy sitting on the deck looking over, and he had dark glasses on. We was all suspicious of anything like that, and I took a good look at him, and I said, 'Well, I know you.' So I went up to him and I said, 'Ain't you So-and-So?' He said, yes. He took his glasses off and I says, 'Where're you going?' He says, 'To Lewiston.' I said, 'Oh, you're going on the American side, eh?' He said, 'Yeah.' I said, 'Where are you off to, Germany?' (*laughs*) I hit him straight. 'No,' he says, 'no, I'm just going to get a job in America.' I went down to the custom man. We had the American custom man on board to search the baggage. I said, 'There's a German on top,' I said, 'and he's coming over to your country. You want to watch out for him.' He said, 'Who is it?' I said, 'He used to work with us, and I *know* he's a German.' 'Point him out,' he said. 'Let's go up and have a look.' I took him, and he looks through the hatch, just put his head above the hatch and looked, and there he is, still sitting over there. He took a good look, and he said, 'I'll pick him up when he gets off. I'll get the immigration to pick him up.' So that's the last I ever seen of him.

It wasn't too bad here in the First War as far as the Germans. We never seemed to have any trouble with them much, but as I say we was all suspicious when we come in at night. At nine o'clock we used to come back from the second trip from Niagara, Queenston, and Lewiston. Then, we had a bunch of soldiers to go back to Niagara to the camp. That was three trips in a day, and of course it'd be midnight or more before we'd get back to Toronto. But we used to have detectives and stuff down at the dock, and they used to look at everybody that come through the gate to go on board, you know, search them and everything, if they thought there was anything on them. It turned out we had quite a bunch of soldiers on there, and a bomb on there would just about do it!

Howard Ainsworth

Mr Spade, who was German, lived at two or four Jersey Avenue in Toronto. At that time we lived at number fourteen. This happened after supper because I didn't see it happen. I overheard them talking about it. But a whole gang of men come around and got him and took him over, out on Clinton Street—that was only about a couple of hundred of feet away from his house—and they tarred and feathered him. Why I don't know, though he never was in trouble of any kind that I know of. He was a carter, he had a horse and wagon. He worked steady, and he never would drink or anything like that.

Was it people on your street that did it?

No, no, a gang of men from somewhere else, I believe. No, all the people around the neighbourhood there, on the street, they liked Spade very well.

Mrs Margaret Hand

I might tell you another story here about one of our gang, one of the girls—a tall, lovely-looking, slim girl who was very interested in one of our boys, the first boy to go. His name was Norm. Norm was killed—missing, as a matter of fact —about two and a half years after war began. And she somehow or other came in contact with a German internee in Toronto, and she married him. And we *cut her dead!* She just didn't belong to us! I look back on this and I'm so *ashamed* of us, at the age we were.

Did you feel this way about anyone in Toronto who was associating with the Germans?

Absolutely! We *hated* them.

Jim Robertson

His family came from Scotland in 1907 and, after working awhile for a farmer in Woodstock, Ontario, his parents bought their own farm.

Some of the Canadians of German background were our friends. We met them in business, buying animals and so on. And my father and mother were very sociable. Before the war there was always this feeling, '*Will* it happen or *won't* it happen? *Surely* they're not going to attack England. Who would ever *dare?*' It happened then of course—it was like a cold shower. I mean, you were just trembling to think, how far will they go? Well, it didn't make the slightest difference. My father solved the problem by taking the pretty sound attitude, 'Well, they are Canadians now and good farmers.' That was the thing, you see: marvellous farmers. 'And they are our friends. We'll visit them and they'll visit us.' But I think it was a little rough when the government decided that Berlin, Ontario, had to become Kitchener, but I think that may have been a few years later. History telescopes a little bit, but I remember it all so well. I don't think you need to labour the point that they were respectable farmers and decent people and very fine people, very industrious, in spite of what was happening in Europe.

CHAPTER TEN

A WORLD TRANSFORMED

The war had been a violent catalyst, and marked a significant break with traditional values and practices. The return to civilian life and the adjustment of industry and agriculture to a peacetime economy did not constitute a return to 'normalcy'; a whole way of life had been destroyed and the new order that replaced it bore little resemblance to what had gone before. The war ushered in a mass society where taste, style, and feeling became components of a market to be manipulated by new advertising practices. The world of the village, small town, and neighbourhood surrendered whole areas of social control to a vibrant new publicity industry armed with the new technology of the radio. A lost generation which included 60,000 dead and countless thousands maimed and crippled could not re-establish the world they had known. The wives, families, and communities to which they returned were part of a new and very different society.

I.   ARMISTICE

Morty Stein

You'd think this place had gone mad, parading up and down Yonge Street. Everybody was down on Yonge Street crying, cheering, screaming, women crying, men crying too. Scenes that you don't forget because they don't happen that often. It was just simply glorious. Even I went down there. Factories closed, nobody wanted to work that day.

You were celebrating the end of the war or the victory?

No, the end of the war, at least I was. The war ended. Everybody was celebrating the end of the war, not the victory. Sure, they were glad they'd won.

Mrs Margaret Hand

I'll tell you exactly what I did, when it finally happened. I went out to the corner of our street with a friend, and somebody in an automobile picked us up and brought us downtown. By nine o'clock there were no streetcars running in Toronto, it was too crowded. The whole city was out! I think all the talcum

'You'd think this place had gone mad....'

'The city was suddenly a mass of flags.'

powder and toilet paper in Toronto was sold out by—well, I wouldn't say by noon—but the streets were strewn, and they were throwing toilet paper. You got talcum shaken on you out of cans! This was rejoicing! You did anything you could do that was different. The city was suddenly a mass of flags. And that night, I was downtown again with my close friend, and they had taken a cart out of The Ward, a rags-and-bones man's cart out of The Ward, and there was a huge bonfire. I can still see it, with the people circling around it. Everybody talked to everybody. There was lots of noise, all kinds of noisemakers, everything you could get your hands on. It was very exciting!

Mrs Roberta White

I went downtown. I was a married woman, and I was grabbed and kissed a million times that day. It was shocking rather, you know. But everybody was exuberant. You just went crazy.

II. TRANSITION

Robert Swan

He returned to his home in Yarmouth, Nova Scotia, and became an apprentice millworker.

Nearly every man had problems, more or less. Everyone had problems but they varied greatly depending on age and background. Some of the men had had some experience in civilian life before they left, and their problem was merely to take off where they left off. In my case (I was 20 when I left), I could have gone back to the bank where I worked before, but I didn't want that. I wasn't concerned with that and I decided to do something else. I had to make my own plans. I had already thought out a little bit while I was in the army what I was to do. I had an idea in my mind which I followed, and happily it worked out. Now there were other men a little older than myself, 23, 24, who had been in actual civilian life for seven or eight years, and were partly up the ladder. They were going into more established positions. There were others who went back to further their education. I know two or three men who wanted to be lawyers, and they studied for two years and picked up in that profession. Men who came from farming communities, who had parents that were farmers, were going back home and resuming life where they left off. It was a foregone conclusion, that's what they were going to do. There were a far greater number of men who didn't have any definite job, and what's more, they didn't have anything to sell to an employer, didn't have any experience. The army experience was no good for them. They had no job, no experience, so they had to start at the bottom. In certain cases, you had men with families who were reasonably well off, who were able to depend on their friends and relatives for financial assistance for the first two to three years until they got re-established through connections. It was a very mixed crowd and I don't suppose there were any two men who had the same conditions to face.

There were some men who just became what you call old soldiers, old bums. They never did settle down. They hung around, spent all their war gratuities, and they bartered. They just went to pieces—men who had trades and occupations. Now one fellow I knew had been working on the railway and he went right back to the railway; he'd been a fireman on the railway and spent the rest of his life as a local engineer. He didn't have any trouble readjusting. Another chap I know was a remarkably talented man, but he didn't have any ability to handle himself. His father had been a taxidermist and a wood carver, and this boy learned a lot from his father. His father had died while he was away, or shortly after he came home, and he took over his father's shop. But he couldn't manage his money. He would go out with the boys and drink a little too much, and eventually he spent his war gratuities and folded up his business one day and went to New York. The first job he got there was painting the checkers on the taxicabs. He did odd jobs and one thing or another, but he died in New York after a year or two. He went to pieces. I know one man who did quite well in the army. He received quite a degree of promotion, but after he came back he lost control of himself and borrowed from every man he could find, and then he embezzled some money, and the last that I heard of him he was peddling vacuum cleaners from door to door. This man had a good military career, he became a colonel, but he reverted to type. He didn't have it to start with. The army had made him, and when he lost out, he lost out. A great many men did well, and others found it impossible to readjust themselves.

Jeremy Phelps

During the war, he was in the medical corps overseas, and his wife worked in a munitions factory. After the war, he bought a farm through the soldiers' settlement plan.

When I was discharged, I got the soldiers' settlement award, and I had to go and take twelve months' training for farming, because I was getting a farm under the soldiers' settlement scheme. I got through in six months and I got the farm in the Parry Sound district. I put eight years on that farm. You see, they had soldier settlement schemes in Canada for soldiers who came back. Some of them were fully qualified for farming. They didn't have to train. I had farming experience, but not enough to satisfy the settlement board. I tell you, I got through in six months anyway. They paid the farmer for the instruction, you see, and I got my room and board there while I had the instruction. And then they got this farm for me, and it was in a little settlement in Parry Sound district, a little place, a German settlement, Meisenhammer, and it was a good farm too.

Was there any hostility towards you in the community?

They boycotted me from the time we went in there. They thought I was getting something when I got this farm through the settlement. It cost me $400 a year for rent there, you know. I foolishly went into purebred stock and that was a foolish move on my part. They wouldn't patronize me at all. I had some good stuff —poultry, geese, and chickens. We used to send eggs to the local store five miles away from there, and they'd go to try to buy these eggs instead of paying me the price for sitting eggs, you see, to get my stock which I was winning all the prizes in the fair with. They boycotted our raising purebred stock and went about stealing some of the stock. I stayed for eight years and then I lost out. I couldn't carry on, and that was my own foolishness in going so deep into pedigree stock.

Mrs Sally Hill

There was an awful lot of dissatisfaction. The government certainly didn't do justice to the soldiers. For one thing, the soldiers that were taken out west and put on that land around Englehart and up around there (they're called the 'prairies of the west' now, and they're beautiful) went through another war of poverty and hunger and cold, because the government put them out there with practically nothing but an axe, and very little provisions and everything. And they had to struggle from scratch with that new ground. It's a credit to them and their courage and perseverance that so many of them did come through. But that was a very bad thing they did. I remember that. I remember the write-ups there used to be in the paper about the struggles those poor boys had out there: no water sometimes for miles, and nothing. Putting the returned soldiers on that absolutely virgin territory, with no arrangements made for provisions, for health, for care in the winter, not giving them even so much as a piece of lumber to make a house out of, just to build it out of sod—nobody but the people that went through it will ever know what that was and what it meant—that was the worst thing, I think, the Canadian government ever did to their returned soldiers!

Larry Nelson

To return to a job behind a desk or a job behind a counter after two or three or four or more years of military life was something that most of the lads just dreaded, unless they were married. If they were married it would be different thing; they had responsibilities and so on. But for those who were not married, they'd had a taste of adventure, and they'd had a taste of travel and a taste of excitement, living without too much restraint. When you put a man in uniform, and he's with a couple of hundred thousand men who are dressed exactly the same as he is, you submerge the personality in the mass. You don't feel that you have any special responsibility, and you lose your identity to some extent, so that your conduct, your morals, and everything else are not what you . . .*(breaks off)* People at home would be rather shocked. But most of us came through that stage, but there's no gainsaying it: it's the truth just the same.

I think as far as the CF man was concerned, he returned and accepted his responsibilities magnificently after this period of restlessness. There was just very small percentage of them who were never able to make the adjustment. They were probably always rebels and never would have been any good anyway. I drank quite a lot in the army but drink was never a problem to me after I came out, and I don't think it was to most fellas. If a chap was well-born, and by that I mean, if he came from good stock in the first place, I don't think very many of them succumbed to the temptations of army life.

Some men never got over their war years. They still lived them—they still do live them now. It was the greatest thing in their life. Others were anxious to throw it off and get back to their way of life and get married and get a good job—that's the main thing—and forget about it. I think perhaps that represents about 90% of the troops. But there are men whose whole life was bound up with the four, four-and-a-half years in the army. It all depends, I suppose, on your background. One particular chap I have in mind—he's really quite a wonderful chap, too—he was a clerk before the war, he was a clerk after the war. He had a clerical state of mind. Out of these years of background of routine nine-to-five business, there's four-and-a-half years that stand out, that were entirely different. But to the rest of us who had a more mixed background, it wasn't like that.

Robert Franklin

He got six months' pay when he was discharged, after serving in the army for three years. He went back to high school in Toronto to get his senior matriculation.

I was tempted to continue on as a soldier. I darn near went to India with the British Army. They wanted volunteers to go to India. I thought about it for a long time before I finally gave it up, which I'm glad now that I did, after having seen people who did go there. Oh, I had no great love for the army, nor I didn't have much against it. I had a lot of good friends; I hated to leave the army, the crowd. It was the crowd I was with, the comradeship, excellent comradeship. I felt awful lonesome leaving it when I got out of the army. I was just as lonesome as could be, because for so long you had always been with the gang, day and night. Come what may, bad or good, you always had your gang around you.

Richard Mills

I felt like a fish out of water. I had civilian clothes: I was used to tight clothes, and civilian clothes seemed so loose. I just felt like a fish out of water. Nearly four years in the army *(he muses)* . . .you feel strange. I had to go to the hospital for an operation, so I was home for two weeks, then I went to London, Ontario for this operation, for something that had developed during the war. I felt really at home, like back in the barracks again, with some of us soldiers there. It was something I was used to.

The civilians seemed to be different, y'know. They insisted that I tell them all about the exploits and this and that, and I didn't want to talk about it. They didn't talk like the soldiers I'd been talking to and living with all year. The neighbours and family friends bugged me about all this. Y'know, it's just a different world, I mean the war world. In the army and the civilian, it's just two different worlds. The best thing I ever did was go to university when I came back, because that was just the best place to adjust back to civilian life. I lived in

North House at the University of Toronto, and half the fellows there were returned men. It was a wonderful place to adjust to civilian life.

Keith Fallis

During the years when I was at university I tried to unfreeze a bit. I used to resent seeing so many luxurious dances in big hotels and so on. I felt these people have all this wealth because they made money out of the war, and they don't know what we went through. I was very influenced by a poem that Alfred Noyes wrote on that question. I can't quote it now, but something about ladies all dressed up in their finery, big fat bodies dancing around, unaware of the sorrows and the tragedies of life. I did cultivate an idealistic belief in the idea that the war had made the world safe for democracy, and I got an oratorical prize or a gold medal or something for a speech on the League of Nations. I remember Salem Bland complimenting me on it—I think he was one of the judges—it had certain 'purple patches' as he called them, such as 'the League of Nations can be the Magna Carta of weak, unprotected countries'—which we hoped. I never unfroze fully. The horror of the war was in the background of my mind, although it was suppressed. Although I praised it as something that had made the world safe for democracy, there was always this inner tension. I never faced it clearly. I was tempted sometimes simply to jump over into the pacifist position, you know, and say, 'War's wrong and I'll never have anything more to do with it,' as many did. On the other hand, I had also an idea of history that that position was too simple.

I'm speaking more from hindsight. At the time I wasn't so clearly aware that I was suppressing these things. One sign of my basic inner discontent was, I was in a special course, an honour course in English, history and philosophy. They tried to combine the three, made it a very heavy course. I reacted almost completely negatively to the philosophy. I felt it was a lot of ratty ostentation on the part of intellectuals who were speculating in pure air, as it were. I remember a couple of books that influenced me towards the end. One was called *Fobbing* and the other was called, I think, *The Slaughterhouse of Philosophy*, in which he said philosophy can't make any claim to be a scientific study because every new philosopher that comes along begins by demolishing all the others. He says that no science does that; they build on what has been found and reject it, and then go on. I had a lot of sympathy with that, with the result that I never did very well in philosophy.

Ben Wagner

Did you talk much about the war with your family after you returned?

I talked about it a lot but in general terms. When you got home, you realized that you were talking about one thing and these people hadn't the basis to understand it. You could go across the road and talk to an old sweat, as we used to call him—an old soldier—and you talked like that. But the families were interested. I remember one case, there was a group of people asking me some questions about the war, and I made this remark: 'I was despatch riding, and I was going to such-and-such a place; it was late at night, so they put me to sleep in their best cow stable.' One of the women was horrified! 'You slept in the cow stable?' I was damn glad to have a roof over my head! Hell, I slept in more cow stables than I did in the house. That was just the viewpoint, they didn't realize these things. They tried to understand, but you gradually got to the point where you only talked about the war with the old sweats.

Dan Vernon

Born in 1895, he grew up on a farm in the Ottawa Valley. The war completely changed his perspective on life, and he felt quite alienated when he returned. He went to university to become a chemical engineer.

I returned to my old world. At that time I was quite alien to it. As a matter of fact, to my astonishment and sorrow, the first thing that my father said to me was, 'You smell of cigarette smoke.' That pierced me. Now I know it was said most kindly. It was said from his heart, it was a wail of woe. As far as he was concerned, here was his white-haired boy come back from the war, and he's smoking tobacco. I did smell of tobacco. I threw my pipe out of the window as we were approaching Ottawa.

Neil Haiste

It was the law that if you left a job and went and enlisted, the boss had to give you your job back when you came out of the army. But that was alright: they could hire you today and fire you next week. That happened in lots of cases where they didn't want you or couldn't afford to keep you. You had to get your old job back, but they didn't say how long you had to keep it.

George Davis

He was 21 when he enlisted, and he was given an indefinite leave of absence from his job with the Toronto Electric Light.

I remembered that I'd been wished good luck at the beginning of the war. The general manager had even said to me, 'Well, George, when you get back, you want a job, you come and see us. It'll be waiting for you.' So, having nothing to do immediately and certainly not having progressed in my experience in business (though I'd certainly learned a lot of other things), I went in to see him. He greeted my warmly, and he said, 'What are you doing? What are your plans?' I said, 'That's what I've come to see you about, sir.' 'Oh, you want a job here?' I said yes. He said, 'Well, I know we promised you one.' (This is the Toronto Electric Light Company.) 'You probably know we are in the midst of handing over to a government-owned body. The Toronto Hydroelectric System has been formed, and they are taking over our business as the TTC is taking over the Toronto Street Railway's business. So we are rather cutting down the staff because the Hydro is taking over our customers. However, there is certainly a job for you.' I said, 'How much will it be, sir?' And he said, 'What were we paying you when you enlisted?' 'Seventy-five dollars a month, sir.' 'Ah well, we'll pay you $75 a month.' I said, 'Just a minute, sir, $75 a month now isn't worth more than $37.50 in buying power. Furthermore I am now married. Now that's not your worry, that's mine, but you are offering me a job at roughly half what you paid me before.' He said, 'I know.' That's *all* he knew about it! 'But you won't be staying here long. You can do a lot better than what we can do for you, but if you want to take it for the time being, you can have all the time off you want to follow up leads, and I'll do what I can.' So I took it up. Seventy-five dollars a month, ha! Peanuts! Though I started as low as four dollars a week. However, it didn't take me long to get a better job as an accountant with a glass manufacturer, and I prospered.

Mark Tanner

I remember after the First World War, I was working for Klute, Peabody & Co., and the president was a very loyal Canadian. Like others at that time, he thought that if you went overseas, why, you were a great patriot and should be looked after. Not too many, certainly not all, of the industrial leaders took that attitude. He met me at the train in Montreal, coming back to Toronto, and shook hands with me and said he was proud of me *(laughs)*, patted me on the back, and he said, 'You're on the payroll as of today. Take a month's holiday, or as long as you like, to get back into shape, and then come down, and we've got a job for you.' He put me out as a salesman. I travelled selling Arrow shirts in eastern Ontario for about a year, and then they transferred me to Winnipeg and I went west.

I was a good Conservative then. I thought the Union Government and the Conservative Party were the winners of the war and the saviours of the British Empire and the country. *(laughs)* It was soon after the Winnipeg General Strike, and the city was divided between those who supported the strikers and those who were opposed, and you couldn't help but get involved in the divisions that existed across the whole city. Listening to Mr Woodsworth, who was there at that time, and some of the labour leaders—there were some really great men in Winnipeg—I began to think maybe I was in the wrong party. *(laughs)* I quickly changed—oh, not quickly, it was over the course of a year or two.

Bruce Cole

The years 1919 and 1920 were good years, so I would think soldiers wouldn't have any difficulty getting work. It was in 1921 that a levelling off took place, and then they would have been in the same position as others. Now what happens then from 1921 to 1925: there was quite a letdown and organizations sprang up against ethnic elements, particularly against Hindus in British Columbia and Greeks in Toronto. Restaurants were smashed. The soldiers that came back and the Anglo-Saxons generally took the attitude that they couldn't find work because of these ethnic groups. In British Columbia there was an organization called the Anti-Asiatic Exclusion League, and in Toronto, if you look back in the newspapers of those days, you would see that there were riots. There were restaurants smashed and other places broken into, on the claim that these foreigners were taking away jobs.

Were these attacks ever directed against Jews?

No, not as such. I don't think that the Jews at that time occupied the place in business that they do today. They were mostly needle trades workers, they were working in factories. But these others: now in British Columbia, the Asiatics (so-called) were prospering farmers, had beautiful farms; here the Greeks had restaurants, had businesses. It was the businesses that were attacked more than the individuals in employment.

Do you think the returned soldiers played a prominent part in these attacks?

I think so, because they had the voice; they had the voice because they had served in the army.

Edward Thompson

A Scot, he was in the British army during the war. He heard glowing tales of Canada from the Canadians overseas, and after the war was sent to Montreal by the British overseas settlement department. He went on to Toronto when he discovered that he would be strikebreaking in Montreal.

I found that when I came to Canada there was an opportunity for a footing. When you went for a job in the Old Country, you went with your hat in your hand, and you sat down, and you had kneepants on and a celluloid collar and a little bowtie on it, and you said, 'Good morning, sir,' 'Yes, sir,' 'No, sir.' When you got a job over there, you were on a permanent basis, more or less, but when you came here it was different. You'd go and you'd tap on the door and some voice would say, 'What the hell do you want?' 'I'm looking for a job.' 'What can you do?' 'So-and-so and so-and-so.' 'Yeah, you can start tomorrow if you like, 50 cents an hour.' Things like that, you know. It was a different kind of a world, a more abrupt kind of a world to come into, and to get used to the changes was kinda hard at the beginning because you were so used to saying certain words, you know.

In Toronto, when you went for a job, you would go down Eastern Avenue and places like that, and they would have signs on the fence: 'No Englishman Need Apply'—this is true—because of the foreign element that were coming in from overseas and things like that. They were picking and choosing the people they were using.

Why didn't they want Englishmen in particular?

Because the others would work for less money. You see, they didn't understand. We'd been fighting to make the world a better place in which to live, and these people were coming here, much the same as they are today, and doing things that they shouldn't...

Undercutting the wages?

Yes.

When you arrived in Toronto were you able to get a job at your trade?

It wasn't too long, no more than eighteen to 24 hours when I got a job at Thompson-Norris, which was a paper-making place out on Jones Avenue. I stayed with them for about a year, and then I got back to the printing industry with *Saturday Night* Press. That was quite an organization. It was run by a lady, but the owner was a Mr Gagné from Quebec. I was reluctant to work for somebody from Quebec after my experience when I first landed in the country—there was a strike on and they were going to employ me as an immigrant and put it over me like that—but I worked there for quite a number of years, until we had a strike. When the strike came, I was put on picket duty outside my own plant. We didn't have a good official in charge of our organization, and he decamped with whatever little money we had. With the outcome that when the boys did return to work, I was one of those that didn't get a job. So I went out west. This was about '21, '22.

Now you could go out west those days on what they called a Harvester Special. This cost you twelve dollars down at the Union Station, and it took you to Winnipeg. At Winnipeg you had to pay another so much a mile, I just forget how much it was, but it was very small. You got on what you might term a local train. It took us about six or seven days to get to Winnipeg from here on these Colonial trains. We used to stop on sidings to let the good trains go by, and we would play baseball and look at stones, to see if we could come up with some gold and stuff on the sidings. When we got to Winnipeg, it was very difficult. There was no hostels or things like they have today. So I just moved from one platform to the other. I think I only paid two dollars to take me to Brandon, in Manitoba. I got to a place called Bagot, it was just outside of Portage La Prairie. There were farmers at the railroad crossing, and the train slowed down, and they were shouting out, 'Five dollars a day, anybody who can drive horses.' Well, being in the army and being on the lead on the gun carriage, and stuff like that, I thought to myself, 'Oh, that'd be up my alley. I can manage this and I'll know about farming.' But I didn't know too much about farming, I found out after I got there, and I didn't get my five dollars a day either.

The man's name was Mr Shore. He was quite an individual, very nice. He had a family of about four, and they all worked on the farm. They had me up at four o'clock in the morning. You had to go out and bring in the cows from the fields and they were milked. While they were doing the milking—the children and the man and his wife—I would have to go and let out the hens and the pigs and water the horses and take them back in and put the harness on. By this time it would be about seven o'clock, and we would go in for breakfast. Breakfast would be pie and meat and everything—things that you didn't look for, not until suppertime at night. And then you would go out and hitch up these horses and so forth.

What did they actually pay you?

Well, I don't know what he paid me, but the man was aged and he wanted to go and live in Winnipeg. He wanted to retire. He thought that I was one of the better men that he'd ever had out there on the Harvest Special, and he wanted me to stay and operate the farm. I forget how many acres it was; he had 640 acres on the one lot and I don't know how many acres he had on the other. He thought I'd be a good man to take it over and share the cost. Well, I was more or less prepared to do this. But one day, it was in the month of October, back end of October. Ploughing was going on well, and I could hear cows and sheep away in the distance. And I found myself sitting on the plough there rolling cigarettes and answering the cows and the sheep back, 'Baa to you' and 'Moo to you.' Then I was down at the store one night and I was listening to the stories of how many farmers were in Brandon in a mental thing—they go mental. I thinks to myself, 'Eddie, you should feel your way back east.' So I went back home that night, and I said to Mr Shore, 'Mr Shore, I gotta go back east. I have friends there, they're in difficulty.' He knew that I was lying because I never got a letter. So he said to me, 'No, you *want* to go back east. You don't like this country, do you?' 'Well,' I said, 'I like the country but I don't like it out here. I'm answering the sheep and the cows back. I gotta get back.' So he said, 'I can't let you back for probably two weeks. I gotta sell a couple of calves to pay you.' So he sold a calf and he give me about $150 for about eight months' work *(laughs).* That was five dollars a day! But he told me that I was one of the family, fed me well and looked after me. I was better fed than the majority of them. He was sorry to see me go and all this kind of stuff. So I came back here and I went back to the trade again.

III.   THE TWENTIES

Mr and Mrs McAffrey

They lived in Peterborough. He taught at the normal school, and she didn't work after their marriage in 1918. They discuss the roaring twenties.

Mr McAffrey: Oh, that was the wild time! Right along towards 1920 and so on, that was when futurist art began, the Dali type of thing. Well, I call it a retreat from reason. Old Ruskin, you know, was highly rational. This outbreak of irrationality—everybody was so repressed through the war that we all just went nuts.

Mrs McAffrey: Oh, yes, all kinds of crazy dances and crazy clothes. That was the Flapper Age. You used to go down the street with your galoshes flapping open. That was where the 'flapper' came from.

Mr McAffrey: Well, the term came from the bird that's out of the cage and flapping but can't yet fly. *(laughs)* But it came to mean a girl that was pretty reckless.

Mrs McAffrey: They flapped their galoshes anyway.*(laughs)*

But that craziness was directly related to how grim things had been during the war?

Mr McAffrey: Yes. There was discussion of experiments with trial marriage and all sorts of things that they're talking about now, you see. It was somewhat the same. The boys had met people from other lands over there, and they came back much more broad-minded than they were when they went over.

Dr Martha Davidson

Trained as a home economist, she worked for Farmers Magazine *and for the provincial Department of Agriculture, and was very active in the Women's Institutes. She never married.*

One way that it affected my life, like the lives of all girls at that time was that in almost no time at all, practically all the boys that you went to college with had joined up and were away. As you know, the slaughter in that war was beyond anything. Someone has said they took spring out of the world, and they expected the other seasons to behave as usual. And that was one of the things that at that age naturally affected me.

Were some of your good friends killed overseas?

Oh, yes, and some were invalided home in a way that made it that they couldn't do what they otherwise would have done. You've taken so many of the young people out, and then peace comes and everyone's hilarious because the war is over. A generation just a bit older gets into doing the things that youth might have done. The people that had never danced before all went wild over it. They started trying to be smart, you know, with their hip flasks and that sort of thing. There was quite a lot of irresponsible living that followed the war.

Jake Foran

He was in high school during the war, and helped out on the family farm in southern Ontario. He became a teacher.

I say that after every war there's a letdown in morals and conduct and dress. It started with the women. Women started wearing shorter skirts. When we were kids, the skirts were right down to the floor, to the ankles, sometimes sweeping the floor. So they came up to the ankles, the calves, and eventually the miniskirt. So in dress, there was a great laxity, permissiveness, in the twenties.

There certainly was a lot of bootlegging because of prohibition. The bootleggers sprung up everywhere and business was still good. During the rehabilitation period there was lots of work. Fellas had money, and they had a hip flask full of liquor almost every time we went to a dance. That was quite daring. Oh, the Roaring Twenties were really wild.

Then they got cars. They'd buy these little old roadsters with rumble seats. Yes, I remember a lot of that. Oh boy, they did a lot in those cars, cruising around the back roads in the country. Maybe I'm exaggerating, but there was a lot of horseplay, immorality, I might say. The girls were more free, permissive, the men more daring. They'd just come back from the war, some of them, and they said, 'What's all this? What's the use?' Life had changed so much. Smoking!—The girls would start smoking. Oh, that was terrible! I was in a school, and a girl was hired, the first time I ever knew one with bobbed hair. You know, when we were kids the hair was always done up; it was unheard-of for a girl to cut her hair off. But I have pictures of the first girls I ever saw with bobbed hair. That was considered wicked almost, bobbing one's hair. The older people thought the world was going straight to hell because they bobbed their hair and shortened their skirts.

Did you yourself take part in this craziness?

Yes, I'd been at dances with a bottle on the hip, and a lot of this crazy touring around. I had a car by that time. Actually, do you know what kept me down a little bit? Teaching. The teacher had to be sort of respectable. A lot of my friends would go off on wild parties that I wouldn't even go to because I had a reputation to stick to straight living.

I think the war at least accelerated the speed of change, but they probably would have happened anyway. I think women would have got tired of long dresses sweeping the floor, whether the war had been on or not. But, oh, the war certainly loosened things up. From a religious standpoint, they loosened up a lot and did things they would never have done before the war. They'd be disgraced before the war if they came home drunk from the dance or something. And I'm not saying there was much of that real drunkenness, but there was an awful lot of drinking in the twenties—in the Roaring Twenties.

Mrs Jane Walters

The twenties weren't so much horribly immoral twenties with sexual vice as they were the Roaring Twenties. Excitement and high spirits, and of course, there was the other too, of course there was. I didn't see so much of it—I was busy bringing up my babies.

Do you think the Roaring Twenties had any connection to the war?

Yes I do think so. It was a relief and it was an excuse for people to have licence. And they sure had it.

A relief from what?

From the war, the tension, and the sorrow. It was a relief and it was an excuse. It was a reason when a whole lot of people, I suppose, just went haywire. The Roaring Twenties perhaps had no reason to it because it was in the air. And the clothes! They were hard to take. Do you know, there was a time at that stage when they wore dresses absolutely straight and flat across here, and some of them used to bind their bosoms to get into these dresses! I had a singer's body and believe me, I had a big bosom, and I had the most awful time getting dresses—all girls did. We just went through that stage of flat bosoms. It was a bad time. You can't buck nature and not get some bad results from it.

There were a lot of fine people in the Roaring Twenties. But most of us settled down to business, getting our homes together and paying for them and bringing up our babies. Most of the girls my age were married and had one baby by then.

IV. REFLECTIONS

Michael Halton

I think that during the First World War, and certainly after it, it was an accepted fact that it was an imperialist war, that the working class had gained nothing from it and couldn't gain anything. Between the First World War and the Second World War the socialist movement was completely anti-war. I can't remember anybody in the Socialist Party debating whether it was just. There was complete agreement that it was a capitalist war for trade and profit. The only thing the workers did was die in it.

Bill Boyd

There's a lot of memories, good and bad. If I was younger, I wouldn't want to go through the same experience again. There are a lot of things I wouldn't want to do that I *had* to do at that time. I won't say it bothered me, but it had an effect on me. In my own case, I was there to do a job, and so you had to do it. You were trained for it. Some people get adjusted, some don't so quick. They go and take young people like us, and they put them in and what did they do? They train you to kill. You get that training for years, and then the war finishes, and they expect you to forget it right away. And if sometime in certain conditions, you get into violence, say, and you react the same way as they've been teaching you, well, anything could happen because you've been taught that. You're taught to fight dirty, to survive, so anything goes. Then when something like that happens, then the person is hardly responsible. Some people can control it, and other people can't control it so easy. It's hard to understand, isn't it? But when you're trained for years to do certain things, then in a breakdown or something, they don't take into consideration the training they've been giving you.

Dan Vernon

My life is divided into three eras: before the war, during the war, and after the war.

Ralph Sharpe

The army straightened me out, you know. Because I couldn't keep a job no time when I was first married. Used to say a lot of them didn't suit me. 'That's it, good day, and goodbye.' But now when I come out of the army, I done 37 years one month on the TTC. And I'm eighteen years on pension now. So figure it out!

Mrs Elaine Nelson

I think it was a good start for young people in marriage if the boy had been overseas and the girl had been doing her share, because you had a lot of things to talk about. And as you talked about them the boy knew that the girl had been carrying her weight at this end, while he was struggling along at the other end. She got a much greater sense of responsibility; she learned how to be economical and took an interest for the first time in cooking and that kind of thing.

I was very much at a disadvantage in that way; my mother had never done anything. I know one time Eaton's sent up whitefish, and they have scales. I thought, 'Oh dear, what a nuisance. We'll have to throw it out.' I said, 'Well, no, some people know how to clean it. I'll try and see if I can.' So I put my finger in and found that the scales ruffled up, and I got a knife. I had scales on the ceiling, on the walls, on the floor, in my hair, everywhere. But I cooked the fish and we ate it. Mother wasn't very happy; she felt I shouldn't have tried to do that. I wasn't supposed to do that. I didn't like that, I wanted to know.

Another time I had a brand new dress. I had to wash it and I didn't know how to starch things. I made this starch—I knew you made it with boiling water—and I put the dress in. I stirred it up and then hung it up. It stood up by itself when it was dry. And Mum said, 'It serves you right. It's just the *plebian* in your father coming out.' *(laughs)* But she said, 'I've never heard of anybody who could be *proud* of washing floors. How *low* can your sights be?' I was a good Canadian and Mother never became one, she just couldn't. When I was travelling years after I realized why: they just don't think; everything can fall around their ears, and they just don't do anything. But anyway, it was all a good school of experience for young people. Some measured up, and some didn't. If they hadn't measured up, had fallen by the wayside in the war, they would have fallen by the wayside somewhere else. So you can't say the war ruined them, they weren't ready to put their sights high enough, to build the kind of a life they wanted.

Craig Pritchard

The effect that the war had on our manner of living; it was the beginning of the end of what I call church life. With the outbreak of war, munitions factories sprung up, and the women started to work in munitions factories. There was no limit to what they could make, we were so hungry for munitions. There was an article in the newspaper at that time which was called 'The Passing of the Sunday Suit.' Up to that time, everybody had their Sunday suit. They wore it on Sunday, then they put it away, and they didn't wear it till the next Sunday. Well, people that had money, they didn't have to do it any more. So that was the end of the Sunday suit, and it was also as I say, the end of people going to church twice on Sunday. This was the beginning of the end.

Why was that?

Up to that time, the father of the home was followed. Now the fathers had gone overseas, you see, because there was a period of unemployment at that time. And the women were going into the factories. They were married women, they got government money, and they had all the money that they needed. So it came into that period of time when everybody was what we say now, 'doing their own thing.' That's when it all started.

Mrs Margaret Hand

It was the First War that shot religion high, wide, and handsome, as far as a great many of us were concerned. We just lost faith in it. I mean, after all, you could pray your head off, but it didn't mean you were going to have your men come home to you. Oh, a great many people stopped going to church. I think most of the people who came home from the war stopped going to church. This was the beginning of what's happened to the churches of Toronto.

It must have upset the older generation.

Yes, it did, but there wasn't anything they could do about it. And I think they themselves must have begun to do a lot of questioning. Because some people who thought God was on our side—well, of course that was such nonsense! God's not on anybody's side in a war.

Mrs Roberta White

So many of the boys were sacrificed in that war—of course, the Germans were too, we know that—that my chances of having another husband were just not there. I was lucky to even have one husband. Hundreds and hundreds of women my age and a bit older never did get married, never had the opportunity to be married, because the loss was so bad. It's what they called the 'lost generation.' And it certainly was.

BIOGRAPHIES

Howard Ainsworth

Born in 1906 on Laplante Avenue in Toronto, he has childhood memories of the war years.

David Allan

Born in 1895 in Surrey, England, in 1912 he was reunited with his mother and father in Toronto where they had emigrated in 1910. He enlisted in 1915.

Christopher Arnold

A black Canadian, he was born in Woodstock, Ontario in 1894 and he worked in the Woodstock Wagon Works and the Thomas Organ and Piano Factory before attending high school and business college. He enlisted in late 1915.

Les Beauchamp

Born in 1906 in London, England, he and his family emigrated to Toronto in 1912.

Sam Beckman

Born in 1887 in the Ukraine to parents who were Jewish farmers, he came to Canada in 1908 to join his uncle who was working as a cabinet maker in Toronto. He worked as a tailor and was active in the Communist Party of Canada in its earliest days.

Frank Bell

Born and raised in Lancaster, Ontario in 1901, he enlisted in the spring of 1916, but was rejected when his age was discovered. He then worked as an electrical apprentice in Montreal.

Alexander Boulton

He was born into a farm family in Napanee, Ontario in 1905.

Bill Boyd

Born in Tiltcave, Newfoundland in 1897, he worked as a deliveryman and then in a furniture company in Toronto before enlisting in 1915.

Scott Brooks

Born in Winnipeg in 1901, he moved with his parents to Toronto two years later. He graduated from University of Toronto School in 1917 and got a job

218

with W.J. Gage, where his father worked as an editor.

Mrs Lorna Browning

Born in Toronto in 1888, she grew up in London, Ontario. She attended Albert College and taught school outside of Arden, Ontario after graduating. She married a storekeeper in 1913, and helped him run his Methodist Sunday School during the war.

Jack Burton

Born in 1901 in New Brunswick, he attended business college in Fredericton in 1916 and 1917.

Mrs Ethel Cameron

Born in Meaford, Ontario in 1899, she worked in a blanket mill during the war.

Mrs Jessie Cartwright

Born near London, England in 1890, she came to Windsor, Ontario in 1911. She then worked for the Salvation Army and was in Winnipeg when war was declared. She also lived in British Columbia during the war.

Charles Casey

Born in 1895 in Limerick, Ireland, he came to Canada in 1912 and worked first as a salesman in Ottawa. He then worked for Burroughs' Adding Machine Company until his enlistment in 1915.

Mrs Melissa Charlewood

Born on a farm outside Kingston, Ontario in 1885, she worked as a stenographer in Kingston and worked in Montreal during the war.

Martin Colby

Born in Toronto in 1896, the son of an Anglo-Irish fireman, he grew up in the Bathurst-Dundas area of Toronto and worked as a driver for breweries.

Bruce Cole

He was born in 1900 in London, England to Jewish parents who had left Poland. His parents came to Toronto shortly after his birth and lived first in the Ward (Elizabeth, Adelaide and Edward Streets) and then moved to the west end in 1907. He followed his father into the Toronto needle trades.

Dr Martha Davidson

Born in Campbellville, Ontario in 1888, she was educated as a home economist at the Macdonald Institute (Guelph). Actively involved in the Women's Institute movement, she served as the editor of the women's section of the *Farmer's Magazine* from 1913 until 1922. She was the author of five books. She died in August, 1976.

George Davis

Born of well-established English parents in Toronto in 1893, he worked as a clerk for the Toronto Electric Light Company before enlisting in 1914.

Andrew Douglas

Born in Scotland in 1892, he came to Toronto in 1910. He worked first for Eaton's and then Tamblyn's before enlisting on the day war was declared.

Albert Dugan

Born in Thunderland, Ontario in 1896, he worked as a farm labourer before enlisting.

Mrs Edna Dupont

Born about 1889, the daughter of an established Toronto family, she attended the University of Toronto. During the war she went into occupational therapy and helped veterans readjust to civilian life.

Mrs Agnes Fairbanks

Born on Spadina Avenue in Toronto in 1892, the daughter of a Toronto real estate man, she attended university and was married in 1916.

Keith Fallis

Born in 1898 in China, the son of a Methodist missionary, he and his family moved to Toronto in 1910, and he enlisted in 1917.

John Fisher

Born in Kent, England in 1890, he came to Canada in 1910 and worked for Simpson's and the Imperial Bank of Commerce in Toronto during the war.

Robert Franklin

Born in Huron County, Ontario in 1898, he grew up in a farming community before enlisting in 1916.

Mrs Helen Gloucester

Born in Wales in 1890, she came to Toronto in 1911 with her husband.

Neil Haiste

Born in 1892 in Sussex, England, he came to Canada in 1910 under the auspices of the Agriculture Society of Canada. He worked on a farm, in a canning factory, and in the Collingwood Shipyards before enlisting.

Mrs Jill Halpenny

Born in Yorkshire, England in 1890, she worked in a mill before coming to Toronto in 1910. She worked at Eaton's until her marriage in 1922.

Michael Halton

Born in Toronto in 1902, he was the son of a teamster. He attended school during the war.

Mrs Margaret Hand

Born in 1897 in Toronto, she attended Jarvis Collegiate from 1914 to 1915, and went to Shaw's Business College. She worked as a stenographer, mostly for the Department of Soldier's Civil Reenlistment in Toronto. She was married in 1922.

Tom Held

Born in Wentworth County, Ontario in 1898, he taught for a year before enlisting in 1914.

Mrs Sally Hill

Born in 1898 in Alliston, Ontario, she married her husband in 1916 just before he went overseas.

Abraham Kuznetz

Born a Russian Jew in 1893, he came to Canada in 1913 and worked as a storekeeper in the West.

Wilfred Lamant

Born in Norwich, England in 1889, he came to Canada in 1912 as a farm labourer. He then moved to Toronto, and worked as a clerk for the William Inglis Company before enlisting in 1916.

Frank Lloyd

Born in Lancashire, England in 1894, he emigrated to Canada in 1913 and worked as a fisherman and then as a machinist in Toronto. He enlisted in 1915.

Duncan MacGregor

Born in Woodstock, Ontario in 1895, he came to Toronto in 1910. A captain of the Jarvis Collegiate cadet corps in 1914, he enlisted in 1915.

Allan MacTavish

Born into a farming family in Oxford County, Ontario, he became a lawyer in 1914 and enlisted at the end of 1915.

Patrick Malone

Born in Dublin, Ireland in 1893, he came to Canada in 1911. He worked as a farm labourer and a factory hand before enlisting in 1914.

Donald McAffrey

Born in St. Thomas, Ontario in 1889, he received his M.A. from Queen's University and taught school in Toronto during the war. He met and married his wife in 1918.

Mrs Sally McAffrey

Born in Woodstock, Ontario in 1889, she worked as a stenographer at the *Daily Woodstock Sentinel Review* in 1910 and was its society editor by 1916 when she left. From 1916 until her marriage, she worked as a stenographer in a Toronto factory.

Mrs Judith McKay

Born in Victoria Harbour in 1900, the daughter of a Methodist minister, she moved with her family to Burke's Falls, Rocklin, East Toronto, Powassen, and North Bay before her father left the ministry in 1912. She worked as a secretary during the war years.

Mrs Miriam McLeish

Born in Beaverton, Ontario in 1894, the daughter of a CNR foreman, she worked in a munitions plant in Lindsay during the war.

Richard Mills

Born on a farm near Petrolia, Ontario in 1896, he taught school in the West before enlisting and going overseas in 1916.

Jake Moran

Born in Wingham, Ontario in 1899, he was the youngest child in a farming family of ten.

Russell Morgan

Born in England in 1890, he emigrated to Canada in 1912 and worked on a farm near Cobden, Ontario. He then worked on the Toronto docks. He tried to enlist twice in 1914, but was refused both times because of the glut of recruits. He remained on the docks and married in 1917.

Bruce Murchison

Born in 1893 in Toronto, he attended the Broadview Boys' Institute and university before enlisting in 1915.

Mrs Elaine Nelson

Born in Parry Sound, Ontario in 1896 of Dutch-English parentage, she was singing in New York when the war broke out. She returned to Toronto and worked first as a Red Cross volunteer and then in a munitions factory.

Larry Nelson

Born in Orangeville, Ontario in 1893, he grew up in a middle class neighbourhood in Toronto. He enlisted in 1914.

Alfred Nevin

Born in 1898 on a farm near Bond Head, Ontario, he lived on the farm until his enlistment.

Mrs Brenda Parsons

Born in 1885 in St. John's, Newfoundland into an established family, she married in 1909 and moved to Toronto. She and her husband ran a farm until 1921, when he went into the tea business.

Mrs Maria Pawel

Born in 1897 in the Ukraine, she came to Saskatoon in 1911 with her mother to join her father, who had emigrated in 1907. She grew up in the Ukrainian section of Saskatoon, working in restaurants and hotels to help support the family.

Jeremy Phelps

He was born in 1884 in England where his mother was a dressmaker and his father was a shoemaker. He worked in various factories before coming to Toronto in 1910, where he worked for the St. John's Ambulance as a first-aid instructor.

Mrs Anita Phillips

Born in St. Andrews, Scotland in 1890, she came to Canada in 1911. Trained as a nurse in New York, she returned to serve in a Canadian hospital in Kent, England during the war. She also served in France.

Craig Pritchard

Born in 1892 in England, he migrated to Detroit, Michigan in 1910, and worked in the auto industry there. He came north to Canada to enlist in 1914.

Bert Remington

Born in Manchester, England in 1895, he came to Montreal in 1910. He got a job with Bell Telephone in 1912 and enlisted in 1914.

Barry Richardson

Born in Montreal in 1895, he lived in Westmount, Outremont, and Maisonneuve. In 1915 he got a job at the Canadian Vickers Shipbuilding Yards.

Charles Riddell

Born in Kearney in the Parry Sound District in 1889, he worked in the lumber camps until his enlistment in 1915.

Jim Robertson

Born in Edinburgh, Scotland in 1904, he came to Woodstock, Ontario with his parents in 1907. His father became a farmer there.

Eric Rosen

Born in 1897 in London, England, he came to Trenton in 1909. He moved to Toronto in 1914 and worked at Dunlop before enlisting in 1915.

Mrs Doris Rosenberg

A Rumanian Jew born in 1896, she emigrated to Montreal in 1907. She eloped prior to 1914 to Toronto with her husband, a presser in the garment industry.

Walter Ross

Born in Rostherne, England in 1894, he came to Canada in 1913. He became an accountant and was working for the Consumer's Gas Company when he enlisted in 1914.

Paul Sawchuk

Born in 1892 in the Ukraine of parents who were Catholic peasants, he came to Toronto by way of Germany in 1913, and worked as a tailor. He was an early member of the Communist Party of Canada.

Ralph Sharpe

Born in Toronto in 1891, he was on his own by 1903. He worked on the lake freighters before enlisting in 1915.

Michael Sheehan

Born in Mimico, Ontario in 1884, he went west at 17 as an unskilled labourer and eventually homesteaded in Saskatchewan. He returned to Mimico in 1914 and enlisted when the war broke out.

Dale Simpson

He was born in Yorkshire, England in 1893.

Mrs Ellen Simpson

Born in Toronto in 1894, she worked as a furrier for Fairweathers.

Anna Smokorowsky

Born in Venlaw, Manitoba in 1902, she was the daughter of Ukrainians who had emigrated to Canada in 1899. In 1910 her parents sold their homestead and moved to Gilbert Plains, Manitoba.

Morty Stein

Born of Lithuanian Jewish parents in Manchester, England in 1894, he came to Canada in 1906. He went to work as a capmaker's apprentice in Toronto and Truro, Nova Scotia. He was an active union organizer in the needle trades.

Mrs Adrienne Stone

Born in Winnipeg in 1898, she moved with her parents to Toronto in 1903. She attended the University of Toronto during the war and served as a VAD at the Davisville Hospital.

Robert Swan

Born in Yarmouth, Nova Scotia in 1894, he enlisted in 1915.

Mark Tanner

Born in Montreal in 1898, he moved to Toronto in 1910 and worked as a messenger and office boy. He enlisted in 1917 and trained as a pilot.

Mrs Edith Thomas

Born in London, England in 1878, she came to Toronto with her husband in

1905. She had worked in a factory in London, but in Toronto she served her community as a midwife.

Edward Thompson

Born in Edinburgh, Scotland in 1896, he came to Canada in 1920.

Dan Vernon

Born in Glengarry County, Ontario in 1895, he got a job in the Department of Agriculture in 1913 and then enlisted and went overseas in 1917.

Ben Wagner

Born in Paisley, Bruce County in 1897 of a farming family, he enlisted in 1915.

Dean Walker

Born in Toronto in 1895, he attended the University of Toronto and enlisted in 1915.

Mrs Jane Walters

Born in 1896, the daughter of a newspaper owner in Welland, Ontario, she served as a VAD during the war.

Peter Watson

Born in Belleville, Ontario in 1899 of a farming family and educated for the ministry at Albert College, he quit to enlist. His father pulled him out before he got overseas.

Stanley Weekes

A Jew born in Poland in 1891, he first went to Argentina, where he worked as a tailor, before coming to Canada in 1912. Living first in Toronto, then Hamilton, where he was married in 1914, he returned to Toronto in 1916, working all the time in the needle trades.

Harold Wheeler

His parents came to Toronto from Birmingham, England some time after his birth in 1883. He enlisted soon after the war started, was captured by the Germans and spent most of the was as a POW.

Mrs Roberta White

Born in 1898 in Northampton, England, she came to Canada in 1905 and worked as a bookbinder.

Mrs Anne Whitelaw

Born in 1902 in Toronto, she grew up in Cabbagetown. Between 1915 and 1920, the year of her marriage, she worked in five factories.

George Wilkes

Born in Toronto in 1908, he has a schoolboy's memory of the war.

Brian Wilson

Born near Owen Sound, Ontario in 1890, he moved to Toronto in 1905. He got a job as a clerk for a music firm and worked there until it failed in 1929.

Burton Woods

Born in England in 1899, he was orphaned at an early age. Sent to Canada in 1911 by the Fegan's Home to work as a farm labourer, he ran away to join the army in 1914.